THE GENIUS OF AMERICA

THE GENIUS OF AMERICA

*How the Constitution Saved
Our Country—and Why It Can Again*

Eric Lane and
Michael Oreskes

BLOOMSBURY

NEW YORK • LONDON • OXFORD • NEW DELHI • SYDNEY

Bloomsbury USA
An imprint of Bloomsbury Publishing Plc

1385 Broadway   50 Bedford Square
New York   London
NY 10018   WC1B 3DP
USA   UK

www.bloomsbury.com

First published 2007
This paperback edition published 2008

ISBN: HB: 978-1-59691-199-4
          PB: 978-1-59691-491-9
          ePub: 978-1-59691-839-9

Library of Congress Cataloging-in-Publication Data has been applied for.

2 4 6 8 10 9 7 5 3

Typeset by Westchester Book Group
Printed and bound in the U.S.A. by Thomson-Shore Inc., Dexter, Michigan

To Joyce Talmadge and Geraldine Baum,
whose love and encouragement made this
book, and much more, possible.

CONTENTS

Introduction

AN EXTRAORDINARY ACCOMPLISHMENT

America! America!
God mend thine every flaw,
Confirm thy soul in self-control
Thy liberty in law!
—KATHARINE LEE BATES, 1893

THE UNITED STATES OF AMERICA is an extraordinary accomplishment. It is the richest, most powerful nation that has ever existed. From a handful of farmers and merchants on the edge of the known world, it has grown, endured, agonized and prospered. Millions have flocked to its shores, and millions more continuously hope to come. Saying that this has become something of a cliché does not make it any less true. Nor does the fact that some people in other parts of the world have come to resent the way America asserts its wealth and power make America's rise any less remarkable or significant. Even America's fiercest critics don't argue that.

But why did this success visit itself on the United States? Certainly it is a land blessed with enormous resources and intrepid people. They have been celebrated many times. But there are other nations with great resources and excellent people. Our purpose is to focus on something so apparent it is often underappreciated. America's extraordinary success is directly related to its unique form of government. Not just to its freedom or its democracy, but to its singularly American form of democracy.

Indeed, one of America's first and greatest inventions was the United States of America itself. This was something wholly new in the annals of government. There had been democracies before. There had been republics before. But what the framers invented was something no one had ever seen before.

They built a system of government entirely self-contained. They looked to neither God nor king for higher authority. This was, as they said, a government of "We the people." Every piece of it represented the people and drew its authority from the people, not, as for example in England, where the king or queen owed their power to the will of God, and the then powerful House of Lords to the lineage of its members.

But for government of the people to really work, the framers had to recognize what people were really like and then design a government around that reality. Through trial and spectacular error, they came to understand that anything less realistic was doomed to fail.

This, then, was their radical breakthrough: their recognition that government had to be designed around a cold-eyed acceptance of men as they really are, not as we might wish them to be. What was that cold-eyed view of human nature? They recognized that people pursue their own self-interests. And in this pursuit, they often regard what is good for them as good for all.

Other political thinkers had, of course, noticed this from time to time before the American Revolution. But before America, proponents of democracy (when they could be found) generally solved the problem of selfishness by suggesting that citizens could rise above their own interests to join in achieving some larger good that they would recognize through reasoning together.

This is an attractive thought. It was nice to believe—it is still nice to believe—that we each have this capacity for public virtue. Indeed, in the heady first days of the Revolution (but neither before nor after, as we describe in Part One), the founders themselves by and large believed this. They generally thought that the simple act of breaking with England would free Americans in their new land from the corrupting values of the old world. In April of 1776, Tom Paine described America as "a blank sheet" on which a freed people could and would script a new start. All that was needed to make government work was virtuous Americans doing the right thing in their new land.

But in the first disastrous years of their independence they came to understand that they had been hopelessly naive. Of course, there were individual examples of self-sacrifice for the larger cause. Yet overall, the framers found, the people could reliably be counted on to do what was best for themselves as individuals, not for some abstract larger whole. As a result, the people had nearly let their army starve in the field of battle. They had competed, one state against another, for the upper hand in trade. They had profiteered and stolen and refused to work together.

The American experiment in self-government was on the verge of failure.

"We have probably had too good an opinion of human nature in forming our confederation," George Washington wrote in 1786.

Then, a quintessentially American thing happened. A group of men, chosen by their states, got together in the sweltering late spring of 1787 to try to fix things. They locked themselves in a room and haggled and brokered and compromised. They went way beyond any instructions they had been given by the states, which had sent them, or by Congress, which had belatedly endorsed their gathering. But they did not do it to impose an ideology or test some social theory. In that pragmatic American way that people all around the world still admire, they were just trying to make it work.

And out of that sweltering room in Philadelphia, out of that crisis of the early American nation, emerged a blueprint for government that was designed to let the people govern themselves despite their imperfections. They called it "this Constitution for The United States of America." It did not count on people to be selfless or somehow bigger than themselves. "If men were angels, no government would be necessary," wrote James Madison, one of the heroes of our story.

Indeed, the Constitution recognized that the great strength of Americans was their drive and ambition. For most, that is what got them to the new world (and still does). The Constitution would make a virtue of this "vice." This new idea for government presumed that people would pursue their own interests. Indeed, it counted on them to do just that. And it created paths for others to disagree, and resist them, or argue for something different.

The framers' invention was a government designed to channel these struggles. To impede change until enough people supported it. To force people to the middle. To encourage compromise. To spread power around so that, in Alexander Hamilton's succinct vision, the few could not oppress the many, and the many could not oppress the few. A lot could get done if people worked together in this system. But if they refused to compromise, it could all grind to a halt.

In other words, what they sent out from Philadelphia was more than just a piece of parchment. They created a set of ideas about government and democracy. Twenty years ago, the scholar Michael Kammen published a marvelous book on the Constitution in our culture. He described both the importance to us of the document itself and of the values and options that surrounded it, what he called *constitutionalism*. At the heart of constitutionalism is an acceptance of "conflict within consensus." Conflict over issues, within a consensus that we are bound one to another by our shared belief in our Constitution and its principles. This crucial tension has both held our country together and driven us forward. For conflict within consensus to be constructive, rather than destructive, Americans had to accept in their political bones several other ideas crucial to the Constitution. One was compromise. The Constitution was a set of compromises and assumed the vital need for compromise for the new government to function. Another crucial idea was representation. The political philosophy of the framers assumed that Americans would accept compromises because they felt properly represented in the branches of government. For a long time this promise of representation was considerably greater than the reality, as we discuss in Part Two.

All of the Constitution's ideas taken together—conflict within consensus, compromise, representation, checks and balances, tolerance of debate—became part of the political conscience of each American. We therefore call this set of ideas, these core political values, the *Constitutional Conscience.* This book describes the development of Americans' Constitutional Conscience and its vital role.

Every nation has a set of political values. But ours are, by comparison, more vital to us, as Americans, than a similar set of values would be to the people of many other nations. Ours is not a country "defined by blood, clan, land origin or religious belief," observed the journalist Ray Suarez. Indeed, said former Harvard president Derek Bok, "more than any other leading democracy, America is a country that preserves its unity through a shared belief in its Constitution, its institutions of government, and its democratic principles." So it is particularly important that we pay attention to our connection to our Constitution, institutions and principles.

We wrote this book because we worry that in recent years Americans have been losing touch with some of these basic constitutional values, most particularly a commitment to compromise and a tolerance for competing ideas. To say it the way Professor Kammen might, conflict has been increasing, and consensus has frayed. Americans' faith in their system is not what it once was. "Our conviction about American greatness and purpose is not as strong today" is the way William J. Bennett describes it on the very first page of his history of the United States, *The Last Best Hope.* Bennett said he wrote his book in part to remind Americans of their debt of gratitude to those who built the country. We share that worthy goal. An antidote to our frustration and cynicism is to remind ourselves from time to time of the principles behind what the framers invented.

Professor Kammen urged Americans to remember "that the founders did not expect their instrument of government to achieve utopia: 'merely' national cohesion, political stability, economic growth, and individual liberty."

They had no idea how effective their work would turn out to be. Many thought the Republic would last for only a couple of decades. Of course, it has not only lasted much longer but thrived. It has not been perfect, of course. Even the best design for government cannot prevent all error of human judgment. One of the central compromises the framers themselves made, to put off to the future the issue of abolishing slavery, nearly tore our country and their intricate design for the national government to shreds.

We linger on this in Part Two. Since we strongly embrace the values on which our system is built, and want to encourage other Americans to do the same, it is important to stare straight into the teeth of the unpalatable element of a system based on compromise. Compromises are by definition imperfect to the people involved. If it is truly a compromise, no one participant is getting everything he or she wants. The more the issue has a moral dimension, the more potentially awful the compromise can look. One of the reasons our politics has become so brittle is that we seem to be seeing so many issues through a moral lens and therefore find it hard to find common ground for compromise.

So it is valuable to remind ourselves that nothing we are struggling through now compares to the dilemma of slavery, which so dominated the nation's first seventy years. It is simple for us to look back and say slavery is wrong and the framers should not have compromised. But the issue for them was far more complicated, both because our age has made the moral judgment about slavery their age was struggling with and because we have the nation they were trying to build. We have no way to know what would have happened had they refused to compromise on slavery in 1787, or at any of several other moments along the march to the Civil War. Perhaps we still would have one nation. Or perhaps we would have two, both ultimately having abandoned slavery. Or perhaps the framers' greatest fear would have been realized, and America would have become a set of feuding, little republics, preyed on and dominated by the great powers of Europe. History is fun to play "what if" games with. But we do not get to rerun history. All we have is the testimony of the participants themselves.

As this original compromise over slavery, America's original sin to some, was finally collapsing, Abraham Lincoln reviewed the history and refused to disown the framers: "We had slavery among us. We could not get our Constitution unless we permitted them to remain in slavery, we could not secure the good we did secure if we grasped for more; And having by necessity submitted to that much, it does not destroy the principle that is the charter of our liberties. Let that charter stand as our standard."

As we look back across all 220 years of our history since the Constitution, it is easy to agree with Lincoln that the overall success, the overall good, is far greater than even the horrifying failings. The constitutional system has lasted longer than any other republic in history. But it has not just survived. It turns out that the framers' insight—that the self-interest of people had to be the basis around which government was designed—had another larger implication.

Until the American Revolution, the general wisdom was that democracies needed to be limited in size. This was because they relied on each citizen to recognize a shared interest with his fellow citizens and sacrifice some of his own desires to that larger good. Just thirty years before the American Revolution, Montesquieu, the French political philosopher whom all the framers looked up to, had contended that republics needed to be small to survive.

But by creating a government that encouraged the pursuit of self-interests, the framers unshackled their new nation from this

philosophical restraint. They made America, to use
our time to describe their invention, scalable. If the cla
and interests would produce better results, they reasone
more ideas and more interests would produce even better res
The old need was to limit the size of a democracy to ensure its
smooth functioning. They turned the argument on its head to encourage expansion and growth.

Expansion and growth, of course, are just what happened.
Americans pursued their interests, and by pursuing their interests
they built the nation. As they did this, alternative approaches to
government came and went around the world, stared down, in fact,
by America with its energy and power. One of the fundamental
differences between those other approaches and the American constitutional system goes all the way back to that sweltering room in
Philadelphia.

The communists, the fascists and the national socialists all put first
the goal of a new and, in their view, better society. Government's
purpose was to enact that better society on behalf of the people.

The end was more important than the means. But to the framers,
the better world, which they believed would come, was a by-
product of their government, not its purpose. The citizens would
decide in common what that better life entailed. Government's
role, under the Constitution, was to channel society's conflicts and
struggles into a field of battle with rules that protected the liberties
of individuals and encouraged compromise. They elevated process
over result. The most venerated artifact in all of American history
is, remarkably, a document laying out governmental process, "this
Constitution for The United States of America."

While the document is quite short (just over seven thousand
words, including the twenty-seven amendments), the process it creates

professor of government before
complex to be understood." But
t was designed that way to make
tion and consensus. A simple ma-
f a point of departure from most
passionate on the point that major-
of what was right or wrong for the

Despite the role the fram... built for government as an obstacle
to rash or speedy change, the American government has, as designed, incrementally allowed much change. Over time, that change
has been extraordinary. Since the Great Depression, a forty-year
consensus among Americans thrust government from a small participant in their lives to a central player. That consensus produced, for
example, Social Security, Medicare, Medicaid and an expansion of
civil rights, voting rights and environmental protections. It also
sharply increased the expectation among the people that government could solve problems.

But in the last decades of the twentieth century, that consensus
unraveled, leaving intact only expanded expectations that government can solve our problems. The country became divided into a
multitude of different interests, each demanding that its own policies
be enacted into law. Discord now demarks the political landscape,
fueled by political "leaders" who reason that they can secure their
own position by promising to support one interest against another.

As the clamor rises, the government cannot accommodate all
these competing demands. Indeed, it was designed to frustrate them.
So, naturally, there is great frustration and anger among many of
these groups whose demands and expectations have been unsatisfied.

None of this would have surprised or upset the writers of the

Constitution. They believed action without consensus was far more dangerous than stasis while searching for consensus. But what might have worried them is how the political frustrations have turned into attacks on the process itself. The values that compose our Constitutional Conscience are meant to reinforce each other. We accept compromise because we feel we are represented in the decision. But many Americans no longer feel well represented. This is due in part to dysfunctions in the Congress that need to be fixed. But, even more, it is also due to our increasing unwillingness or inability to appreciate a central principle of the Constitution: American government was not established to satisfy our specific wants, but to sort out all our desires and demands and find some common good.

What have you given us? Benjamin Franklin was asked as he left the Constitutional Convention. "A republic, madam, if you can keep it."

Quoting Franklin's warning in this context may seem alarmist. Certainly, we have never been richer or more powerful as a nation. Yet within we harbor deep doubts and divisions that undercut our unity. A key element of this has been a tendency to blame the process of government, the one the framers gave us, for our problems. This attitude is corrosive and threatening for the reason Learned Hand, the great jurist, once explained: "Liberty lies in the hearts of men and women; when it dies there . . . no constitution, no law, no court [can] save it . . . A society in which men recognize no check upon their freedom soon becomes a society where freedom is the possession of only a savage few; as we have learned to our sorrow." Our Constitutional Conscience, what we believe in our hearts and minds, is more central even than the document itself and all the rulings of the Supreme Court. Certainly, it is not dead in us. But we do believe it is ailing.

In Part Three, we trace back to the late 1970s the rise of an unhappy attitude toward government and recall how Ronald Reagan crystallized it in his first inaugural address in 1981.

It had been a long journey for Reagan—actor, Roosevelt Democrat, union leader, corporate spokesman, Barry Goldwater advocate, conservative governor of California. Through a lifetime of experience he had honed his view that government needed to be limited. Now he looked out on a nation in turmoil. At home, inflation had sapped the country's economic will, and the rift of Watergate was still raw. Abroad, for all its power, the nation had been humiliated by an Iranian cleric who after 444 days was just at that moment releasing the hostages he had held in the American embassy in Tehran. Reagan, speaking for the first time as president, went beyond just the idea that government was too big.

> In the present crisis, government is not the solution to our problem; government is the problem. From time to time, we've been tempted to believe that society has become too complex to be managed by self-rule, that government by an elite group is superior to government for, by and of the people. Well, if no one among us is capable of governing himself then who among us has the capacity to govern someone else? . . . We hear much of special interest groups. Well, our concern must be for a special interest group that has been too long neglected . . ."we the people," this breed called Americans.

It was an important moment at the outset of what became one of the most important presidencies of the twentieth century. Reagan's vision of a united American people, blocked from the realization of their dreams by an entrenched political system, signaled the start of what became known as the Reagan Revolution. One of the themes of this book is the striking extent to which much of our political debate can be traced back to either Tom Paine's idealistic vision or James Madison's cold-eyed pragmatism. We are not America without both.

Reagan strongly echoed Paine 205 years earlier. In times of crisis, times that try men's souls, turn to the People, that breed called Americans, who unfettered by government will have the wisdom to govern themselves on that blank slate called America. It is a cry raised repeatedly through American history, by reformers and radicals and just plain restless folk seeking to foment change. Its revival is a constant through our history. Particularly in times of turmoil, we fall back on the ultimate source of the nation's authority, the people.

Talk of the people strikes a chord in each American because it connects to the story of the American Revolution as we receive it in school. But the call to the people leaves out half the history of the Revolution. When Reagan set the people as the antithesis of the government, he was returning to the spirit of 1776. But the story of 1776 is incomplete without the story of 1787 and the writing of the Constitution, which rescued the heroism of 1776 from the dustbin of history. Whereas 1776 was the triumph of liberty, 1787 was the triumph of a new wisdom that to preserve liberty there must be a process for making choices and taking action. That process is laid out in the Constitution. The Constitution's writers drew their government's authority from the people, and from nowhere else. But they also rejected, quite clearly, the notion that the people could, mystically, solve the nation's problems without a process of government to bring them together. Their own experience had violently disabused them of that notion.

As Reagan spoke, the men behind him represented the majority leadership of the House of Representatives and the Senate. So his words about rule by an elite group might have been understood as a bit of political hyperbole meant to suggest that the problem was the specific people or the Democratic Party, which had been in control of the government just then. But this would be to miss the much larger antigovernment sentiment gathering strength in those years among Democrats and Republicans, left and right, a force that carries forward to this day.

Two years before Reagan was elected president, the voters of California adopted a proposition, number 13 on that year's ballot, to limit the spending authority of their legislature. This reinvigorated a process, initiative and referendum, that allowed Americans to vote directly on issues and circumvent their state legislatures (or even the Congress under a version now being pushed by former U.S. senator Mike Gravel). That is, philosophically, exactly the opposite of the view of the framers, who gave process a central role in their vision of democracy.

This historical context would not have occurred consciously to many of the spokesmen for the gathering effort to take power from government. Reagan believed profoundly in America, and one of his important contributions was a revival of what he called "informed patriotism" steeped in an understanding of our history. Certainly, Reagan would not have accepted the idea that he was arguing across the years with the writers of the Constitution.

But there were those who explicitly acknowledged that they wanted to undo what the framers had invented. A few months before Reagan took office, in the frustrating final days of Jimmy

Carter's presidency, Carter's counsel, Lloyd Cutler, a consummate Democrat, called for the scrapping of the essential elements of the process created by the Constitution. "Whatever its merits in 1793, American Government has become a structure that almost guarantees stalemate." He proposed a Parliament whose members would be more responsive to the president.

We can see from the perspective of twenty-five years later that Reagan's analysis of government as the problem and Cutler's call for the abolition of the independent Congress were just the beginnings of a period of stalemate in America and consequent frustration.

It is an irony of our age that one of America's greatest triumphs, one of Reagan's greatest triumphs, the collapse of the Soviet Union, coincided with a growing disillusionment at home with the American process of government, the very process which has proven so much more resilient and lasting than any of its competitor systems.

To maintain the essential legitimacy of democracy, government must *ultimately* respond to the demands of its people. But America's government is designed to slow such response, to resist, as Hamilton put it, "an unqualified complaisance to every sudden breeze of passion, or to every transient impulse." This inevitably creates tension between the people and their government. This tension has intensified as the country's politics have fractured. We are living through "the growth of a politics based upon narrow concerns, rooted in the exploitative division of class, cash, gender, region, ethnicity, morality and ideology—a give no quarter and take no prisoners activism that demands satisfaction and accepts no compromise." In other words, a period of strife and disunity much like the early days of America out of which the framers invented the process of government in the Constitution.

Faced with the growing divisions of our age, Congress has done less, just as the framers designed it to do. The result is ever-growing criticism of the government as an obstacle to change. People of all ideological and political stripes, frustrated by government's incapacity to provide what they want, have found common ground in blaming the design of the government for their failure to get their way.

But the fault, to paraphrase Cassius, is not in the government (or at least not only in the government). The government is doing what the framers designed it to do when a divided country "accepts no compromise." It is waiting for compromise to seem more palatable than political warfare.

Americans are always free to reject what their forefathers bequeathed them. The South tried that once. The Constitution ingeniously includes a process for its own amendment, which could even include its own undoing if enough Americans agree.

Many Americans talk as if they want that now. *Power to the people*, a term coined by the left during the 1960s, has now become a slogan for disaffected groups of all political stripes. Their question is why should we have a government that frustrates the demands of so many people?

America's greatest strength and greatest weakness are the same thing. We are not burdened by a sense of history, our own or anyone else's. Our sense of the past is, to be polite, thin and growing thinner. The evidence for this is all around us. We opened this introduction with the third stanza of "America, the Beautiful" to make the point. Everyone knows the first stanza, with its appeal for God's grace and brotherhood. But virtually no one knows this later stanza, which honors the core idea of our Constitution. Our detachment from history has liberated us as Americans to focus forward. We look to the future in a way that many other societies envy. But it can also disconnect us, as is the case now, from an understanding that would comfort and guide us.

The framers did what they did for carefully thought out reasons. Their choices made sense then. We think understanding them better would help us understand our present predicament better. To do that, we need to revisit the most important eleven years in American history. Those are the years from 1776, when the colonies declared themselves free and independent, to 1787, when a group of men gathered in Philadelphia and, as William Bennett summed it up, "devised the most miraculous political document in history just as the young nation seemed to be falling apart."

An extraordinary intellectual revolution took place in the minds of America's leaders during those years. In 1776, most of them believed that self-interest was a threat to democracy, but that Americans, free of England, would rise above their self-interests to create the new nation. By 1787, they had changed both ideas. They recognized that while America was a special land, Americans were like everyone else, motivated by their own interests. But they could still make their new nation work by reinventing democratic government to channel those self-interests into the larger good.

It is to the saga of those eleven years that we first turn.

Part One

THE INVENTION

It is evident that no other form [of government other than a Republic] would be reconcilable with the genius of the people of America; with the fundamental principles of the revolutions; or with that honorable determination, which animates every votary of freedom.

—JAMES MADISON, 1788

1

THE MORE FATAL PROBLEM LIES
AMONG THE PEOPLE THEMSELVES

> *A* people *is traveling fast to destruction, when* individuals *consider* their *interests as distinct from those of the* public. *Such notions are fatal to their country, and themselves.*
>
> —JOHN DICKINSON, AMERICAN PATRIOT, 1768

> *Experience has taught us, that men will not adopt & carry into execution, measures the best calculated for their own good without the intervention of a coercive power.*
>
> —GEORGE WASHINGTON, AMERICAN PATRIOT,
> EIGHTEEN YEARS LATER

ONE OF THE ENDURING lessons of our own age is that what happens in men's minds can be more powerful and lasting than what happens on the field of battle. No event in history illustrates this any more clearly than the American Revolution. What we think of as the Revolution actually occurred in two parts, as one of the nation's founders, Dr. Benjamin Rush of Pennsylvania, pointed out in 1787. The first was a military rebellion in which King George III lost control of part of his North American empire. It was a remarkable event, the first time in many years that a British army had been defeated. But for all that sense of a world turned upside down, this war might well have become a footnote to world history (if perhaps not British history) were it not for the second, intellectual, revolution that took place among the colonists between 1776 and 1787. Those eleven years are the most important in the history of the invention of the United States and quite possibly the most important in the history of the idea of democracy. Because during those years the framers of the Constitution redefined what it meant to be a democracy and what it would take to stay a democracy. They established something totally new. To understand the government they gave us, we need to understand the experience that caused them to create it.

Americans declared their independence from England in 1776, of course, and eleven years later, in 1787, wrote our Constitution. The two documents they produced are the touchstones of American democracy. Both are dedicated to the preservation of liberty. But the two documents enshrine remarkably different notions of how to do that. In 1776, the founders were focused on throwing off bonds and giving the people (at least white males with property) the right to participate in the political system. By 1787, the framers understood that liberty could not survive unless joined to a system that could balance one group's self-interests against another's.

Events changed the framers' minds. Human nature wasn't quite what they had thought and hoped. In 1776, on the eve of independence and war, Americans viewed themselves as capable of suppressing their individual self-interest for the public good, in the conduct of their public affairs. They called this ability public virtue. America was a blank slate, Tom Paine declared in 1776, and Americans would write with virtue on it. All they needed to do was declare liberty from the corrupt and aging empire that subjugated them.

By 1787, the framers along with many Americans had a different self-assessment. Americans, it turned out, were like people everywhere and at all times, mostly self-interested and self-regarding and, in the public arena, usually unable to suppress their self-interests for the greater good.

What explains such a dramatic reversal of their view of human nature in a mere eleven years? In a word: reality. The reality of American conduct during the war and the ensuing efforts to build the new nation had demonstrated to the founders that self-interest, not public virtue, was the citizenry's most compelling motivation. Simple liberty from Great Britain had not been adequate to ensure success of the new nation. Real people simply could not sustain the life of public virtue envisioned in the revolutionary fervor.

This change of view would have a profound effect on the shape of our government as laid out in the Constitution. Americans needed a new form of government based on this new acceptance of what people are really like. "But what is government," James Madison, the father of the Constitution, wrote in 1788, "but the greatest of all reflections of human nature?"

A UTOPIAN MOVEMENT

Gordon Wood, the eminent historian, described the Revolution as "one of the great utopian movements of American history." This sounds puzzling at first, because we have come to think of the founders as such practical, pragmatic men. But Wood is starting the conversation in the mid-1700s with an examination of the decision to rebel in the first place. That decision was built, centrally, on a belief that human beings can improve. Or, more specifically, that Americans in their new land could be better citizens—*more virtuous* is how they would say it—than they had been under their British rulers. Virtue was an important political concept to the colonists. Their reading of history, particularly classical history, led them to conclude that liberty was "fragile" and required public virtue for its maintenance. Public virtue was an ability to see the larger, common good and sacrifice some of your own interests to achieve it. "When virtue is banished, ambition invades the hearts of those who are capable of receiving it, and avarice possesses the whole community," observed the philosopher Montesquieu. It was self-interest, the decline of virtue, which had destroyed the Greek and Roman republics. Without public virtue, tyranny would prevail, the founders believed, but with it greatness was possible. The framers themselves would come to recognize the utopian nature of this faith.

Avarice possessing the whole community would not be a bad description of America in the 1760s and early 1770s. It certainly was not a harmonious place. The entire country seemed to be in a self-destructive uproar. The colonists were "a quarrelsome, litigious, divisive lot of people." People seemed to sue each other "almost as regularly as they ate or slept." Such contentiousness also marked the behavior within and between the colonies. Western North Carolina went to war with eastern North Carolina. The farmers of western Massachusetts were at odds with the commercial interests of Boston. Among the colonies there were constant disputes over boundaries. For example, rival settlers from Pennsylvania and Connecticut almost shed blood over claims to land in northeastern Pennsylvania. Discord among colonists was so prevalent that even some of the most independence-leaning leaders saw it as a threatening problem. James Otis, a Massachusetts revolutionary, warned in 1765, "Were these colonies left to themselves tomorrow, America would be a mere shambles of blood and confusion."

Yet despite this discord, over the next ten years, the colonists moved steadily if not inexorably toward separation from England. How was this possible? In large measure it was because they believed the chaos, the decaying virtue, was caused by their relationship to Great Britain. England was their prime modern-day example of a fallen country, like the Greeks and Romans. As viewed from the Atlantic seaboard, the English had dissipated the liberty brought by the Glorious Revolution (1688) through an obsessive desire for wealth, power and position, social rank and refinement. This pursuit of self-interest, according to John Dickinson, had sunk the English into a "tameness and supineness of spirit" and, as a result, servitude to both Parliament and king. Dickinson worried the same thing was happening already in America.

Among the leaders of the American Revolution, John Dickinson was an important figure. He was involved in every debate from the opposition to the stamp tax in 1765 to the ratification of the Constitution in 1788. He drafted the Articles of Confederation, America's first, ultimately failed, constitution. Yet he has been largely lost to us, compared to the prominence of his colleagues. Perhaps that is because he was more conservative than some of them. He was a forceful defender of American rights, yet until the bitter end he argued for reconciliation with Great Britain. On July 2, 1776, he said that declaring independence was premature (although once done, he immediately joined the Revolutionary Army).

But to understand the ideas that motivated the colonists in those years, we must excavate John Dickinson's powerful and articulate voice. He was a master wordsmith. Indeed, it was Dickinson, not Thomas Jefferson, who was known as "the penman of the Revolution." In the prewar years, he was the most brilliantly articulate spokesman for that faith in public virtue that gave Americans the confidence to rebel.

John Dickinson was a lawyer by trade, an American "aristocrat" by birth and a conciliator by nature. In 1765, he had gained a national reputation, at the age of thirty-three, as a leader of the resistance to the Stamp Act, England's imposition of a direct tax on such things as newspapers, almanacs, legal papers, and playing cards. The colonists won the Stamp Act fight, but almost immediately Parliament enacted new measures that Dickinson considered a new threat to American freedom. The Quartering Act required the colonies to house and supply British troops. The Restraining Act suspended the New York State Assembly for refusing to obey the Quartering Act. And the Townsend Acts imposed various duties and tariffs on colonial trade.

In the winter of 1767, Dickinson published fierce arguments against these burdens. More important, in terms of the intellectual evolution of America's ideas of government and public virtue, he lectured the colonies themselves for their poor response to these acts, particularly the Restraining Act. They had been selfish, he believed, refusing to support each other. "He certainly is not a wise man, who folds his arms, and reposes himself at home, viewing, with unconcern, the flames that have invaded his neighbor's house." This lack of concern of one colony for another, one group of persons for another, echoed what Dickinson believed had undermined liberty in both England and in all of history's republics. The colonies needed to be warned that selfishness, failure to stand together, and failure to display public virtue were threats to liberty.

Dickinson's medium was a series of letters, titled "Letters from a Farmer in Pennsylvania to the Inhabitants of the British Colonies." Dickinson was a farmer in only the loosest sense. He was actually one of the largest property owners in Pennsylvania, wealth he inherited on his father's death in 1760. But that detail did not interfere with the enormous impact of his writings.

First published in the *Pennsylvania Chronicle* between December 2, 1767, and February 15, 1768, these letters proved so popular that they were quickly reprinted in all but four of the twenty-three colonial newspapers and in pamphlet form. They contained a sharp critique of British policy and the deterioration of British politics. But more, they are a brilliantly articulate record of the belief in the importance of public virtue that was taking hold among the intellectual classes of revolutionary-era America. In his letter of January 15, 1768, he described the fatal vice of the English people that most Americans believed was destroying English freedom:

My Dear Countrymen,

Some states have lost their liberty *by particular accidents*: But this calamity is generally owing to the *decay of virtue*. A *people* is traveling fast to destruction, when *individuals* consider *their* interests as distinct from those of the public. Such notions are fatal to their country, and to themselves. Yet how many are there, so *weak* and *sordid* as to *think* they perform *all the office of life*, if they earnestly endeavor to encrease their own *wealth, power*, and *credit*, without the least regard for the society, under the protection of which they live.

A Farmer

THE BREAK WITH ENGLAND

Over the next ten years, repeated efforts by Parliament in London to tax and regulate the internal relations of the colonies convinced many Americans that Dickinson was right about the decay of British political society and the threat of that decay to Americans. John Adams observed that official corruption in England was a "Cancer" that had become "too deeply rooted, and too far spread to be cured by anything short of cutting it out entire." In fact, this notion of the corrupting influence of British politics was so strong that it helped scuttle an effort to find a middle ground to avert separation. In 1774, Joseph Galloway of Pennsylvania proposed, in effect, a two-house legislative system. Parliament in London and a national legislature in America would act together on issues concerning the colonies. Parliament would continue to have authority over America, but the colonists could no longer be taxed without the consent of their own representatives as well. The compromise drew considerable support in the Continental Congress, the single house assembly of state representatives that governed America from independence through ratification of the Constitution and the establishment of the new government. But Patrick Henry rose in opposition. This solution would accomplish little, he said. "We shall liberate our Constituents from a corrupt House of Commons, but throw them into the Arms of an American Legislature that may be bribed by that Nation [Britain] which avows in the Face of the World, that Bribery is a Part of her System of Government." By a vote of 6 states to 5, Galloway's compromise was killed. Imagine if that vote had gone the other way. The rise of America, and the evolution of democratic government, might have followed a very different path.

Yet having rejected compromise, separation from England was still a frightening and radical prospect. On the eve of war many Americans, including Dickinson, still favored reconciliation with England. To them, separation was "a leap in the dark." It was not enough just to believe that virtue was in decay under British rule, as Dickinson had argued. To sever their ties to the most powerful nation on earth, to their motherland, Americans had to believe they could do better on their own. If they made this leap in the dark, they asked, "where would they land?"

The man who proclaimed the answer more powerfully than anyone else was a new arrival to America. He would become the best-known and most articulate revolutionary polemicist of the late 1700s, on both sides of the Atlantic. His name was Thomas Paine. "We have it in our power," Paine instructed, "to begin the world over again." Independence now from England could save America from its discord and conflict, Paine wrote in a tract he called *Common Sense*. To Paine, the very word *republic* meant the public good. "Youth is the seed time of good habits, as well in nations as in individuals, the present time is the true time for establishing it [an American republic]. The intimacy which is contracted in infancy, and the friendship which is formed in misfortune, are, of all others, the most lasting." And the good habit Paine expected of liberated Americans was public virtue, the capacity of citizens of the new

Republic to suppress their individual interests for the public good. This is, of course, exactly what Americans had proven unable to do under British rule.

But then again, Tom Paine had not been in America the past ten strife-filled years. He had arrived from England only in the fall of 1774, so sick with typhus that he had to be carried ashore. It is hard to say what would have happened to the penniless and friendless Paine if not for the letter he brought with him from England. It was from the most famous man in America, Benjamin Franklin, who was then serving in England as America's representative. Improbably, based on Paine's record of failure in England, Franklin vouched for Paine, whom he had met in London. That was enough for Robert Aitken, a bookseller, who hired Paine to write for his inaugural issue of the *Pennsylvania Magazine,* probably the most important hire of a freelance writer in the history of America.

In the age of revolution, Tom Paine was a remarkable, recognizably modern, presence. His almost complete lack of formal education somehow freed him from the more formal writing style of most of the other founders. He wrote, Paine once said, so those who could barely read could understand him.

Paine would serve in the Revolutionary Army, coauthor the radical Pennsylvania Constitution of 1776, serve as a member of the French National Assembly as a delegate from Calais, author the *Rights of Man* and the *Age of Reason* for which he was inaccurately condemned as an atheist (he was merely an opponent of all organized religion), be imprisoned in France for treason against the French Republic, be liberated through the efforts of James Monroe, and finally return to America, where he would die poor and unheralded.

In our story he plays a crucial part. In 1776, this new immigrant to America became America's most convincing voice for independence and for the claim that with independence would come the public virtue English rule did not permit.

If you accept Gordon Wood's notion that the decision to rebel was a utopian movement that rose above the reality of colonial disunion, then it was Tom Paine's vision that rallied the movement.

Once in Philadelphia, Paine entered the environment of political tumult he always sought. The First Continental Congress had just completed its eight-week session, and the questions of tyranny, freedom and independence dominated the many papers and cafés of America's largest city. Paine became the editor of the *Pennsylvania Magazine*, writing numerous articles advocating freedom and rebellion. In January 1776, he had published *Common Sense*, a pamphlet of "breathtaking boldness," that offered "sound doctrine and unanswerable reasoning," as George Washington put it, "upon the propriety of a separation." So popular was this pamphlet that over 120,000 copies were in circulation by the end of 1776. Even today, that would be a big best seller.

By April 1776, he resigned as editor of the magazine and was writing again, attacking the critics of *Common Sense* and pushing again for independence and republican government. Under the Arcadian-sounding pseudonym "the Forrester" (a job he never held), he wrote four letters for the Pennsylvania press. In the third of these, published in the *Pennsylvania Packet* on April 22, 1776, he told Americans of the great opportunity that independence offered them. He understood that colonists feared this leap. So he posed the central question: "Can America be happy under a government of her own?" The answer is "short and simple," he said. "As happy as she please; she hath a blank sheet to write upon."

Paine's faith in the people of his new land was boundless. Past was not prologue. Given a blank slate, Americans would rise to the responsibilities of a free people once the burdens of Britain were gone. "We are young, and we have been distressed; but our concord hath withstood our troubles, and fixes a memorable era for the posterity to glory in."

Americans rallied around Paine's vision of a virtuous America. A poem in the *New Jersey Gazette* in May of 1778 captured the sentiment.

Here Governments their last perfection take.
Erected only for the People's sake:
Founded no more on Conquest or in blood
But on the basis of the Public Good.

The idea of independence drew Americans together against a common enemy and provided a powerful force for suppressing the colonists' quarrelsomeness. The revolutionary colonists were Americans with a common American interest. A mood of optimism infused even the men who would be far more skeptical ten years later. "Would any Man two Years ago have believed it possible, to accomplish such an Alteration in the Prejudices, Passions, Sentiments and Principles of these thirteen little States as to make every one of them completely republican, and to make them own it," wrote John Adams in 1776.

Despite all the history of conflict among them, the revolutionary colonists saw independence from England as freeing them to live the virtues they idealized. Independence would lead to the spread of public virtue, which then rooted would seed itself and reseed itself in following generations. "If there is a form of government . . . whose principle and foundation is virtue," Adams wrote, "will not every sober man acknowledge it better calculated to promote the general happiness than any other form?" Even a young James Madison chimed in: "A spirit of Liberty and Patriotism animates all degrees and denomination of men." America would be a place populated, predicted Thomas Jefferson, by "sensible, hardworking, independent folk secure in their possession of land, free of the corruptions of urban poverty and cynicism, free of dependence on a self-indulgent aristocracy of birth, responsible to the common good as well as to personal betterment, educated in the essentials of free government and committed to the principles of freedom—peaceful, self-reliant, self-respecting, and unintimidated people."

The colonists filled their public documents and writings with an almost religious proclamation of their belief in their own special pubic virtue and the central role of that virtue to their hope for liberty. Pennsylvania's Constitution of 1776 declared, "A firm adherence to justice, moderation, temperance, industry and frugality are absolutely necessary to preserve the liberty, and keep a government free."

As the colonists saw it, English freedom, like the freedoms of the classic republics, had been destroyed by the absence of public virtue and with it the hope for American freedom under English rule. Only through independence could American public virtue flourish and consequently American liberty exist. "As the possibility of a break with England approached," one historian summed up, "the American mind seemed almost relieved, as though the Revolution would finally do 'away with the flimsy excuses suggested by avarice and mistaken self-interest' and 'bring the unanimity, the firmness, and wisdom' that had so long seemed lacking in American society."

This faith in public virtue had a practical and direct effect on the national and state governments the colonists established as they declared independence. Simple government was best, and all that was needed. For if government was, as Paine wrote, only a "necessary evil" for "restraining our vices," then a simple government would suffice for a people with few vices and strong virtue. Simple government would be one that expressed and acted upon the will of the majority. In fact, anything more complicated could undermine the realization of the public good. "The more simple any thing is," wrote Paine, "the less liable it is to be disordered, and the easier repaired."

Remarkably, some of this same sentiment was expressed in 1777 by a twenty-two-year-old officer in the Continental Army by the name of Alexander Hamilton. New Yorkers were debating the structure of their new state government. Hamilton wrote that adding a second house, a senate, to the New York legislature was unnecessary. Having two houses would "occasion delay and dilatoriness," Hamilton wrote, and, of "much greater evil," would, "from the very name, and from the mere circumstance of it being a separate member of the Legislature, . . . be liable to degenerate into a body purely aristocratical." For Hamilton, the "danger of an abuse of power from a simple Legislature, would not be very great," if such body was based on an "equality and fullness of popular representation." In the course of the dramatic intellectual revolution that occurred between 1776 and 1787, perhaps no one would more radically alter his view than Hamilton.

This reliance on public virtue to ensure the public good influenced the drafting of many state constitutions immediately after the Declaration, most clearly through the transfer of powers from royal executives to legislatures, leaving executives with very little authority.

The Pennsylvania Constitution of 1776 went the farthest in placing its faith on the virtue of the people. That constitution contained every imaginable means of anchoring the exercise of power in the will of the majority of the state's voters. The legislature had only one house, members served one year at a time, and their maximum term was limited. The executive was a committee with no veto power.

Most significantly, faith in public virtue was central to America's first "Constitution," the Articles of Confederation and Perpetual Union, drafted by John Dickinson in 1776.

The Articles granted the Congress exclusive power over the war effort, foreign affairs and monetary policy, but not the power to tax or to regulate commerce among the states. In other words, the Congress could borrow money for the war, but it had no means to pay it back. It had to rely on the states, which, as the Pennsylvania Constitution illustrated, were tied to the will of the majority of their electorates. Congress had no power to coerce the states to repay its war debt, muster troops or to conform to any of its requirements.

This omission of coercive powers in the Articles of Confederation was intentional. Madison noted that the Articles of Confederation were drafted with "confidence that the justice, the good faith, the honor, [and] the sound policy" of state legislatures would compel their compliance. Coercive power was therefore unnecessary. A decision of Congress would reflect the public good. The public virtue of the citizenry and their state legislators would then ensure that the states would cooperate. "The Articles contained no provision empowering Congress to use coercive authority against the states because, quite simply, it was difficult to believe they would willfully defy its decisions."

THEN REALITY

Then reality set in. Not only was the War of Independence a time "that tried men's souls," in Paine's memorable phrase; it also tested the faith that sound government could rest on public virtue. And faith in virtue failed.

Americans charged into war and limped home from it, miraculously victorious. To be sure, the war had shown the extraordinary qualities of some Americans. But it had also demonstrated that Americans could be extraordinarily selfish. "Out of a population of 2.5 million people, fewer than 1 percent were willing to join the regular army fighting for their country's independence." State after state refused, as they could under the Articles of Confederation, to supply clothing, food or money for the troops. So scarce were the resources that one of America's great generals, Nathanael Greene, complained, "A country overflowing with plenty [is] now suffering an army employed for the defense of everything dear and valuable to perish for lack of food." An enraged Colonel Ebenezer Huntington, who was to become a general and then a member of Congress from Connecticut, wrote to his brother, "I wish I could say I was not born in America . . . The insults which the army has met with from the country beggar all description."

No one expressed this deprivation more pointedly than Joseph Plumb Martin, Private in the Continental Army. Born in Massachusetts in 1760, he had entered the Connecticut State militia in 1776 at the age of fifteen and fought in the battles of Brooklyn and

White Plains. By the end of 1777, America's first national army, the Continental Army, established by the Continental Congress in 1775, was mustering, and Martin, done with his state militia service, enlisted. He would serve until the end of the war. At that time each state government provided for its own state's protection through a state militia. Once the War of Independence broke out, states in effect lent their militias to the national government, the Continental Congress, to fight the war, but under the term of service the states set for them. Throughout his enlistment Martin made notes that he would ultimately convert into an almost philosophical journal, published some fifty years later as *A Narrative of a Revolutionary Soldier: Some of the Adventures, Dangers, and Sufferings of Joseph Plumb Martin*. His remembrance of one Thanksgiving vividly captures the cynicism with which one revolutionary soldier viewed his national government.

> While we lay here, there was a Continental thanksgiving ordered by Congress . . . We had nothing to eat for two or three days previous, except what the trees of the fields and forests afforded us. But we must now have what Congress said—a sumptuous thanksgiving . . . Well—to add something extraordinary to our present stock of provisions, our country, ever mindful of its suffering army, opened her sympathizing heart so wide, upon this occasion, as to give us some thing to make the world stare. And what do you think it was, reader—Guess—You cannot guess—I will tell you: it gave each and every man half a gill of rice and a table spoon full of vinegar!! . . .
>
> The army was now not only starved but naked; the greatest part were not only shirtless and barefoot, but destitute of all other clothing, especially blankets. I procured a small piece of

raw cowhide and made myself a pair of moccasins, which kept my feet (while they lasted) from the frozen ground, although, as I well remember, the hard edges so galled my ankles, while on a march, that it was with much difficulty and pain that I could wear them afterwards . . . But hunger, nakedness and sore shins were not the only difficulties we had at that time to encounter; we had hard duty to perform and little or no strength to perform it with . . . However, there was no remedy—no alternative but this or dispersion;—but dispersion, I believe, was not thought of—at least, I did not think of it,—we had engaged in the defense of our injured country . . . and we were determined to persevere as long as such hardships were not altogether intolerable . . . we were now absolutely in danger of perishing . . . in the midst of a plentiful country.

The colonists won the war anyway. Certainly, the perseverance of Private Martin and his fellow soldiers was part of the reason. But so was the inattentive and uncoordinated British leadership and, of course, the intervention of the French, who trapped General Charles Cornwallis at Yorktown.

THE WEAKNESS OF AMERICA'S GOVERNMENT

The wartime deprivations had dramatized the weakness of a national government that rested on the belief that individual citizens and their states would be adequately motivated by public virtue to rally around national goals. Individual states effectively could either block or opt out of any decision of the Continental Congress. And they did. The newly independent states saw themselves more as small, jealously independent nations than as members of a large united one. The war's end in 1781 not only freed the states from England but freed them to pursue their competition with each other. Numerous and growing problems, contained beneath the surface initially by the spirit of 1776 and by the immediacy of the war, erupted. How to protect the frontier men and women, how to settle competing claims to the vast western lands, how to repay the growing revolutionary war debt, how to maintain American access to the Mississippi River. This latter issue almost caused the southern states to withdraw from the union, as it seemed the northern states were willing to cede use of the river to Spain. Additionally, the determination of states to maintain their own paper money and to impose state taxes on the products of other states denied the possibility of a national economy. And the freedom of each state to enter into agreements with foreign nations not only undermined the national economy but reintroduced competing foreign governments into American affairs and threatened America's security.

The weakness of the national government under the Articles of Confederation required urgent repair. The problem was magnified by the weakness of most of the state governments. The framers saw the state governments, tied as they were so tightly to the will of their majorities, as too weak to preserve liberty or order within their own borders or to resist actions that undermined stable society.

Of particular concern was legislation in almost every state that reduced the debt of its farmers and others small entrepreneurs. Legislation in some states even blocked the judicial enforcement of debt, overturned jury verdicts, canceled fines and usurped other judicial functions. The peace treaty with England (the Treaty of Paris) called for the repayment of prewar debts. But Virginia, the state with the largest debts to British merchants, closed its courts to British creditors.

All of this stirred great concern among the framers, who wondered whether they could actually create a coherent country capable of living up to commitments, making treaties with the outside world or even consistent rules for all its citizens. Most of the state governments were too weak and too tied to majority votes to resist the demands for watering down debt. For a country, failure to pay debts because a majority demanded it was a big problem.

But in one state, Massachusetts, the opposite happened. The state refused to resolve the problems of some of its farmers and small merchants, and a rebellion broke out. Its leader, Daniel Shays, was a veteran of the Continental Army. Most Americans today would not know the name Daniel Shays. But to the framers in 1787, he represented their worst fears. The rebellion that came to bear his name shattered any remaining belief that citizens could be called on to set aside their own needs and interests for a larger good. The nation could not be preserved without radical change.

Daniel Shays had been a farm laborer in western Massachusetts when fighting broke out at Lexington and Concord. He rushed to enlist and saw action at Bunker Hill in June of 1775. Articulate and brave, he quickly rose to sergeant, but then waited four long years for promotion to captain. That delay, frustrating as it was to Shays, was only a prelude to further delay in receiving his final pay, after he was mustered out in 1780. He came home to Hampshire County and like many of his fellow farmhands sunk deeper in debt and deeper into bitterness. He seemed to be reaping none of the rewards of the Revolution many of them had helped win.

By January of 1787, Captain Shays, who was thirty-nine years old, found himself at the head of a ragtag force of men who called themselves "regulators" to express their goal of "moderating government" to serve their needs. For some of these men, these needs were real and immediate. A postwar recession and British restrictions on trade with the British West Indies had set off a chain reaction of attempted debt collections by English manufacturers against Massachusetts importers, then by those importers against inland retailers and those retailers against western farmers. The creditors wanted hard money (gold, silver or copper), which was legally required, rather than paper money, produce or property, which, in better times, they had commonly accepted.

The regulators' first response had been to petition the state government for relief from their debt through enactment of legislation requiring debt collectors to take paper money. But their request was rebuffed by the state legislature, which then adjourned. Enraged, the regulators forcefully blocked the operation of a number of courts, which were foreclosing on mortgages, and intimidated store owners throughout western Massachusetts.

The state of Massachusetts attempted to secure help in suppressing the rebellion from the Continental Congress, but in a familiar story most of the other states refused to commit resources. So a state militia under the command of General Benjamin Lincoln was sent west to crush Shays's Rebellion. The regulators had planned to capture the federal arsenal in Springfield, Massachusetts, and use the vast quantity of muskets, powder, shot, and shells to resist General Lincoln's expedition. But a militia force beat them to the armory. The fighting continued for more than a month, before finally the rebellion was crushed.

Shays's Rebellion terrified the framers. James Madison wondered if the outcome for Massachusetts would have been more dire if the rebels had had a stronger leader than Captain Shays. "Who can determine what might have been the issue of her late convulsions, if the malcontents had been headed by a Caesar or by a Cromwell? Who can predict what effect a despotism established in Massachusetts would have upon the liberties of New Hampshire or Rhode Island or Connecticut or New York?" So threatening did the rebellion seem that George Washington wrote to James Monroe declaring that the British seemed correct in their prediction about postwar Americans: "Leave them to themselves, and their government will sure dissolve."

Action was needed. Nathaniel Gorham, a representative from Massachusetts to the Constitutional Congress, and later its president, is reported to have written to Prince Henry of Prussia inquiring if he would be interested in assuming "regal powers" over America. The prince declined.

George Washington had been wavering on whether to attend the grand, or federal, convention, later called the Constitutional Convention, that Virginia and other states had called for in Philadelphia. The "threat" to the new nation helped convince him to come out of his Mount Vernon retirement. The Continental Congress, which up to that moment had not yet fully warmed to the federal convention, acted quickly after Shays's Rebellion to endorse it.

To the framers in 1787, America was in chaos, disintegrating. The entire country was "groaning under the intolerable burden of . . . accumulated evils," noted John Quincy Adams in his commencement address at Harvard in 1787. The framers saw in America "mistrust, the breakdown of authority, the increase of debt, the depravity of manners, and the decline of virtue." These were, as they understood it, the very societal conditions that had historically destroyed efforts at self-government.

TOO GOOD AN OPINION OF HUMAN NATURE

Madison said that the framers had been "mistaken" to believe that the states would support the general government because "sound policy" would make them realize they should. The Articles of Confederation became a symbol for what in retrospect seems evident—a government built on a reliance on public virtue would fail. Indeed, to some Americans, the Revolution itself seemed to have failed.

The framers identified the problem as their misjudgment of what motivates people. "We have probably had too good an opinion of human nature in forming our confederation . . . We must take human nature as we find it. Perfection falls not to the share of mortals," Washington wrote to John Jay in 1786. By 1787, that "too good opinion" had been replaced by a more realistic one. Utopianism was destroyed by Shays's Rebellion and the general state of chaos throughout the fledgling nation. It fell to one of Washington's most trusted military aides, Alexander Hamilton, an immigrant from the Caribbean, to lay out the new vision of human nature as he, his commander and the other founders had experienced it since 1776.

Back in 1777, Hamilton, echoing Tom Paine, had favored a simple New York legislature, with one house, where the voice of the people could be represented without encumbrances. But the ensuing ten years sharpened his views of people and the kind of government needed to channel their drives. Many of his specific ideas about government, like an elected but life-tenured president, would be too authoritarian for the framers. But his foundational observation about human nature would crystalize the intellectual transformation that had taken Americans from a faith in public virtue in 1776 to something radically different, as Hamilton summarized it, in 1787: "Men love power . . . Give all the power to the many, they will oppress the few. Give all power to the few, they will oppress the many."

That men loved power and would use it to get their way was not a new observation about human nature. But Americans had thought they could be different. Now, after eleven years of painful experience, they knew they could not be. Public virtue had proved an insufficient guard against the power of self-interest.

Madison wrote that the "more fatal" cause of the new nation's crisis "lies among the people themselves." Similarly, Washington observed in a letter to John Jay, dated August 15, 1786, "Experience has taught us, that men will not adopt & carry into execution, measures the best calculated for their own good without the intervention of a coercive power." Americans did not conduct themselves according to a shared vision of the common good, but were motivated by their own self-interest, which they often viewed as the common good. "It is a just observation that people commonly *intend* the Public Good," wrote Hamilton. But, he concluded, "this often applies to their very errors." Or as Benjamin Franklin noted, "Most men indeed . . . think themselves in possession of all truth, and that whatever others differ from them it is so far error."

In the pursuit of their self-interest, Americans frequently joined similarly interested people. Factions, the framers called them, or groups "united and actuated by some common impulse of passion, or of an interest adverse to the rights of other citizens." And, as the framers viewed the American landscape in 1787, factions were at war. "So strong is this propensity of mankind to fall into mutual animosities, that where no substantial occasion presents itself, the most frivolous and fanciful distinctions have been sufficient to kindle their unfriendly passions, and excite their most violent conflicts." And these tendencies toward conflict were enhanced by ambitious leaders who "inflamed" their factions "with mutual animosity, and rendered them much more disposed to vex and oppress each other, than to co-operate for their common good."

The crisis was enormous. The very basis on which they had built their separation from England and their new democracy—that Americans set free would work together—had been wrong.

This conclusion raised a basic question for the framers. Where could they find the coercive power Washington said was needed without giving up the liberty from monarchy they had just won? Did the weakness of public virtue mean that a democratic republic was impossible? Some of their own supporters thought the answer to this question was yes. Richard Price, an English minister and political essayist (invited by Congress in 1778 to become an American citizen because of his support of independence), wrote that he had been "mortified" by accounts of "dissipation," "excessive jealousy" and "clashing interests" in America, which threatened "that the fairest experiment ever tried in human affairs will miscarry and that a revolution which had revived the hopes of good men and promised an opening to better times will become a discouragement to all future efforts in favor of liberty and prove only an opening to a new scene of human degeneracy and misery."

Many others shared this view. Nathaniel Gorham's letter to the prince of Prussia was one of several suggestions for restoring a monarch in America, a thought which horrified Washington. As Washington described in a letter, the national turmoil was feeding a call for tyranny. "What astonishing changes a few years are capable of producing! I am told that even respectable characters speak of a monarchical form of government without horror. From thinking proceeds speaking, thence to acting is often but a single step. But how irrevocable and tremendous!"

When we recall the courage of the revolutionary generation, we usually think of Private Martin's shivering through the winter at Valley Forge or Washington on that scow crossing the Delaware. Brave they surely were. But in many ways the greatest act of courage in the entire revolutionary saga was this moment eleven years later.

Faced with the collapse of the very idea on which they had built their new nation, the framers refused to give up. They had already fought too hard and sacrificed too much. They refused to accept that Americans could not govern themselves. "It is evident," wrote James Madison, "that no other form" of government other than a republic "would be reconcilable with the genius of the people of America; with the fundamental principles of the Revolution; or with that honorable determination, which animates every votary of freedom." James Wilson of Pennsylvania said, "The citizens of the United States, however different in some other respects, are well known to agree in one strongly-marked feature of their character—a warm and keen sense of freedom and independence."

But if they were to go forward, if they were to preserve the liberty they had fought for, they had to invent a new kind of government. "The American war is over," Dr. Benjamin Rush of Pennsylvania wrote in January of 1787 in his address to the people of the United States. "But this is far from being the case with the American revolution. On the contrary, nothing but the first act of the great drama is disclosed. It remains yet to establish and perfect our new forms of government; and to prepare the principles, morals, and manners of our citizens, for these forms of government, after they are established and brought to perfection."

They needed a new government based not on the romantic ideal of public virtue but on recognizing people as they really are. They needed a government that guaranteed liberty, while protecting people from the excesses of liberty. They needed a government that would channel self-interests, rather than counting on people to set them aside. They needed, Madison said, "a republican remedy for the diseases most incident to republican government."

And so they gathered in Philadelphia and invented one.

2

APPROACHING SO NEAR TO
PERFECTION AS IT DOES

> *Is it not time to awake from the deceitful dream of a*
> *golden age and to adopt as a practical maxim for the di-*
> *rection of our political conduct that we, as well as the*
> *other inhabitants of the globe, are yet remote from the*
> *happy empire of perfect wisdom and perfect virtue?*
> —ALEXANDER HAMILTON, 1787

A N E S S A Y O N Thomas Jefferson once defined *genius* as the capacity to see ten things where the man of talent sees two or three, plus the ability to then apply those perceptions to the material of his art. Rarely has there been a man who better illustrates this definition of genius than Jefferson's friend James Madison. Madison's grasp of the political world of 1787 was unsurpassed. He then applied those perceptions to a work that was to the art of government as brilliant and inventive in its age as Einstein's rethinking of time and space, and Picasso's reshaping of form and image, were in theirs. Madison wrote the blueprint for American democracy. Then he did even more. He carefully guided his plan through the convention in Philadelphia. To succeed, the delegates, Madison included, had to compromise on many specific points. By modifying his own proposals, even if sometimes grudgingly, Madison became both the father of the Constitution and the midwife of the most important principle underlying the nation's success: His new political structure only worked if its participants were willing to compromise. The spirit of America, as drafted by James Madison and revised by the delegates at Philadelphia, was a spirit of compromise.

The story of the convention at Philadelphia has been told many times. Each generation finds its own meaning. The framers meant to give the states great power, or no power at all, went the arguments before the Civil War. The framers were heavily motivated by mercantile interests, or barely motivated by them at all, raged the debate as the frontier closed and the nation's industrial might rolled.

We touch on the story again to recall what we think is valuable and relevant to our age: this spirit of compromise at the moment of creation. For it isn't just what they wrote that mattered, as important as the document has become to us. It is how they worked and argued and revised and, amazingly, produced a Constitution "approaching so near to perfection," in Benjamin Franklin's subtle description, despite the imperfections, narrow interests, selfish motives, prejudices and outright errors of each individual delegate. Out of many voices came one nation. It is that spirit we need to recover.

THE RIGHT MAN AT THE RIGHT MOMENT

James Madison was the right man at the right moment. It is a very lucky thing for America that he was there on May 25, 1787, when delegates convened in Philadelphia for the first session of what is now known to us as the Constitutional Convention. America was in crisis. Americans had won their liberty from Great Britain, but they had failed to establish a successful self-governing country. Their utopian notion in 1776—that all they needed was simple government, free of England and relying on the public virtue of the people—had failed.

Instead, the country was riven by factions, each intending to impose its interests on others. Self-interest, not public virtue, dominated public conduct. The pursuit of happiness had become the pursuit of individual and group interests and not those of the community or nation. Neither the national government nor the state governments were strong enough to create order out of the chaos these competing groups created.

The fear that their country was failing produced in the framers a new attitude that sounded very much like humility. Take, for example, Alexander Hamilton, who has rarely been thought of as a humble man. "Is it now time to awake from the deceitful dream of a golden age," Hamilton said of the failed promise of simple government resting on faith in public virtue, "and to adopt as a practical maxim for the direction of our political conduct that we, as well as the other inhabitants of the globe, are yet remote from the happy empire of perfect wisdom and perfect virtue?" Many delegates to the convention held this new attitude. They all believed Americans had been given exceptional opportunity. Perhaps they even had exceptional ambitions for themselves and their new nation. But, the framers had come to realize, as individuals in a political or civic setting, Americans were not actually exceptional in their ability to rise above their own interests. Accepting this reality, that we are just as flawed and self-motivated as "the other inhabitants of the globe," made all sorts of compromises and agreements possible.

In fact, the convention itself would become a first test of their new thinking about democracy. Almost all the delegates agreed on the need for a stronger national government. But what kind of government? On this question they had, Franklin wrote, "ideas so different, . . . prejudices so strong and so various, and . . . particular interests, independent of the general." Could men with such varied ideas, prejudices and interests come together, fight for their views, and then accept the outcome of the process?

In answering yes to this question, the framers created a new definition of *public virtue*. Before, *public virtue* had meant setting aside a self-interest to accept a general public interest. Now it assumed that Americans would pursue their self-interest within the halls of government. But if their voices were meaningfully heard, they would respect for the greater good decisions even when adverse to their views. Participation, compromise and respect for process would become the new measures of public good. Good decisions, wrote James Wilson, would require "mutual concessions and sacrifices . . . mutual forbearance and conciliation."

The delegates viewed the convention as the last chance to rescue the American experiment. Its task, wrote Madison, was "to secure the public good and private rights against the danger" of faction and self interest, "and at the same time to preserve the spirit and the form of popular government." If the delegates failed, Franklin wrote to Jefferson, "it must do harm as it will show that we have not wisdom enough among us to govern ourselves; and will strengthen the opinion of some political writers that popular government cannot long support themselves." "Wise measures," wrote

Washington, were required, "to avert the consequences [tyranny] we have but too much reason to apprehend."

Wise measures would require wise men able and willing to create a new model of government that would answer two fundamental questions: How could liberty be maintained without the high level of public virtue and simple government they had earlier agreed were necessary? How could a democracy protect individual liberty if a majority wanted to impinge on it?

Madison's answer was a new system that limited what had been previously considered the hallmark of democracy, the will of the majority. The conduct of state governments since the Revolution had convinced them that their commitment to simple government had been, well, simplistic. The will of the majority, the framers now understood, did not automatically produce the common good. Recent history had proven to them that a government too susceptible to the majority voice of its citizens could not protect liberty. "There is no maxim in my opinion which is more liable to be misapplied, and which therefore more needs elucidation than the current one that the interest of the majority is the political standard of right and wrong," Madison wrote to James Monroe. For the interest of the majority, Madison added, was the "immediate augmentation of property and wealth," and its realization would compel "the majority in every community to despoil and enslave the minority of individuals; and in a federal community to make a similar sacrifice of the minority of component States."

The fear in 1787 was not the potential for despotism by the few, although that remained a concern, but, paradoxically, despotism by the many and particularly by majorities. "It is much more to be dreaded that the few will be unnecessarily sacrificed to the many."

Most Americans would be surprised to be told that at the heart of the invention of our country was a rejection of pure majority rule as the basis for democracy. We so often turn to the majority to answer our questions, from school yard votes on what games to play to Supreme Court decision making. We are brought up on the phrase *majority rules*. But this is not how our government works or was intended to by Madison and the framers. Its purpose is to stop or at least slow actions that were supported by merely a majority. It does so by dividing political power among the various branches of government and allowing one to check the other in ways we will later describe.

In 1880, Lincoln Steffens, a radical, muckraking journalist, was so shocked to discover what he viewed as the antidemocratic motives of the framers that he promised to write a "true history of the making of the American Constitution." He never did, which is too bad. It would have certainly been an interesting book. You can disagree with the framers, as Steffens did, or you can feel they brilliantly solved the crisis of their age. But either way it is not possible to understand our present government without understanding Madison's and the other framers' thinking at the convention 220 years ago.

The Convention's Conductor

James Madison, a delegate from Virginia, took one of the best seats in the house for the convention. "I chose a seat in front of the presiding member, with other members on my right and left hands. In this favorable position for hearing all that passed, I noted in terms legible and in abbreviations and marks intelligible to myself what was read from the Chair or spoken by the members." This was May 25, 1787, the first meeting day of the Constitutional Convention. As the delegates drifted into Philadelphia, a quorum of seven states had arrived. (Eventually there would be twelve. Rhode Island never made it.) Their first order of business was the election of General Washington as president of the convention, which Madison recorded in his famous notebook, later published as *Debates of the Convention*.

Madison was more than the convention's "semiofficial" reporter. He was its conductor and its intellectual engine, a combination of "the profound politician, with the Scholar . . . the best informed man of any point in debate." Those who knew him were not surprised. He had always been diligent and studious. The oldest of ten children, and the first son of a successful Virginia planter, Madison had been the right age to fight in the Revolution. But his health, which he complained about all through his long and largely healthy life, had not been strong enough. Instead he devoted his energies to the politics of the young country, both in Virginia and as the youngest member of the Continental Congress. He was thirty-six years old at the time of the convention. Young perhaps for the inventor of a nation, but many of the delegates were not much older.

At the Constitutional Convention, he took on the arduous reporting role, no doubt, to better remember the arguments of his colleagues in preparation of his own arguments and to provide for American history firsthand the "truth and lessons" of the convention.

Since at least the fall of 1786, Madison had been thinking deeply about the problems that confronted the governance of the new country. As he watched its decline into chaos, he studied the experience of historical and more current nations to determine the causes that had helped or destroyed them. Madison, like many of the other framers, was a "modern" thinker, one who believed that history should inform decision making. "Where we see the same faults followed regularly by the same misfortunes, we may reasonably think that if we could have known the first we might have avoided the others." Or as Washington had earlier written, "The treasures of knowledge . . . are laid open for our use, and their collected wisdom may be happily applied in the establishment of our forms of government."

From this study, Madison reached a conclusion about the causes of the American crisis. Public virtue, he concluded, simply could not moderate self-interest, particularly that of majority factions, at least when it came to the governmental tasks of regulating peoples' conduct and redistributing their wealth.

That was the conundrum Madison set himself to solve. The people had won the right to govern themselves, yet the people were not "virtuous" enough to do so.

To address this problem, Madison drafted a plan for a new government. Both as proposed and as ultimately adopted, it was radical. First, it proposed a national government with coercive powers over the states and not simply a revision of the Articles of Confederation. This caused concern for even some supporters of a strong national government. For example, the ardent nationalist and Revolutionary War hero Charles Cotesworth Pinckney of South Carolina on May 30 "expressed a doubt whether the acts of Congresss recommending the Convention, or the Commissions of the deputies to it, could authorize a discussion of a System founded on different principles from the [Articles of Confederation]."

The plan completely reversed the earlier notion, underlying the Articles of Confederation, that liberty could only be protected by public virtue and simple government. In the place of public virtue, Madison's republican principle substituted a complex form

of government built around new ideas of representation and separation of power.

Its "pivot," as he described it, would be a new notion of how
people were represented in the government. Unlike in England,
where only the House of Commons was elected, in America all
governmental power—legislative, executive, and judicial—was to
be vested in the people. As Madison's ally Pennsylvania delegate
James Wilson would write, "the executive and judicial powers are
now drawn from the same source, are now animated by the same
principles . . . with the legislative authority: they who execute, and
they who administer the laws, are so much the servants, and therefore as much the friends of the people, as those who make them."
Then, after placing all of the power of government in the hands of
the people's representatives, that power was to be divided among the
different branches of government to avoid the accumulation of too
much power in any one branch.

The federal government would have the power to conduct foreign affairs, protect the nation and regulate trade among the states
and with other nations. The states would have general legislative
power to regulate the conduct of their citizens.

The federal power to make laws or to declare war would belong
to a two-house Congress. The executive would enforce the laws
and conduct any war. And the judiciary would resolve disputes
over the application or meaning of law.

Each branch would have power to check the actions of the others to keep any one branch of government from exceeding its authority. "The separation of this governmental power, rather than
simply the participation of the people in a part of the government,
became the best defense of liberty." In short, a reliance on public
virtue was to be replaced by a "policy of supplying by opposite and

rival interests, the defect of better motive." Or more bluntly put, "ambition must be made to counteract ambition."

Madison applied this new approach aggressively. For example, legislative power, the supreme power of government, was to be further subdivided between the Senate and House of Representatives, whose members would, Madison believed, have different interests based on the difference in size between Senate and House districts and terms and qualifications for office. This proposal was not intended by Madison as a means for giving small states a larger voice in the new government, as is commonly thought. That idea, as we shall see, would emerge later as a crucial compromise that probably saved the convention. Madison's purpose behind the two-house legislature was for the Senate to cool the passions of the House, Washington reportedly told Jefferson years later. For a bill to become law, it would have to receive a majority vote in each house of Congress (and then be subject to the executive's veto), creating many opportunities to stop legislation and many hurdles to its enactment. According to Madison: "In republican government the legislative authority, necessarily, predominates. The remedy for this inconvenience is to divide the legislature into different branches; and to render them by different modes of elections, and different principles of action, as little connected with each other, as the nature of their common functions and their common dependence on the society, will admit."

To Lincoln Steffens (and to others more recently, as we shall see in chapter 8), this complicated system, requiring more than a simple majority to get action, was undemocratic. But to Madison, it was the solution to their fundamental problem: how to create a working government, one that both protected the rights of individuals and minorities while possessing enough authority to take effective action across a territory larger than most of the nations of the old world.

Just a few years before the American Revolution, the great French philosopher Montesquieu, whose writings on democracy and separation of power were very important to Madison and the other framers, had argued that, at best, a democracy could only work in a "small territory" because "in a large republic the public good is sacrificed to a thousand views." Conversely, he wrote, "in a small one, the interest of the public is easier perceived, better understood, and more within the reach of every citizen; abuses have a lesser extent, and of course are less protected." The wisdom of the age, as reflected by Montesquieu, was that size was the enemy of orderly democracy, making it harder for citizens to agree on the public good. Everything about the chaos in America between 1776 and 1787 seemed to prove him right.

But if democracy required a small territory, America was hardly an ideal vineyard in which to grow it. For America was expanding rapidly in both size and population. Between 1770 and 1790, the population had doubled from two to four million, and settlement was expanding from the Atlantic seaboard toward the Mississippi River. The incipient nation was growing so fast that the great economist Adam Smith, from his perch in Scotland, predicted it would eclipse the mother country in wealth within a hundred years.

Madison's new vision of democracy turned that growth from an obstacle to democracy into an asset, indeed, into a virtue. Under his plan for a new government, the presence of a "thousand views" meant more opportunity for different views to be heard and less opportunity for a single view to dominate the others. Indeed, this approach introduced what became a basic thread in the story of the nation. Growth was good. Integrating new citizens was, ultimately, positive (although often complicated and painful).

"In the extended Republic of the United States, and among the great variety of interests, parties and sects which it embraces, a coalition of a Majority of the whole society could seldom take place on any other principles than those of justice and the general good." Madison was quite a precise man. His choice of words was interesting. Not just a majority of the whole society, but a coalition of a majority. Two separately elected legislative bodies and a separately chosen executive all had to concur.

For Montesquieu, the ideal democracy, indeed, the only possible democracy, was a small one such as the city-state of Athens where everyone had supposedly similar interests and could work out their problems together. Madison saw a way to create democracy on a continental scale through representation that forced coalitions of a majority.

At least, that was his theory.

But, as Madison knew, many theories of government had ended up on the dust heap of history. He knew that he would have to orchestrate its enactment. He understood what a challenge this was going to be. He told Washington that he knew his proposal was radical: "Temporising applications will dishonor the Councils which propose them, and may foment the internal malignity of the disease, at the same time that they produce an ostensible palliation of it. Radical attempts, although unsuccessful, will at least justify the authors of them."

Madison would leave nothing to chance. By the eve of the convention he knew that many of the delegates shared the broad view that a stronger central government was needed. But the success of the convention depended not only on a shared vision of the broad outlines of a new, stronger central government but on its details. Here the going would be rough, for as Washington noted, the states of America were "different from each other in their manners, circumstances and prejudices." "On the need for change . . . the delegates were like-minded men. But on what kind of change—there the temple of accord became the Tower of Babel."

Madison, a master political craftsman, understood the importance of creating an agenda upon which the convention would focus. He had arrived early in Philadelphia, staying as he always did at the House-Trist lodgings at Fifth and Market just down the block from the Pennsylvania state house, where the convention would be held. He wanted time to take the political temperature of the delegates as they arrived and to informally meet and talk with as many as possible.

He seemed particularly interested in the Pennsylvania Federalists: Robert Morris, James Wilson, Benjamin Franklin, and Gouverneur Morris.

Madison also wanted time to sell his friend Governor Edmund Randolph of Virginia on his plan. He could not succeed without the support of his own state, Virginia, whose delegation also included his ally George Washington and George Mason (who would later oppose the Constitution). But Randolph was the key. "It was axiomatic with Madison that Virginia would go no farther into federalism than Randolph would but how far he would go sometimes depended more on Madison than on himself." Travel was slow in those days, and the delegations took time to arrive. Madison used that time to full effect. The Virginia delegation met daily to discuss Madison's proposals.

The fruits of Madison's politicking became clear on the convention's first day of real business, Tuesday, May 29, 1787. Madison himself, from his seat near George Washington, took notes as his plan was presented by the governor of Virginia, ensuring that ever-more the young Madison's ideas would be known to history as the Virginia Plan.

> Mr. Randolph opened the main business . . . [t]he character of such a governme[nt] ought to secure 1. against foreign invasion: 2. against dissentions between members of the Union, or sedi-tions in particular states: 3. to procure to the several States vari-ous blessings, of which an isolated situation was incapable: 4. to be able to defend itself against encroachment: & 5. to be para-mount to the state constitutions . . . [h]e then proceeded to the remedy; the basis of which he said, must be the republican principle.

IN CONVENTION—SETTING THE AGENDA

In politics, as in so much of life, timing is crucial. So it was with the presentation of Madison's Virginia Plan for a new government. Madison, the Virginia delegation and other allies were aware that the plan's radical features would cause upset, and that the other del-egates would need time to see its wisdom. They would go first, set the agenda, to accomplish this end. Randolph, expressing "his re-gret" that he should be the one to "open the great subject of their mission" rather than others of "longer standing in life and political experience," claimed the right to open on the basis of Virginia's origination of the convention.

It took fully two weeks for the more conservative opposition forces to organize themselves. During that time, the only agenda item was the Virginia Plan. It was not until June 15 that William Paterson of New Jersey offered a far less radical formula. Supported by the small states of Connecticut and Delaware and the strongly Anti-Federalist delegates from New York, it proposed only to remedy the narrow failures of the Articles of Confederation: giving Congress power to raise revenues through certain taxes, to regulate trade and commerce with other nations and between the states, and to enforce these laws.

But the comforting modesty of the New Jersey proposal was too late. According to Max Farrand, the great historian of the convention, "It is altogether possible, if the New Jersey plan had been presented to the convention at the same time as the Virginia plan, that is on May 29th, and if without discussion a choice had then been made between the two, that the former would have been selected." History may seem inevitable when viewed backward. But it rarely looks that way at the time.

During the prior two weeks the delegates had discussed much of the Virginia Plan and had, broadly, become comfortable with its boldness, although they had already started tinkering with the details in telling ways, as we shall see (for example, shifting the selection of senators from the House of Representatives to state legislatures). On June 19, after several days of debating the New Jersey Plan, the delegates agreed with Madison's view that the New Jersey Plan "contained no remedy for [the] dreadful class of evils" which had brought America to the precipice of chaos, and rejected it 7–3 in favor of considering in detail the Virginia Plan. This vote cleared the way for the discussion of the new government.

The Virginia Plan, which, under Madison's guidance, Randolph had presented on May 29, with many small changes, but only a

few very substantial ones, became the Constitution of the United
States.

It is worth lingering for a time on those substantial changes, because their achievement illustrates the very philosophy and values
that Americans would call on throughout their history to maintain
the Republic and protect the Constitution. The power of Madison's proposed new government, although divided, was expansive.
In many ways, it is remarkable how easily the delegates embraced
the fundamentals of Madison's plan, given its sharp break from
anything they, or anyone else, had known. But there was fierce debate and dissension. And two things stand out. First, that in each
case a compromise was found. And these compromises, at least in
retrospect, reinforced Madison's larger theory of dividing power to
foster liberty, although Madison himself didn't necessarily see it
that way at the time.

The Sharpest Debates

The sharpest debates among the framers revolved around two
questions, both relating to the division of political power: Would
the states continue to have a meaningful independent role as a balance to federal power, and would the president be independent
enough to keep a check on the new Congress? The delegates
would answer yes to both of these questions, changing Madison's
Virginia Plan, before its ink was truly dry. But these changes would
not come easily. Madison and his allies would resist, exhibiting the
same fierce pursuit of self-interest their proposed government was
meant to modulate. But in the end they would compromise and
move on, exhibiting the conduct that their proposed government
demanded of its participants for progress. Madison's principles

would remain intact, but the details of the plan would change to accommodate the variety of interests that would be expressed by the delegates.

The debate over state power was the most difficult. Madison and many of the like-minded delegates were disgusted with the state legislatures. As a result, the Virginia Plan as Randolph presented it envisioned near total federal dominance over the states. Congress would be authorized to legislate on all national matters and even say no to all state laws that it, Congress, determined to be contrary to the proposed Constitution.

But the convention would not go that far. Over the weeks, the delegates rolled Madison's plan back and increased the power of the states, creating a dual sovereignty (federal and state) that is one of the distinctive features of American government.

First, the convention quickly killed the idea that the Congress could negate state laws. Next it decided that the powers of the federal government would be limited to those explicitly granted, such as the regulation of national and international commerce, foreign relations and the declaration and management of war.

But then there was the question of whether states would be equally represented in the Congress, regardless of their population, which is how the Continental Congress worked under the Articles of Confederation. The subject nearly destroyed the convention, and might have, had it not been for a former shopkeeper from the little state of Connecticut.

In Madison's plan, there were two houses in Congress, to keep an eye on each other, but in each house representatives would be in proportion to population.

The states with the biggest populations, however defined, would have the most representatives. On this subject there would be no easy resolution. Delegates from the smaller states—Connecticut, Delaware, New Jersey and Georgia, as well as New York and Maryland—were ferociously opposed to this proposition, wanting equal representation for each state in the new legislature. Their argument ironically mirrored Madison's claim that majority factions in the states were snuffing out the liberty of minorities.

Roger Sherman, a self-trained lawyer from Connecticut, made the point forcefully: "As the States would remain possessed of certain individual rights, each State ought to be able to protect itself: otherwise a few large States will rule the rest." This view was amplified by Gunning Bedford of Connecticut on June 30, after several votes on the topic revealed the large states' unwillingness to compromise on the issue. "If political Societies possess ambition, avarice, and all the other passions which render them formidable to each other, ought we not to view them in this light here? Will not the same motives operate in America as elsewhere? If any gentleman doubts it let him look at the votes. Have they not been dictated by interest, by ambition? Are not the large States evidently seeking to aggrandize themselves at the expense of the small?"

But neither Madison nor his allies acknowledged the parallels between their view of human conduct and their own immediate conduct. In fact, many shared Benjamin Franklin's confusion over "what advantage the greater States could propose to themselves by swallowing the smaller." Whatever the real substance behind the small states' fear of the larger ones, there was no question that it generated ferocious sentiments and almost imploded the convention until a compromise was struck.

Roger Sherman had the solution. It was June 11, 1787, and the delegates were in their second week of debating the Virginia Plan. Sherman, sixty-six, had been a shoemaker, a store owner, a surveyor, a Connecticut official in various branches and levels of government, a member of both the First and Second Continental Congress and a signer of the Declaration of Independence. He would also sign the Constitution, lead the ratification battle in Connecticut and serve in the Congress as both a representative and a senator until his death in 1793.

Sherman had arrived late for the convention. Connecticut had waited until the last minute to answer the convention call, and Sherman, on the way, had stopped to shop for two days in New York. Arriving on May 30, he missed Randolph's presentation of the Virginia Plan. But on the very next day he appears to have expressed Connecticut's initial position that change, but only a little change, was necessary. As Madison noted: "Mr. Sherman . . . admitted that the Confederation had not given sufficient power to Congress and that additional powers were necessary . . . he seemed however not to be disposed to make too great inroads on the existing system."

Roger Sherman became a wonderful example of that great American tradition of the man from a small state finding a big voice. Throughout the debate Sherman spoke 138 times, third only to Madison and Gouverneur Morris. He would be a constant voice for small-state power, but also a committed nationalist looking for compromise in the service of that latter goal.

On this day, June 11, the delegates focused on the Virginia Plan's proposal for a "national Legislature." They had already decided for the first time, and without debate, that the national legislature would be divided into two houses and, with considerable debate, that members of the House of Representatives would be elected directly by the people. Sherman had opposed the latter decision, arguing instead that members of the lower house ought to be

chosen by state legislatures because the people are without "information and are constantly liable to be misled." And on June 7 the
delegates, on a motion by John Dickinson, had voted in favor of a
motion that senators be chosen by the state legislatures, rather than
by the House of Representatives.

Now the question was the proportionality of representation, or,
as Franklin put it, whether "the number of Representatives should
bear some proportion to the number of the Represented." The day
had started with the adoption of a motion that the lower house of
the new legislature be proportioned on the basis of a state's population. Connecticut, alone among the small states, had supported it.
Sherman then offered his idea as a compromise between the big
states, which wanted proportionality in both houses, and the small
states, which wanted each state to have equality of voting in both
houses. He moved "that a question be taken whether each State
shall have one vote in the 2d. branch [Senate]. Every thing he said
depended on this. The smaller states would never agree to the plan
on any other principle than an equality of suffrage in this branch."
This warning was not Sherman's alone. Only two days earlier Paterson had complained that proportional representation would
strike "at the existence of the lesser states," and had warned, according to Madison's notes, that "N. Jersey will never confederate
on the plan before the Committee. She would be swallowed up.
He [Paterson] had rather submit to a monarch, to a despot, than to
such a fate. He would not only oppose the plan here but on his return home do everything in his power to defeat it there."

But Madison and his allies were not listening. Their passion for
their own view on the issue (self-interest) and certainty of their
own position (self-regard) drove them first to defeat Sherman's
compromise motion and then to immediately pass a motion (6–5)

for proportionality in the upper house of the new legislature. This move ended any chance for a quick resolution of the issue. As Franklin observed on June 11, "It has given me a great pleasure to observe that till this point, the proportion of representation, came before us, our debates were carried on with great coolness & temper." But not on this issue.

Here the gloves were off. Anyone troubled by the supposedly negative nature of modern political discourse should read the convention notes for June 30, 1787. The usually very decorous Madison charged that Mr. Sherman's Connecticut had shirked its responsibilities during the Revolutionary War and afterward by refusing to comply with requisitions from the Continental Congress. To which Oliver Ellsworth of Connecticut responded by assuring the delegates that "the muster rolls will show that she had more troops in the field even than the State of Virginia." Clearly, serious discussion had come to a halt. Elbridge Gerry of Massachusetts "lamented" that the delegates, "instead of coming here like a band of brothers, belonging to the same family, . . . seemed to have brought with [them] the spirit of political negotiators." The stakes were high. The "fate of America," wrote Gouverneur Morris, "was suspended by a hair."

Nevertheless, the debate continued, for two reasons. First, substantively, the convention could not succeed without large majorities (consensus) on fundamental questions. Nothing but a state's own vote could make it subject to the new Constitution, and proportional representation was the type of issue that could result in either no Constitution or two nations. It fact, several times in the debate delegates on both sides of the issue suggested the option of more than one nation. But the vast majority of delegates agreed with Nathaniel Gorham of Massachusetts, who on June 29 declared "that a rupture of the Union would be an event unhappy for all," and with Madison's view that such a rupture could lead to "the same causes which have rendered the old world the Theatre of incessant wars and have banished liberty from the face of it." The delegates wanted a national government and shared the hope of Ellsworth "that some good plan of Government would be devised and adopted."

Second, procedurally, the June 11 votes were not final. The delegates would have to vote again. This round of votes had taken place in the Committee of the Whole House, which was simply the convention (that is, all the delegates) acting under far more informal rules than those that they had adopted for their formal processes. This informality allowed members to test ideas, proceed without rigid quorums and speak more frequently. But a vote of the Committee of the Whole House did not constitute a vote of the convention. The convention itself would have to reconsider every matter sent to it by the committee. In this case it meant that there would have to be another vote on the makeup of the Senate, hopefully after deliberation had cooled passions.

And that is exactly what happened, although it took until deep into summer.

After the delegates had spent weeks considering other provisions of the Virginia Plan, they returned to the question of proportional representation. Now the two June 11 votes of the Committee of the Whole House were before the convention. The first, proportional representation in the House of Representatives, was adopted by a 6–4 vote, with one state, Maryland, divided and New Hampshire's delegates absent from the convention. Then on the second question, proportional representation in the Senate, Sherman's Connecticut colleague Ellsworth reoffered the compromise, moving that the rule of suffrage in the Senate be equal votes for each state. "We were partly national, partially federal. The proportional representation in the first branch was conformable to the national principle and would secure the large states against the small. An equality of voices was conformable to the federal principle and was necessary to secure the Small States against the large."

On July 2 the convention voted. From the 6–5 vote in June for proportional representation in the Senate, the delegates now shifted to a 5–5 vote for one state, one vote. The convention was deadlocked. "We are now at a full stop," and nobody thinks "that we should break up without doing something," Sherman observed. The convention responded by resorting to a time-honored legislative tradition. It sent the issue to committee, a committee composed of one member from each state "to take into consideration both branches of the legislature."

The committee reported to the convention on July 5 "that in the second Branch of the Legislature each State shall have an equal Vote." Perhaps as a sweetener to the larger states, the committee also recommended that revenue bills must start in the House of Representatives. On July 16, after much wrangling on other parts of the committee's report, which required again another committee to review, the convention voted in favor of what effectively was Sherman's original proposal, now called the Great Compromise, or the Connecticut Compromise.

The Great Compromise, which would save the convention, finally passed by only a 5–4 vote. Massachusetts divided. The five supporting states were Connecticut, Delaware, New Jersey, Maryland and North Carolina. Georgia, which had divided in the past, opposed the measure, even though it was among the smallest states. New York's delegates were absent. Two, Robert Yates and John

Lansing, who had always supported the small states because they wanted to limit federal power, were gone, leaving in protest over the direction in which the convention was heading. Hamilton would return. New Hampshire's delegates had still not arrived.

Many important big-state delegates took their defeat badly, at first. Randolph claimed that "the vote of this morning (involving an equality of suffrage in 2d. Branch) had embarrassed the business extremely." The session then adjourned to allow the larger states, in Randolph's words, to "take such measures . . . as might be necessary."

A PRIVATE MEETING BRINGS AGREEMENT

The next day, the seventeenth, Madison reported that delegates from the larger states, along with some fewer members of the smaller states, gathered informally before the actual meeting to once again discuss the proportional representation vote. Some of the larger states remained extremely upset, claiming that "no good government could or would be built on that foundation." But their time had passed. "Others," according to Madison, "seemed inclined to yield to the smaller States, and to concur in such an Act however imperfect and exceptionable, as might be agreed by the Convention as a body . . . It is probable that the result of this consultation satisfied the smaller States that they had nothing to apprehend from a Union of the larger, in any plan whatever against the equality of votes in the 2d. branch."

The message was simple. A solution viewed as perfect by every delegate was not possible. Either there would be compromise, or there would be no country. The topic had been fought over exhaustively. The big states had lost, and that decision should be respected.

In fact, it was. The subject was not discussed again through the end of the convention. Later, Madison, being the consummate politician, embraced the decision he had fought fiercely against. Division of power between state and federal governments, he said, was "double security" for "the rights of the people."

With the resolution of the upper-house question, the convention was able to resume deliberation on the remaining resolutions of the Virginia Plan. Compared to the battle over the upper house, the rest of the convention must have seemed quite calm. But there was a continuing argument that shed light on the nature of the system they were building, and which resulted in another memorable compromise that we live with to this day. This debate was on how to elect the chief executive.

"This subject," according to James Wilson of Pennsylvania, was "the most difficult of all on which we have had to decide." Underlying this struggle was a widely shared view that a critical role for the new executive was to check the legislature. "One great object of the Executive is to controul the Legislature," proclaimed Gouverneur Morris of Pennsylvania on July 19. Most of the delegates were in accord. Legislative tyranny was as great or greater a threat to liberty as was executive tyranny. For most of them, this was the lesson drawn from the years since independence. Madison, like many others, foresaw the reintroduction of monarchy as a real possibility if the federal legislature became, as he described on July 17, "omnipotent" like state legislatures (which, for the most part, would all provide for strong executives in ensuing years). "If no effectual check be devised for restraining the instability and encroachments of the latter [the legislature], a revolution of some kind or other would be inevitable." Some delegates may have actually supported such a restoration. James McHenry of Maryland reported that on

August 6 he witnessed his Maryland colleague John Mercer create a list of delegates "with for and against marked opposite most of them." McHenry questioned Mercer about the list, and Mercer told him "laughingly that it was no question but that those marked with a 'for' were for a king." Was he joking? The historian Max Farrand posits that with so many problems attending the election of the president, some of the delegates "may have been circulating rumors of establishing a monarch in order to try out public opinion."

Despite Madison's desire to keep restraints on the legislature, under the Virginia Plan the executive was to be elected by the legislature. The legislature's power over the executive would then be limited by limiting the executive to one term. "If he ought to be independent," Randolph argued on July 19, "he should not be left under a temptation to court a re-appointment. If he should be re-appointable by the Legislature, he will be no check on it."

But why did Madison, that savvy thinker and operative, propose this dependence in the first place? Why grant to the new legislature the power to elect the executive if the executive was needed to check the legislature? The answer was straightforward. Madison and his supporters of the plan doubted the capacity of the public to make such an important choice directly. "The sense of the Nation would be better expressed by the Legislature, than by the people at large," who "will never be sufficiently informed of characters," Sherman proclaimed on July 17. "It would be as unnatural to refer the choice of a proper character for chief Magistrate to the people," George Mason argued, "as it would, to refer a trial of colours to a blind man."

But many delegates were more forward looking, more democratic if you like. Gouverneur Morris thought the legislative election of the executive would be "the work of intrigue, of cabal and of faction." And limiting the executives to one term was no solution, said Rufus King of Massachusetts on July 19, because "he who has proved himself to be the most fit for an Office, ought not to be excluded by the constitution for holding it." Perhaps ironically given the widely shared skeptical view of human nature, many delegates agreed with King's support for an executive elected directly or indirectly by the people. The people, according to Gouverneur Morris, "will never fail to prefer some man of distinguished character, or services; some man, if he might so speak, of continental reputation."

Back and forth they went on this topic from July 17 onward. Numerous ideas were explored: election by the national legislature, by state legislatures, by governors, by electors, by the people directly and, ultimately, by combinations of those. "In every Stage of the Question relative to the Executive, the difficulty of the subject and the diversity of the opinions concerning it have appeared. Nor have any of the modes of constituting that department been satisfactory," reported Mason on July 26.

Finally, in late August, this matter was taken up by the Committee of Eleven, whose job it was to report on things "postponed" or "not acted upon." That committee, comprising one delegate from each state present (New York's delegates were still absent, and Rhode Island was not in attendance), included important delegates on various sides of the issue, such as Madison, Sherman, Morris, Dickinson and King. On September 4, these delegates made a surprising proposal that would become the basis of the convention's final compromise. Each state was to appoint electors equal in number to their number of senators and representatives. The electors were to meet in their own state and select their nominees. Thus, from a summer-long debate over how to pick a president, the electoral college was born.

When asked by Randolph and Pinkney to explain the reasons for changing the mode of electing the executive, Gouverneur Morris, a member of the Committe of Eleven, sent a list. The first was "the danger of intrigue & faction if the appointment should be made by the Legislature," Morris told them. Another was that many delegates "were anxious" about "an immediate choice by the people." A third was "the indispensable necessity of making the Executive independent of the legislature."

If a camel is a horse designed by committee, the electoral college is the camel of American government. However anachronistic it may seem to us today, the electoral college still serves one role: It is like a bronze monument to the spirit of compromise that suffused the Constitutional Convention of 1787. This proposal was clearly an attempt to draw something from each of the many proposals the convention had been considering in order to arrive at not necessarily the best plan, but the best achievable plan.

Indeed, that notion of the best achievable plan became a kind of informal motto for the convention. On September 17, after numerous sessions, a multitude of proposals and many difficult compromises over hard, substantive issues, the convention agreed to a new Constitution. It was unanimously adopted by the twelve states. Not every delegate agreed, but a majority of every delegation did. Only Hamilton, who had returned, was present for New York, so his vote alone put New York into the yes column. Neither Randolph of Virginia, who introduced the Virginia Plan, nor his colleague Mason were willing to support the final product, although

Randolph would come around and support its approval at the Virginia ratification convention.

Madison recorded the final day as he had virtually every day.

Monday Sepr. 17. 1787. In Convention
The engrossed Constitution being read,
Doctor Franklin rose with a speech in his hand, which he had reduced to writing for his own conveniency, and which Mr. Wilson read.

In 1787, Benjamin Franklin was eighty-one, the convention's oldest delegate and probably the country's most famous person. He was now too frail and ill (with gout and stones) to transport himself to the state house or to speak before the convention, so he was carried there in a sedan chair by four prisoners from the local jail and his speeches were read by his fellow Pennsylvania delegate, the influential James Wilson, like Franklin a signer of the Declaration of Independence. Wilson read Franklin's memorable words.

I confess that there are several parts of this constitution which I do not at present approve, but I am not sure I shall never approve them: For having lived long, I have experienced many instances of being obliged by better information or fuller consideration, to change opinions even on important subjects . . .

In these sentiments, Sir, I agree to this Constitution with all its faults, if they are such; because I think a general Government necessary for us . . . I doubt too whether any other Convention we can obtain may be able to make a better Constitution. For when you assemble a number of men to have the advantage of their joint wisdom, you inevitably assemble with those men all their prejudices, their passions, their errors of opinion, their local interests, and their selfish views. From such an Assembly can a perfect production be expected? It therefore astonishes me, Sir, to find this system approaching so near to perfection as it does.

Franklin's view was as close as we have to a perfect summary of the spirit of the moment among many of the framers. Washington, for example, wrote to the Marquis de Lafayette, "It appears to me, then, little short of a miracle, that the Delegates from so many different States (which States you know are also different from each other in their manners, circumstances and prejudices) should unite in forming a system of national Government, so little liable to well founded objections."

Of course, the framers had an extraordinary amount about which to be proud. They had established an entirely new form of government based on new theories of government. They had, they thought, saved their country from chaos or tyranny.

They had developed a far more mature notion of public virtue, one which denied the possibility of—and, more important, eliminated the need for—perfection in human political behavior. In its place through representation and separation of powers, the framers substituted struggle among competing ideas, interests and egos. They no longer pretended they could fix human nature, so they harnessed it. Under this scheme the process would replace the product as the test of lawmaking legitimacy. "The founding fathers . . . saw conflict as the guarantee of freedom . . . The Constitution thus institutionalized conflict in the very heart of the American polity."

From the perch of history, the framers' judgment about their own efforts seems very wise. The historian Bernard Bailyn put it this way: "The Founders of the American nation were one of the most creative groups in modern history . . . Since we inherit and build on their achievements, we now know what the established world of the eighteenth century flatly denied, but which they [the framers] broke through convention to propose—that absolute power need not be indivisible but can be shared among states within a state and among branches of government, and that the sharing of power and balancing of forces can create not anarchy but freedom."

But in September of 1787, this was not the view shared by all Americans. And this was very significant, for not only did Americans have to live under the new Constitution, they had, as we discuss in the next chapter, to support its ratification in order for it to go into effect.

Some Americans believed that the convention had gone too far by not just repairing the Articles of Confederation. To this group of critics, the convention had exceeded its authority by creating a new, powerful, national government. Other groups of Americans simply thought the states should have more power than the Constitution provided, an argument that would continue until 1861 and beyond. Many also thought that the convention had not gone far enough in the protection of individual rights, that despite elected representatives, separation of power and checks and balances, the new governmental institutions and processes were still no guarantee against actions that trampled on individual liberties. "You are not to enquire how your trade may be increased nor how you are to become a great and powerful people, but how your liberties can be secured; for liberty ought to be the direct end of your government," thundered Patrick Henry of Virginia in opposition to ratification at the Virginia ratification convention in 1788.

Ratification was far from assured. In the end, it would require an extraordinary effort by many of the framers in the constitutional conventions of their own states. And in the spirit of the whole constitutional project, it would require yet one more compromise by Madison and his colleagues. That compromise produced something they originally thought unnecessary. It produced the first ten amendments to the Constitution, the Bill of Rights.

3

THAT POOR LITTLE THING—THE EXPRESSION *WE THE PEOPLE*

> *Is it not the glory of the people of America, that, whilst they have paid a decent regard to the opinions of former times and other nations, they have not suffered a blind veneration for antiquity.*
>
> —JAMES MADISON, 1787

PATRICK HENRY, THE revolutionary hero whose "give me liberty or give me death" speech fueled the war for independence, now opposed the new Constitution that had been drafted in Philadelphia. Three words explained his enmity. Those three words are the most resonant in American history. If schoolchildren learn anything about their Constitution these days, they learn these three words as a statement of the nation's unity and egalitarian democracy. Those words are *We the People*.

Yet to Patrick Henry, those words proved that the Constitution was the framers' grab for national political power that would, if ratified, recklessly endanger Americans' liberty. Why else, he thought, would they weaken the power of states, which to this point had so

well protected the freedom of their citizens? "Is this," Henry asked
of the new Constitution, "an association of a number of independent states, each of which retains its individual sovereignty?"
Clearly no, he answered. The proposed new government, Henry
roared, was "most clearly a consolidated government." To prove his
point, he cited the first three words of the new Constitution's pre-
amble, which were, he noted, "that poor little thing—the expression, We the People, instead of the states of America."

"We the People of the United States, in Order to form a more
perfect Union . . ."

To modern Americans, the phrase has lost its original radical-
ness. We don't see why it inflamed Patrick Henry. But indeed the
proposed new Constitution did inflame him and "a great number"
of other Americans, as Madison put it. They fought to kill the
Constitution and in the process spurred one of history's greatest
debates about democracy.

That debate accomplished a great deal beyond just the ratification of the Constitution itself. Supporters mounted a defense in
which they laid out a new philosophy of government. They acknowledged, ultimately, that Henry was right in his description of
the new government but wrong in his criticism. This new government was more centralized and covered a far larger territory than
any democracy had ever previously covered. That was true. But
supporters of the Constitution were able to convince Americans
that this document laid out a system that was not only possible but
necessary. To assuage the fears, raised by Henry and other opponents, that this centralized government would threaten liberty, the
framers also addressed what in retrospect can only be seen as their
biggest mistake at Philadelphia. And in making this adjustment
they offered the first tangible demonstration of the genius of the

new system. It could adapt to political need. It could channel lofty dreams and base politics into one process. And out of that process, driven by the individual interests and even selfish purposes of each citizen, could emerge something larger, even better, than the sum of what went in. In this case, what emerged to ensure ratification of the Constitution was its first ten amendments, what we now call the Bill of Rights.

THE PEOPLE WILL DECIDE

"You are called upon to deliberate upon a new Constitution for the United States of America," announced Alexander Hamilton to the people of New York and the new nation on October 27, 1787, in the first of a series of missives, known now as *The Federalist Papers*, that he, Madison and John Jay wrote to persuade the people to support the new Constitution. It was the people of the United States, not the state legislatures, who were to judge the value of the proposed new Constitution through "Conventions of Delegates chosen in each state by the People thereof."

The framers' decision to submit the Constitution to the people was groundbreaking, "the most audacious and altogether unqualified appeal to the notion of popular sovereignty and majority rule that had ever been made, even in America." No other nation had ever submitted its Constitution to its people. Nor had Americans submitted the Declaration of Independence or most of their state constitutions to popular vote (only Massachusetts and New Hampshire had sought popular approval). This decision for popular ratification was somewhat ironic given the framers' skeptical view of human nature and the divisions at the convention over whether the people could be trusted to directly select the president and members of Congress.

But, in fact, circumstance made them feel there was no real choice.

The ratification of the Constitution is a wonderful example of the way in which the framers merged their lofty visions with pragmatic politics. That is a lesson we need to keep drawing from their experience. Good ideas alone are no substitute for wise action rooted in reality. Looking back on their work, we have no way of knowing whether the framers' lofty vision grew out of their understanding of pragmatic politics, or whether their lofty vision was articulated just to rationalize their pragmatic politics. Perhaps it is a distinction without a difference, but it certainly applies to the decision to submit the Constitution to ratification by convention in each state. Madison declared that a constitution's legitimacy was rooted in the approval of its people. Perhaps these were lofty ideals speaking. Governor Edmund Randolph offered a more practical reality. There was little chance state legislatures would ratify a new Constitution that so reduced their power. They decided to go around the state legislatures and appeal directly to the people.

A DIVIDED PEOPLE

But in the fall of 1787, the people were divided. The convention had been conducted behind closed doors. The debates, which Madison recorded and we can now study, were unknown to Americans. (Madison's notes on the convention were published more than fifty years later.) The framers had carefully argued over every clause, in private, but had done virtually nothing to share their thinking or prepare other Americans for what they had done. They had invented a new form of democracy designed to allow the people to govern themselves. But they had not explained it to the people. This certainly would not be the last time in American politics when leaders faced a backlash when they left the people out of the process.

Most Americans favored a strengthening of the Articles of Confederation, which is what they thought the convention was doing. But they were far less certain about the proposed new government that actually emerged. This was not a mere reform but an extraordinary shift of political power from individual states to a new national government. While the framers saw this shift as the only means of protecting the liberty of Americans from the current chaos, many Americans were not convinced.

This produced an extraordinary ratification debate—a clash of ideas, to say nothing of occasional fists, egos, self-interests, agendas and visions, on a continental scale. It was one of the most vigorously contested electoral processes in the nation's history. "There were some fifteen hundred official delegates to the twelve state ratifying conventions, where every section of every clause and every phrase of the Constitution was raked over." And while the voting mandate was restricted throughout the country to free adult males who owned property, several states liberalized their property ownership requirements to allow more men to vote.

The opponents, the Anti-Federalists, understood that the proposed Constitution was favored by many of America's most trusted citizens. To defeat or amend it would require extraordinary exposition. For more than a year the words flowed relentlessly. "Judging from the newspapers," wrote Madison, "one would suppose that the adversaries were the most numerous and most in earnest." (Of course, many articles in support of the new Constitution were also published, the most famous being *The Federalist Papers.*)

One of the most articulate opponents, Samuel Bryan, entered the fray in Pennsylvania on October 5, 1787, and his numerous columns, under the name Centinel, were published in newspapers throughout the country. The new government, he wrote, was a means for America's elite (defined in various ways) to impose their views on the rest of America. Through this, America would lose its democratic character, and Americans their liberty. "The proposed plan of government . . . is a most daring attempt to establish a despotic aristocracy among freemen, that the world has ever witnessed." Despite the claims that the new government was of the people and for the people, it was too complex and, no matter where it was to be located (the federal District of Columbia was not created until 1790), too distant to allow for their participation, at a time well before cars, trains, planes, telegraphs, telephones and e-mails.

Beyond these broad thoughts, the Anti-Federalists had no unifying agenda. "They had no plan whatever," noted Madison. "They looked no farther than to put a negative on the Constitution and return home." Nor did they all have the same motives. The Federalist James Wilson caricatured an Anti-Federalist as a self-interested American "who either enjoys, or expects to enjoy, a place of profit under the present establishment." For some that was surely true. But for many their motivation was as well intentioned as the Federalists. In general, opposition to the proposed Constitution represented a profound fear of its then unique centralization of power, a depersonalizing distancing of government from its citizens and the potential for abuse from both. It is an argument that has recurred repeatedly through American history. Even today Americans debate between Paine's vision of simple government and Madison's complex system of checks and balances.

The goal for most opponents was to stop the proposed transfer of political power from the states to the new national government. They argued against the Constitution in general, as well as against many of its specific provisions. How could liberty be protected over such a large territory? Why was there no "bill of rights" to guard Americans from what the framers themselves had argued was the inevitable tyrannical nature of majorities? Why a single executive, and why make him commander in chief of the army and navy, too? Onward the objections rolled through the vice presidency, the possibility of a standing army, Congress's power to alter the state's power over congressional elections, the power of taxation, the small size of the House of Representatives (only sixty-five members for the entire nation of around three million people, not counting the half million or so slaves), the Senate's power to confirm executive appointees and the requirement that the Senate consent to treaties. Some wanted a new convention, and some wanted to amend the proposed Constitution in various substantive ways. Some wanted amendments before ratification. Others were willing to support ratification if the Federalists promised to support postratification amendments.

Dissenting delegates to Pennsylvania's ratification convention captured broadly most of the Anti-Federalists' concerns. "We dissent because it is the opinion of the most celebrated writers on government, and confirmed by uniform experience, that a very extensive territory cannot be governed on the principles of freedom, otherwise than by a confederation of republics" and because of "the omission of a Bill of Rights, ascertaining and fundamentally establishing those unalienable and personal rights of men, without the full, free, and secure enjoyment of which there can be no liberty, and over which it is not necessary for a good government to have the controul."

The odyssey of Patrick Henry from a supporter of a stronger national government to an opponent of the Constitution illustrates how events of the day influenced the views of many Americans on the question of ratification. Henry, the first and many-time governor of the State of Virginia, member of the Continental Congress and Virginia legislature, had, in early 1787, been chosen as a delegate to the Constitutional Convention but had refused his appointment. Although he had long favored a stronger national government, he was now in opposition. He "smelt a rat." That rat was, in his mind, a "cabal" of northern states intent on dominating the South and denying southerners their freedom to pursue their own self-interests.

The cabal for Henry had been exposed through a prospective treaty giving Spain control of the Mississippi, negotiated on behalf of the Continental Congress by John Jay of New York. As Madison worriedly wrote to Washington in December of 1786, "Mr. Henry, who has been hitherto the Champion of the federal cause, has become a cold advocate, and, in the event of actual sacrifice of the Mississippi by Congress, will unquestionably go over to the opposite side."

The problem was that Jay, America's minister of foreign affairs, had, in violation of his instructions, negotiated the treaty with Spain. In return for favorable trade terms, desired by east coast, mostly northern, merchants, the treaty agreed to close American access to the Mississippi River for at least twenty-five years. Virginia and the southern states were depending upon lands west of the Appalachian Mountains and navigation rights on the Mississippi River for their growth. The treaty would end any such efforts. Indeed the Jay affair had even shaken the indomitable nationalist Madison, who warned Jefferson that the treaty could justifiably lead to a dismemberment of the new country. In fact, James Monroe reported to Henry that such a split was the goal of certain northern legislators who were considering the formation of a northern confederation.

The treaty, in the end, was not approved, but Patrick Henry still changed sides. On October 19, he rebuffed even George Washington's plea for his support. "I have to lament that I cannot bring my mind to accord with the proposed Constitution." And later to the Virginia delegates he would say:

> Here is a resolution as radical as that which separated us from Great Britain. It is radical in this transition; our rights and privileges are endangered, and the sovereignty of the states will be relinquished . . . : It is said eight states have adopted this plan. [Henry was unaware that New Hampshire, the ninth state, had ratified it on June 21.] I declare that if twelve states and a half had adopted it, I would, with manly firmness, and in spite of an erring world, reject it. You are not to inquire how your trade may be increased, nor how you are to become a great and powerful people, but how your liberties can be secured; for liberty ought to be the direct end of your government.

THE PEOPLE IN CONVENTION

It was clear from the beginning that supporters of the new Constitution had a fight on their hands. But the strategy for winning that fight evolved in the test of ideas and wills that developed after the

Philadelphia convention sent the Constitution to the states for ratification on September 28, 1787.

The Pennsylvania legislature had been in session on September 28, and the very next day Pennsylvania became the first state to call a ratification convention. But like much in Pennsylvania politics, the path to this decision was not pretty. Pennsylvanians were deeply divided over a number of social, economic and religious issues, and much of this division had been etched more deeply by the fight over its constitution of 1776. That state constitution was the antithesis of this new federal Constitution. It was the model of simple government. A one house legislature, for example, and no independent executive. The opponents of that constitution, like James Wilson, the second most influential delegate to the Constitutional Convention, were the leaders of the fight to ratify the new federal Constitution. On September 29, the Anti-Federalist members of the Pennsylvania Assembly intentionally absented themselves from the state house to prevent a quorum on a vote to call the ratification convention. Their goal was to slow down consideration of the Constitution. A mob of Federalists found some of the absent members at their Philadelphia lodgings and dragged them to the Pennsylvania state house. There they were forced to sit until the assembly acted favorably on the convention call. After that show of force, the ratification debate settled into a more traditional clash of ideas.

James Wilson dominated the Pennsylvania convention. No one could have been more suited for leading the debate on ratification. Wilson, a Scottish immigrant, had arrived in America in 1765, moved to Philadelphia, where he was hired to serve as a tutor at the College of Philadelphia (after 1779, the University of Pennsylvania). Now he was one of America's most eminent lawyers, scholars and politicians. At the Constitutional Convention, many judged him near to Madison in his vision, mastery of history and political acuity. He was one of only six men to have signed both the Declaration of Independence and the new Constitution and one of a fewer number who had also been elected as a delegate to his state's ratification convention.

Again and again he rose at the ratification convention to explain the Constitution's virtues and defend against the multitude of defects the Anti-Federalists identified. Wilson's message was that we needed the new Constitution to grow, in every sense, strong as a new nation. Like most of the Federalists, at least early in the national debate, he argued against a bill of rights, finding it unnecessary, given the proposed new government's limited powers. Why, he asked, would there be, for example, a need for a provision protecting freedom of the press if Congress had not been given power to enact legislation affecting the press.

At the heart of Wilson's case for the Constitution was a proclamation of the new public virtue of compromise that had emerged from the convention debates. In October of 1787, he gained national attention by the publication throughout much of the country of his "State House Yard Speech," called by one historian "the single most influential and most frequently cited document in the entire ratification debate." Wilson echoed Madison, Washington and, particularly, his fellow Pennsylvanian Franklin as he said of the Constitution:

> When I reflect how widely men differ in their opinions, and that every man (and observation applies likewise to every State) has an equal pretension to assert his own, I am satisfied that anything nearer to perfection could not have been accomplished. If

there are errors, it should be remembered, that the seeds of ref-
ormation are sown in the work itself, and the concurrence of
two thirds of the Congress may at any time introduce alterations
and amendments. Regarding it then, in every point of view,
with a candid and disinterested mind, I am bold to assert, that it
is the best form of government which has been offered to the
world.

Wilson's speech reflected the initial strategy of the framers. This
was the government the country needed, not perfect but the best
that could be achieved. And it could be made better through
amendment if that turned out to be necessary. It quickly became
clear, however, that more was needed than the possibility of amendment. The Federalists' vague reassurance that the Constitution
could be amended would transform into a promise that it would
be, and fast.

On December 12, Pennsylvania, by a vote of 46–23, became the
second state to ratify the Constitution, following only Delaware,
which had unanimously ratified it on December 7. But the Pennsylvania Anti-Federalists did not concede. Nine states were needed to
ratify, and they knew that if they could stop the Constitution any-
where, particularly in New York or Virginia, they could keep it
from going into effect.

Wilson and the Federalists had won the ratification vote in
Pennsylvania, but they had not persuaded the Anti-Federalists in
Pennsylvania or elsewhere to a take a chance on the new government. Opponents remained livid over "that violence and outrage"
by which the Pennsylvania Assembly, controlled by Federalists, had
prematurely forced a vote in the legislature to convene the ratification convention, as well as the subsequent speed of the ratification

process. At a ratification celebration in Harrisburg in December of 1787, a mob of Anti-Federalists reportedly attacked Wilson. Elbridge Gerry of Massachusetts, signer of the Declaration of Independence, delegate to the Constitutional Convention and Anti-Federalist, warned the nation that Pennsylvania had "adopted the system, and seen some of its authors burnt in effigy—their town thrown into riot and confusion, and the minds of the people agitated by apprehension and discord." Those twenty-one Anti-Federalist delegates published their dissent in the *Pennsylvania Packet and Daily Advertiser* on December 18, 1787. This dissent would frame the terms for the debate that would continue elsewhere through the ratification process.

The framers realized the fight was not going well. They feared they were losing the debate and that ratification was in the balance. "The Public here continues to be much agitated by the proposed federal Constitution and to be attentive to little else," Madison wrote to Jefferson on February 19, 1788. In Massachusetts Oliver Ellsworth judged it "doubtful" that "the Constitution will be adopted at the first trial in the conventions of nine states."

Madison pleaded with Americans to set aside their fears and embrace the new plan: "Hearken not to the voice which petulantly tells you that the form of government recommended for your adoption is a novelty in the political world . . . Is it not the glory of the people of America, that, whilst they have paid a decent regard to the opinions of former times and other nations, they have not suffered a blind veneration for antiquity, for custom, or for names, to overrule the suggestions of their own good sense, the knowledge of their own situation, and the lessons of their own experience?"

But it was becoming clear that all the fine words about how this was the best possible government might not be enough to win the day. Supporters needed a new strategy. To win votes for ratification, they offered to support something they had originally thought was unnecessary: a bill of rights.

The Bill of Rights

In retrospect, it seems odd that the framers ignored a bill of rights, which in the minds of most Americans is the Constitution's most important protection of liberty. There seemed no principled or pragmatic reason for its exclusion. The idea of a bill of rights was entirely consistent with the American experience with Britain and the framers' skeptical view of human nature. It would have added another layer of protection against what most Americans thought was "the experience of all mankind . . . , the prevalence of a disposition to use power wantonly." In fact the proposed Constitution already contained protections for some of the most fundamental individual rights, namely protections against arbitrary imprisonment (habeas corpus), against legislative trial and imposition of penalty (bill of attainder), and against the enforcement of ex post facto criminal laws. Madison at one point in 1788 claimed that his "own opinion has always been in favor of a bill of rights," although it was an opinion not recorded at the convention.

In fact, the topic received little discussion at the Constitutional Convention, and then only late into its proceedings. Charles Pinckney first recommended the Committee on Detail consider freedom of press and several other rights on August 20, 1787, but this went nowhere. On September 12, Elbridge Gerry of Massachusetts urged a guarantee of trial by jury, which was unanimously defeated. Two days later a motion on press freedom was defeated.

It is not that the delegates opposed these rights, not even press freedom. No, something more interesting was at work here, and it illustrates why political debate and conflict are so important to producing the best outcomes for the country.

Even great ideas can stand scrutiny and usually can be improved. Moreover, the genius of an idea is not always the same as the comfort people feel with it. In this case, the fundamental reason for not including a bill of rights in the Constitution as it was sent out from Philadelphia was that Madison and his colleagues were really quite enamored of what they had invented. "I have not viewed it in an important light," Madison acknowledged to Jefferson about a bill of rights. Madison and his colleagues at Philadelphia had believed that the very point of their new design of government was that it did protect rights, in a more fundamental way than just listing them.

A bill of rights was superfluous at best, Madison argued. Enumerating those rights was, Madison said scornfully, creating mere "parchment barriers" that could be violated at any time by "overbearing majorities." The real protection was their new system of checks and balances, said Madison, and he explained why.

> Wherever the real power in a government lies, there is the danger of oppression. In our Governments the real power lies in the majority of the Community, and the invasion of private rights is *chiefly* to be apprehended, not from acts of Government contrary to the sense of its constituents, but from acts in which the Government is the mere instrument of the major number of the Constituents. This is a truth of great importance, but not yet sufficiently attended to . . . Wherever there is an interest and power to do wrong, wrong will generally be done, and not less readily by a powerful & interested party than by a powerful and interested prince.

The new Constitution did not need a bill of rights because its system of checks and balances protected the rights of individuals from that most dangerous oppressive force, the will of the majority.

The ratification debate forced the Federalists to reassess this position against a bill of rights. By the time of Patrick Henry's speech to the Virginia ratification convention, the Federalists had already decided they were wrong. A bill of rights was necessary, substantively and most assuredly politically. Substantively it provided appropriate, if perhaps redundant, protection, the Federalists reasoned, and politically it would split the opposition. Those who actually favored a bill of rights could now be won to the Federalists' side, and those for whom favoring a bill of rights was simply a tactic to protect state power by defeating the Constitution would have fewer arguments on which to stand.

The question then became the timing of such amendments. Here the Federalists were adamant. There could be no bill of rights until after the Constitution was ratified, for otherwise the ratification process would be derailed, a new convention required, and its product very much uncertain. Their strategy became to promise support for a bill of rights in the first Congress in return for ratification support at the various state ratification conventions.

Madison himself became a key spokesman for the new strategy. Traveling home to Virginia, in early March of 1788, to stand for election as delegate to that state's ratification convention, he was challenged by an important Baptist minister who opposed the Constitution for its failure to affirmatively protect freedom of religion. Madison argued that such a demand would doom the new Constitution and not guarantee that a new convention would produce a new national government, let alone one that protected religious freedom. Rather, he argued for supporting ratification on the

basis of his promise, along with that made by other Federalist leaders, that a first order of business in the new Congress would be a
bill of rights, including religious freedom. (Both would live up to
their side of the bargain.)

By the time of the Virginia convention, this Federalist strategy
was working. Massachusetts went first. On February 6, it became
the sixth state to ratify the Constitution. The debate in Massachusetts had been fierce. On a daily basis, Anti-Federalists such as Elbridge Gerry and Agrippa (James Winthrop of Massachusetts) fired
away at threats the new government would pose to individual liberties. And the relatively close vote of 187–168 evidenced the
power of that argument. In the end, victory was only ensured by
the agreement of Federalists to support a future bill of rights. "I
give my assent to the Constitution," declared Massachusetts's convention president and state governor John Hancock, "in full confidence that amendments proposed will soon become a part of the
system." The Massachusetts convention recommended a list of
amendments to the Constitution that, it said, "would remove the
fears, and quiet the apprehensions, of many of the good people of
this commonwealth, and more effectually guard against an undue
administration of the federal government." This same strategy was
then adopted by South Carolina and New Hampshire.

Virginia followed suit. Despite Henry's extraordinary efforts, he
could not stop the momentum for ratification, fueled by Madison's
influence with the delegates generally and particularly with his old
friend Governor Edmund Randolph, who in the end supported ratification. On June 25, Virginia's delegates voted 89–79 (Henry voted
no) to support the Constitution. But that ratification also charged
Virginia's future members of Congress to "exert all their influence,
and use all reasonable and legal methods, to obtain a ratification of

the foregoing alterations and provisions, in the manner provided by the fifth article of the said Constitution; and, in all congressional laws to be passed in the mean time, to conform to the spirit of these amendments, as far as the said Constitution will admit." Those foregoing alterations consisted of a list covering a number of topics including a bill of rights, which provided, among other things, for freedom of speech and religion, freedom to assemble and petition government, freedom from undue search and seizure, and trial by jury.

Virginia's ratification strengthened the Federalists in New York. The most pressing question at the convention's end seemed to be whether New York would stand alone among the influential states in opposing ratification. Many New York delegates in fact were willing to take that position. On July 26, 1788, New York voted to join the new nation by the slimmest of margins (30–27), and only after a bill of rights was recommended.

On September 13, 1788, the Continental Congress resolved that the Constitution had been ratified and commanded that the first Wednesday in March 1789 would be the time and that New York, seat of the old confederation Congress, would be the place "for commencing proceedings under the said Constitution."

The new Constitution had survived its first test and shown its resilience before it even took effect. But there was a lot of political blood on the floor, and the partisan rivalries were only just beginning. Patrick Henry and his fellow Anti-Federalists in charge of the Virginia legislature, using the power to select senators given them by the new Constitution, denied Madison a seat in the new Senate. But Madison campaigned and won a seat in the House of Representatives, whose members were directly elected, beating a friend, James Monroe. Madison, fulfilling the promise he had made to that Baptist minister and other Americans, asked the first Congress on June 8, 1789, to enact a bill of rights he had culled from the over eighty provisions that had been suggested: "It will be a desirable thing, to extinguish from the bosom of every member of the community, any apprehensions that there are those among his countrymen who wish to deprive them of the liberty for which they valiantly fought and honorably bled . . . There is a great body of the people falling under this description, who at present feel much inclined to join their support to the cause of federalism, if they were satisfied on this one point."

Getting a bill of rights through Congress took a bit of work.

Madison's own enthusiasm to see the work through was not exactly matched by his fellow members of Congress. For many new congressmen, it was a minor matter compared to the more tangible task of establishing the new government. At the same time, the Anti-Federalists in Congress continued their campaign against the powerful centralized government by trying to block the very bill of rights many of them had argued for. If they could block a bill of rights, they reasoned, they could force a new constitutional convention where they could strengthen state power. Both New York and Virginia, in ratifying the Constitution, had called for a new convention. That thought terrified and galvanized the Federalists, who knew a new convention could reopen everything in Madison's delicately balanced government plan.

Finally, five months after Madison asked Congress for a bill of rights, Congress transmitted twelve proposed amendments to the states for approval. One amendment, to immediately enlarge the membership of the House of Representatives, died. Another, to block congressmen from raising their pay during their current term of office, was eventually enacted—203 years later, on May 7, 1992, as the Twenty-seventh Amendment.

On December 15, 1791, Madison's Virginia provided the final votes needed for ratification of the other ten amendments, the ten we all now know as the Bill of Rights.

The new government was in place, and the Constitution, as amended, was in effect. The ratification of the Bill of Rights completed America's progress from an independent but shaky confederation to a republic with an innovative new government that would eventually prove to be a model of democratic stability.

But few Americans were paying close attention to this last stretch of the opening journey. For most, the drama of the creation had already faded into the background of their everyday life. But in this background the framers' vision would be tested again and again. The battle over ratification and the Bill of Rights was just the first such test. Americans would demand more from their Constitution than the text alone allowed. In this case the Constitution accommodated those demands. The question would be: Could it do so in the future?

Part Two

THANK GOD, IT WORKED

Our Constitution works. Our great Republic is a government of laws and not of men.

—GERALD FORD, 1974

4

TO MEET EXTRAORDINARY NEEDS

It is patriotism to write in favor of our government and sedition to write against it.

      —*ALBANY CENTINEL*, 1798

Perhaps it is a universal truth that the loss of liberty at home is to be charged to provisions against dangers real or pretended from abroad.

      —JAMES MADISON, 1798

THE DAY GERALD FORD became the thirty-eighth president it was obvious history was in the making. His predecessor, Richard M. Nixon, had just resigned in scandal. The chief justice of the Supreme Court, Warren E. Burger, administered the oath prescribed by the Constitution. Ford pledged, as every president before him had, to "faithfully execute the Office of President of the United States, and . . . to the best of my Ability, preserve, protect and defend the Constitution of the United States."

Completing the oath, Ford moved to the podium and declared "our long national nightmare" of Watergate was over. "Our

Constitution works. Our great Republic is a government of laws and not of men." As Ford left the podium, the chief justice, a Nixon appointee, turned to Senator Hugh Scott of Pennsylvania and in a far more personal expression of relief exclaimed about the constitutional system, "Hugh, it worked. Thank God, it worked."

But what, exactly, is it that had worked? Certainly, the checks and balances as the framers had written them in the Constitution had proven sound. But just as surely, there was something more important than just the words on parchment, as Madison had once characterized the idea of a bill of rights. No, from the beginning our Constitution was more than just a document. What developed around it—and then what worked—was Americans behaving in a manner consistent with the larger ideas, values and principles behind the Constitution.

These responsibilities that the Constitution bestows on us is what we have called our Constitutional Conscience. It was this unwritten sense of the Constitution that empowered Republican Senator Howard Baker to put his institutional role as a member of Congress above his partisan duties and demand of a Republican president: What did he know, and when did he know it? It is what gave a judge, John Sirica, who had voted for that president, the strength to issue a ruling in uncharted legal territory that ultimately helped push the president from office. They exercised authority beyond the four corners of the written document—authority that had evolved after the Constitution was written and without any formal amendment of it. When Chief Justice Burger thanked God that it had worked, he was saying in a much pithier way the same thing Franklin Delano Roosevelt had said forty years earlier: "Our Constitution is so simple and practical that it is possible always to meet extraordinary needs by changes in emphasis and arrangement without loss of essential form. That is why our constitutional system has proved itself the most superbly enduring political mechanism the modern world has produced."

In the name of national security and presidential prerogatives, Nixon had attempted to thwart the constitutional obligation of the legislature and judiciary to oversee his activities. It was neither the first nor the last time the country faced such a struggle. Indeed, within seven years of the Constitution's ratification, there was a crisis in which the party in power suppressed domestic dissent in the name of national security. Richard Nixon and his Republican allies spied on their enemies and lied about it. John Adams and his Federalist allies had taken one step further in 1798, criminalizing criticism of their own activities and then arresting their critics.

That early crisis, triggered by enactment of the Sedition Act, revealed that the checks and balances of Madison's system were less than foolproof and that the country had no agreed-upon way to decide when the Constitution had been transgressed. Within years, the country developed one, an independent judiciary, unique in the world at that time. The threads from those early days to our more recent history are easy enough to follow. President Nixon was checked, in good measure, by a federal judge exercising judicial power developed after the Constitution was written, but within its framework.

The simplicity of the Constitution has made it adaptable. Without constitutional amendment, both the federal courts and the presidency have emerged from surprisingly unclear beginnings to help stabilize the Constitution and the Republic against a variety of difficult challenges. That is the genius of its design.

The framers, of course, could not have anticipated the break-in at the Watergate or many other events and changes across the nation's history. That is why adaptability was and is so vital. But what the framers did anticipate was the fundamental nature of men and of politics, which is what their essential form of government was designed to control. Self-interest and self-regard have motivated those with political power to seek more power than is granted to them. The invention of a representative government with divided powers has repeatedly checked the excesses of the powerful, although sometimes, as in both 1798 and 1974, only after national crisis.

Chief Justice Burger's palpable sense of relief, his implicit recognition that a very different outcome to the Watergate scandal might have been possible, would have baffled most Americans in 1974. Of course it worked. What else would you have expected? Americans experienced Watergate as a "nightmare" of continuing revelations of criminal activity by a president (and his staff), for whom an overwhelming majority had voted in 1972.

But to most Americans, the working of the Constitution is assumed. Americans admire, even revere, the Constitution. Times of crisis, like Watergate, remind us of its role in helping to define and unify us. But our knowledge of its goals, its institutions and their processes, or its history is thin. It is part of our lives but not really part of our education. Most Americans probably could not see Nixon and Watergate as a modern version of exactly what the framers feared. Americans could not perceive a different America, an America in which power was seized and tyranny prevailed. To Americans living in the Watergate era, or today, tyranny is something that happens in other times or other places. It couldn't happen here.

But to the framers, tyranny was something that could, and had, happened here. Fear of men with too much power, of the tyranny of a king, of an established church, of a despot, of aristocrats and, at least as important, of a popular majority dominated their thinking from independence through ratification of the Constitution and the Bill of Rights and the early years of the new nation. George Washington warned in his Farewell Address to the nation of a future in which "cunning, ambitious, and unprincipled men" would attempt "to subvert the power of the people and to usurp for themselves the reins of government, destroying afterwards the very engines which have lifted them to unjust dominion." They would often do so believing that what was good for them was good for America, as when President Nixon declared that his decision to obstruct the various inquires into the Watergate affair "were made in what [he] believed at the time to be the best interest of the Nation."

This conflation of personal and national interest is exactly what the framers feared would bring down their new government. If in fact the framers had witnessed President Ford's inauguration, their biggest surprise, at least governmental surprise, would have been the continuation of the Republic itself. This fear of its failure, resulting from self-interest and self-regard, was behind Franklin's famous characterization of the new government as a "republic, if you can keep it." Indeed, many delegates to the Constitutional Convention shared Franklin's worry that only "with luck" could the framers "produce a government that could forestall, for a decade perhaps, the inevitable decline of the Republic into tyranny."

Indeed, in less than a decade, the fears were proved right, and one of the signers of the Constitution, John Adams, was at the heart of the crisis.

THE CRIME OF POLITICAL CRITICISM

Under the threat of war and in the name of national security, one political party in 1798 tried to destroy the other, and the nation

almost unraveled. At the heart of the matter was a piece of legislation, a blight on American constitutional history, known as the
Sedition Act.

The Act created for John Adams what history would measure as
the most pivotal decision of his career. Adams had become the second president of the United States on March 4, 1796. His victory
had been razor thin, three electoral votes, over his opponent,
Thomas Jefferson, who then became vice president. (Until the ratification of the Twelfth Amendment in 1804, the candidate who
received the second-most votes for president became the vice president.) While neither candidate had campaigned for office, their
supporters had waged brutal campaigns on their behalf in this first
contested presidential election. In fact, this race was the first in
which political parties vied for power, the Federalists for Adams
and the Democratic Republicans for Jefferson. The closeness of the
race reflected a serious divide in the American electorate over
whom to favor in the ongoing war between England and France.

The choice of England or France, both predators circling their
desired American carcass, reflected the divide between the newly
emerging political parties. The Federalists, under Adams and Hamilton, were even more suspicious of human nature and more distrust-
ing of the "people" and democracy than Madison's and Jefferson's
Democratic Republicans. The Federalists favored more order and
more concentrated power. They wanted that power in the hands of
the nation's elite. The Democratic Republicans stood for more liberty and a broader dispersion of political power to the nation's
many yeomen and artisans and to the states, or, as one of the Republicans' most ardent critics had it, to the "mobocracy." Through
those ideological screens the Federalists favored England and the
Democratic Republicans favored France, and through those screens

emerged the development of "clearly recognized Federalist and Democratic Republican points of view on all political questions."

America's policy of neutrality had upset both the English and the French. England responded by seizing American ships, forcing American sailors into the British navy and refusing to honor a number of terms of the Treaty of Paris, which had officially ended the War of Independence. To resolve these matters, President Washington sent John Jay to England. The result was the Jay Treaty.

The Jay Treaty was, at first, enormously unpopular. Most Americans shared the view that it had not accomplished the nation's primary goals of ending English intrusiveness. Even the Federalists considered it only a means to avoid war with England. The Republicans saw it as betrayal of American liberty. Jay was hung in effigy many times over. Alexander Hamilton, a strong treaty supporter, was stoned by a mob in New York. Even George Washington could not avoid attack.

The Jay Treaty was unpopular with the French as well. They saw it as an American alliance with England. In response, France threatened America with a break in diplomatic relations and then seized American ships. President Adams dispatched a mission to France to reduce the tensions. The French foreign minister, in what became known as the XYZ Affair, demanded a bribe and a loan from America as conditions for commencing negotiations. When that demand was rebuffed, the French refused to meet with the American delegation.

The news of the XYZ Affair roiled Americans, many of whom wanted Adams to declare war. Support of France became anti-American. Everyone was now a Federalist. The Republican Party was left sputtering.

President Adams, now a hero for the first time in his political career, resisted calls from other Federalists for war against France. Americans were not yet ready for war with such a powerful country, the conqueror of much of Europe. Adams adopted the view that, in the words of his son (and future president) John Quincy Adams, "the government can never carry through any war, unless the strong unequivocal and decided voice of the people leads them into it." Rather, President Adams prepared Americans for a war through a broadly supported military build-up but hoped that he could avoid one.

Thanks to the XYZ Affair, the Federalists had won the ideological war with the Republicans, but this was not enough for their hard-liners, who viewed opposition to their policies as opposition to the Constitution and America. "Jacobins," they called the Republicans, after the radical French political club that had instituted the Reign of Terror in France in 1793, and they acted to destroy their opposition.

On July 10, 1798, the Federalists passed the Sedition Act, which in effect criminalized criticism of the president and Congress. The target was the press, in particular the nation's many Republican newspapers. The Republican press, wrote one ardent supporter of the Act, "has inspired ignorance with presumption, so that those who cannot be governed by reason are no longer to be awed by authority." Adams himself complained that the Republican press would go to any length to defame "our government." Of course, the Federalist press, in the manner of the times, was equally as strident in its assault on Republicans.

The goal of the Act was simple: "to muzzle dissent and browbeat the Republicans into submission." And it was to be enforced by Federalist prosecutors and judges throughout the country. For the Federalists, "force and coercion rather than reason and argument were to be the ultimate arbiters of political controversy."

The Act's design was hardly subtle. It was to expire on March 3, 1801, the last day of Adams's first term of office. This would "ensure that the act would not be turned against the Federalists" if they lost the 1800 presidential election. Also, the Republican vice president was excluded from the act's protection. The never-ending criticism of Jefferson in the Federalist press could be continued. And this criticism was lurid. Observed Hamilton about his enemy Jefferson, "To be the proconsul of a despotic Directory over the United States, degraded to the condition of a province, can alone be the criminal, the ignoble aim of so seditious, so prostitute a character."

On July 14, President Adams took his fateful step. Despite his earlier sentiment that "a free press maintains the Majesty of the People," he signed the bill. The "most reprehensible act of his Presidency," according to his otherwise sympathetic biographer David McCullough.

The Sedition Act caused enormous uproar. Only seven years after the ratification of the First Amendment, intended to protect freedom of speech and the press, Congress enacted legislation to prosecute Americans for the expression of their political views. And the statute was enforced. Congressman Matthew Lyon of Vermont and many newspaper publishers were prosecuted or threatened with prosecution. No Federalist was even charged despite the equal malice and misrepresentation from the Federalists.

On the surface, the justification for the Sedition Act was the threat of war. Adams and other Federalists viewed criticism of the government as national weakness and a dangerous invitation to the French to attack. Congressman Harrison Gray Otis of Massachusetts saw the Republicans as "crowd[s] of spies and inflammatory agents" everywhere "fomenting hostilities" and "alienating the affections of our own citizens." One Federalist newspaper, the *Albany Centinel*, wrote without apparent irony, "It is patriotism to write in favor of our government and sedition to write against it." For the Federalists, silencing these critics would strengthen the country. But silencing them would also end political debate over the central issue of the time, an outcome frequently attractive to people in power. Noted Madison, "Perhaps it is a universal truth that the loss of liberty at home is to be charged to provisions against dangers real or pretended from abroad."

But whether or not the French threat was real or imagined, beneath the surface the issue was political power. Confusing or obscuring their self-interest with the national interest, the Federalists, through the Sedition Act, saw the opportunity to maintain their hold on America's governing institutions. "By leveraging a moment of high patriotism, they managed to enact a legislative program designed to cripple, perhaps even destroy, the Republican Party." In the end, the country would defeat their attempt.

But first the Republicans deepened the constitutional crisis and almost pulled apart the country. The Republicans were in a bind. They could not challenge the Sedition Act by going to court. Jefferson had once expressed to Madison the hope that the Bill of Rights would "put into the hands of the judiciary" a legal check on the acts of the government. But this role of the courts as the independent guardian of the Constitution had not yet evolved. The views of most federal judges corresponded with those of the Federalists who had appointed them. The "entire Federal bench joined in the crusade against 'Jacobinism.' "

Yet the Republicans had to counter the Federalists' attack. The course they chose, under Madison's and Jefferson's guidance, was to have the states respond. In an argument that would reverberate strongly through the Civil War (and in weaker notes even today), the Republicans proclaimed that states had the right, indeed the responsibility, to protest and perhaps reject (nullify) congressional acts that they judged unconstitutional.

This was a strange position for Madison, who at the Convention had deplored any meaningful roles for the states in federal governance. But Madison's view of strong national government did not include the authoritarian stance the Federalists, like Hamilton, had added to the original model. He saw the Federalists' conduct as a threat to his most fundamental Constitutional principle. "Information and communication among the people . . . is indispensable to the just exercise of their electoral rights." In Madison's words arguing for a state's right to effectively nullify a federal statute was a "calculation," one necessitated by a majority's usurpation of power (that is, ignoring the First Amendment) and the "oppressive exercise on a minority by a majority" of that power. But in this case the calculation would prove wrong.

Two states, Virginia (under Madison's guidance) and Kentucky (under Jefferson's), responded. Both adopted resolutions declaring the Sedition Act unconstitutional under the First Amendment. Virginia's recommended course of action was argument alone. Kentucky wanted more. "That the several states who formed that instrument, being sovereign and independent, have the unquestionable right to judge of its infraction; and that a nullification, by those sovereignties, of all unauthorized acts done under colour of that instrument, is the rightful remedy."

Both state resolutions caused an enormous uproar. George

Washington, historically one of Madison's closest allies, charged that the Virginia resolution would "dissolve the union or produce coercion." And some Federalists saw the resolutions as close to a call for war.

No other states joined Virginia and Kentucky, but a number of states adopted resolutions condemning them. "No State government," declared Maryland, has the power "to declare an act of the Federal Government unconstitutional." That power, according to Vermont, was "exclusively vested in the judiciary courts of the Union." (A contention that would not be realized until the Supreme Court itself ruled that it had such power in 1803.) The federal government considered indicting the governor of Kentucky for sedition.

The nation was headed for a schism. But then suddenly the crisis was over, not through indictment, nullification, the courts or civil war, but through the most fundamental check on what Jefferson called the "evil propensities of the government." The voters threw the incumbents out.

The English defeated the French, but, even with the war over, the Federalists kept pushing for more enforcement of the Sedition Act. With their fear reduced, Americans could more calmly view the political landscape, and they judged it ugly. In the election of 1800, the voters overwhelmingly ousted the Federalists from power. Vice President Thomas Jefferson became the third president of the United States, and the Republicans took control of both the House and the Senate. One day before the Republicans took power, the Sedition Act expired.

At one level the Constitution had worked, and the country moved on. But the crisis had revealed a weakness in the system.

There was no consensus on an institutional means for judging whether a law or the act of a government official was constitutional.

THE RISE OF THE COURTS

For many Americans today, the Republicans' failure to challenge the Sedition Act in the Supreme Court might seem strange. The Court's power of constitutional review has become an accepted part of American governance. But this was not the case from the beginning. No nation then gave their courts the power to overturn laws. And the Constitution did not clearly grant the courts such power.

Article III provides only for a single Supreme Court and such other lesser courts that Congress determines the country needs. These lesser courts now number in the hundreds with each state having federal trial courts (district courts), whose work is reviewed by a far fewer number of appellate courts (courts of appeals). The number of Supreme Court justices was also left for Congress to decide, and that number (nine now) has varied over our history. Article III provides that the power of the Supreme Court shall extend to cases "arising under this Constitution." But, at the beginning of the Republic, it was unclear whether the framers' had intended this language to allow the Court to declare an act of Congress unconstitutional or had some narrower reach in mind, for example, declaring state legislation that clashed with federal power unconstitutional.

The framers had spent little time on the courts at the convention. But some later indicated they had supported a broad view of judicial review as a barrier against the feared tyranny of all legislative majorities. Hamilton had argued in *The Federalist Papers* that "a Constitution is, in fact, and must be regarded by the judges, as a fundamental law." From this, Hamilton had reasoned that the job of the Supreme Court and other courts of the United States was "to ascertain [the Constitution's] meaning, as well as the meaning of any particular act proceeding from the legislative body." And then, Hamilton had continued, to apply the Constitution if there was an "irreconcilable variance between the two."

Some other Americans had opposed this political role for the courts. To them, it was undemocratic or even tyrannical—particularly for the Court to be able to declare an act of an elected legislature unconstitutional. In the end, the Constitution itself left the question vague.

But within a few years of the Sedition Act crisis, the Supreme Court itself answered the question. In 1803, Chief Justice John Marshall and the Supreme Court decided that a particular federal statute was unconstitutional.

President Jefferson, notwithstanding his earlier letter to Madison seeming to support this role for the Court, complained to Abigail Adams, "The opinion which gives the judges the right to decide what laws are constitutional, and what not, not only for themselves in their own sphere of action, but for the Legislature and Executive also, in their spheres, would make the Judiciary a despotic branch."

But, most important, while Jefferson carped, he took no action against Marshall and the Court. Neither did Congress under Republican control. In theory, Congress could have impeached Marshall for overstepping his authority. In those days, before the Court's role had been as publicly accepted as it is now, an effort by the Republican Congress to impeach the Federalist John Marshall for a particular decision would not have seemed as violative of the constitutional principle of separation of power as it would today. But they let the ruling stand.

And through these two decisions, the Court's and the Republicans', a critical change in the Constitution was made. Judicial power was broadened to clearly cover the right of the Court to declare an act of Congress unconstitutional. Once planted, the seeds of this idea rooted in the Constitutional Conscience. By the mid-1830s, Alexis de Tocqueville matter-of-factly reported on the "great political importance" of the federal judiciary resulting from a judge's power to strike down a law the "judge holds to be unconstitutional." In the late 1800s, a constitutional historian wrote that the courts were the "most peculiarly American feature" of the Constitution and largely responsible for the "stability" of the Republic, a view echoed by the historian David McCullough in 2006. And Woodrow Wilson compared the Supreme Court to "a constitutional convention in continuous session."

While the federal courts, and particularly the Supreme Court, have over their history issued a number of decisions that have been more politically destabilizing than stabilizing, overall the courts have served as a very useful drag against the excessive political impulses of the other branches.

By the time President Ford took his oath to defend the Constitution, the federal courts had been called on many times to settle fundamental questions concerning the breadth of constitutionally protected individual rights, the extent of federal and state power, and the line between legislative and executive power. In fact, it was just such an issue that put a federal judge, John Sirica, in a very tough place and ultimately led to the elevation of Ford to the presidency.

A JUDGE STANDS UP TO THE PRESIDENT

Judge John Sirica was struggling. He needed to decide the most important case of his career, whether he should order the president of the United States, Richard Nixon, to provide the court with tapes of the president's conversations in the Oval Office. On July 23, 1973, Sirica had signed a subpoena at the request of the Watergate special prosecutor for these same tapes. And, within several days, the president had refused to comply. In a letter to Sirica, Nixon stated: "With the utmost respect for the court on which you are the Chief Judge, and for the branch of government of which it is a part, I must decline to obey the command of that subpoena. In so doing I follow the example of a long line of my predecessors who have consistently adhered to the position that the President is not subject to compulsory process from the courts." Separation of power was the president's justification. "The independence of the three branches of our government," he wrote, made it "inadmissable" for the court to compel any "particular action from the President." He claimed that all communications he had with his aides were privileged, and executive privilege was absolute. This refusal triggered the start of a constitutional crisis between the judicial and the executive branches of government that would ultimately be resolved by the president's resignation and Vice President Ford's assumption of office.

The tapes were critical to the Watergate inquiry. No longer the simple investigation of burglary of the Democratic headquarters, the investigation now focused on a broad array of criminal behavior and, most significantly, the president's role in any of it or in any attempt to block the investigation. Earlier in the summer, the president's former counsel, John Dean, had testified before a Senate committee that Nixon had been involved in a cover-up, but until this point it was only his word against the president's. And Sirica himself had been "skeptical of Dean's allegations." But later in the summer, the testimony of a former presidential assistant exposed the tapes, which Archibald Cox, the Watergate special prosecutor, and the Watergate grand jury believed would reveal the truth of Nixon's complicity.

As Sirica considered the matter, he was, in his own words, "nervous." He had good reason. Despite the political importance of the federal courts, they do not have the power to enforce their own decisions, relying on the other branches of government for their implementation. If those branches, in this case the executive branch, choose to ignore or make little effort to enforce a decision, there is little a court can do. In fact, the court's real power rests on the public perception that a constitutional referee is needed and that it acts independently, fairly and wisely in performing that role.

This reliance on public opinion was clearly on Sirica's mind. No court had ever enforced a subpoena against a president. The president had argued that a decision to require the tapes would severely alter the presidency and structure of American government. And he had suggested that he was under no obligation to follow an order that contradicted his judgment of what was in the public interest. Nor, he argued, could the court enforce such an order against him. His responsibility was directly to the people, who could demonstrate their disfavor through the electoral process or by supporting his impeachment.

The president's argument was not surprising. The Constitution separated the branches of government and assigned each its general powers. It did not answer the particular question Sirica had to confront: whether the president could protect his tapes from a criminal investigation. And in such circumstances, the president's strong assertion of presidential power to protect his own conversations, whether offered to protect principle or self-interest, would prove unsettling to any judge. Indeed Sirica was deeply affected by the uncharted waters he was about to enter. "No judge wants to step off into new legal territory, if he can avoid it," particularly in a case such as this. "It's difficult to describe how worried I was . . . What if I was wrong? . . . Nixon was the President of the United States; he deserved the benefit of the doubt . . . Millions of people had voted for [him]. I had voted for him."

"What if I was wrong?" asked Sirica, pointing to one of the most misunderstood aspects of judging. Although judges are supposed to apply the rules of the Constitution, not make them, the reality tends to be more complicated. The Constitution often does not provide a clear answer to the particular question asked, and the court must fashion one. In these instances, a judge's sense of right or wrong, sensibilities and experience, his own version of the Constitutional Conscience, will all come into play, along with judicial precedents and other institutional considerations. "My own instinct was to follow Cox's argument that no man is above the law. But my judicial experience told me that I needed the support of previous cases before venturing too far in challenging the president."

On August 29, 1973, Judge Sirica issued his order and opinion. The president was required to turn over the tapes for the court's review of their relevance to the investigation. Judge Sirica wrote: "That the Court has not the physical power to enforce its order to the President is immaterial to a resolution of the issues. Regardless of its physical power to enforce them, the Court has a duty to issue appropriate orders. The Court cannot say that the Executive's persistence in withholding the tape recordings would 'tarnish its reputation,' but must admit that it would tarnish the Court's reputation to fail to do what it could in pursuit of justice. In any case, the courts have always enjoyed the good faith of the Executive Branch, even in . . . dire circumstances."

Sirica's decision did not end the controversy, but began its ending. The president would cling to power for another year. He continued to withhold the tape recordings and fired the attorney general and the special prosecutor in order to halt the investigation. But ultimately—after Judge Sirica's opinion had been upheld on appeal, after numerous members of Congress had supported impeachment resolutions and after the public had clearly turned against the president—the tapes were provided. "I was overwhelmed with relief," Sirica wrote. "The President had backed down. He had stepped away from perhaps the worst clash between two branches of government in our history." The tapes revealed the president's participation in a cover-up. Nixon then resigned.

Watergate was as bad a presidential scandal as our country has faced. But it is also one of the most heartening examples we have of the strength we can draw from our Constitutional Conscience as we have developed it through experiences, from the battle over ratification, to the Sedition Act crisis and on through Watergate. That Constitutional Conscience is why voters turned the Federalists out in 1800, and it is where Judge Sirica found the common sense and strength to stand up to a president in 1973. Indeed Sirica was not alone. On Capitol Hill, Republicans put their institutional obligations to provide a check on the presidency ahead of their political need to help a member of their own party. The Senate Watergate hearings gained much of their credibility from the decision of Howard Baker to demand the facts. And the House Judiciary Committee's articles of impeachment, which ultimately convinced Nixon he had to go, were approved by members of both parties.

Michael Kammen defined the penumbra of ideas surrounding the Constitution, what he called *constitutionalism,* as a belief that the Constitution "embodies a set of values, a range of options and means of resolving conflicts with a framework of consensus." That is our most important political possession, our Constitutional Conscience.

This conscience has limited, though not eliminated, the impulses of Americans to pursue self-interests at any cost. "Americans have bitterly disagreed with one another on matters of constitutional interpretation, but respect for the Constitution and the system of government it created has restrained the behavior of most citizens, especially those who have held public office."

It hasn't always worked perfectly, or without struggle, but it has always, ultimately, worked, thank God. We, the people, have worked out our problems, often without changing the Constitution's text. We just expanded its meaning. But it turned out our hardest problem was deciding who "We the People" would be. That would take more than one hundred years and several amendments to the Constitution.

5

THE RIGHT TO ALTER THE
ESTABLISHED CONSTITUTION

*No country ever has had or ever will have peace until
every citizen has a voice in the government. Now let us
try universal suffrage. We cannot tell its dangers or delights until we make the experiment.*

—ELIZABETH CADY STANTON, 1865

A T THE HEART of the Constitution is an idea about representation. It was, as we have seen, a radically new idea in 1787.
It is also an idea that has taken most of the span of our history to
live up to. Under the framers new vision, every branch of the government drew its authority from the people and represented them
and only them. The more people who participated, the framers argued, the better and more representative would be the actions that
emerged from the process. But at the creation there was a contra-
diction between their rhetoric and reality. In the political world of
the framers, only a small slice of the population participated. Small
by our standards, to be sure, and well short of the potential for the
"greater variet[ies] of parties and interests" they espoused.

But the theory nevertheless sunk in. The notion of broad representation entered the nation's Constitutional Conscience, becoming, as Martin Luther King would one day call it, "a promissory note" on the Constitution's fundamental promise that government would be based on the consent of its citizens and that America's many voices would be heard through a representative system.

Much of our history can be seen as a struggle to fulfill that idea.

The struggles have been intense and sometimes bloody. Those with power have not wanted to share it, as the framers predicted. Those who historically were without power, like African Americans and women, have sometimes been allies in the fight for enfranchisement. But at other times, demonstrating the framers' insight that people pursue their own interests first, they have gone separate ways. But consistently they have used the language of the Constitution, and the larger Constitutional Conscience it created, to bolster their cause.

It does not deepen our understanding to read history backward or impose our moral judgments on our predecessors. But clearly, we find it hard to accept a world that could deny women or African Americans citizenship or the vote. But in 1787, the norm was that only white men with property were judged competent to participate.

The problem of participation under the Constitution is subtler and more interesting than just whether they lived up to our standards. By excluding parts of the population, the framers undercut their own theory of their system. Earlier we noted that for the framers, the product of their deliberative process was less important than the process itself. That is what has made the system so much more resilient than alternatives that place the ends ahead of the means. "But what," a critic might rightfully ask, "if the product was absolutely morally indefensible?" The framers would suggest the impossibility of such an outcome in a system of representative government, divided powers and checks and balances. "But what if the voice that would have opposed such a product was excluded from representation?" This would undermine the legislative product because the process itself was not representative.

At the ratification of the Constitution, women and slaves were not represented, and white male votes in slave states counted more than white male votes in nonslave states. So slavery would be preserved, and for the next seventy years the country would struggle to maintain this distortion that the framers knowingly allowed in their system in order to hold the Union together.

AMENDING THE CONSTITUTION

As proud as they were of their new design for government, the framers recognized that, in Washington's words, "the People of America" might find the Constitution "less perfect than it can be made." To address this probability, the framers provided an amendment clause. Through it, Americans could exercise their "right . . . to alter or abolish the established Constitution, whenever they find it inconsistent with their happiness," wrote Hamilton. The wisdom of this clause was immediately apparent when enactment of the first ten amendments, the Bill of Rights, became the quid pro quo for enactment of the entire Constitution.

The framers made enactment of amendments very difficult. They did not want the nation's basic law to be changed lightly. The door to what Washington called constitutional "amelioration" is not easy to open. The framers' fear of majority rule and desire for consensus compelled them to create high barriers for constitutional amendment. Two thirds of each house of Congress must first approve a resolution for amendment. Only then can it be submitted to the states for their consideration. Three fourths of the states (now thirty-eight states) must ratify the submitted proposal through their state legislatures for a proposed amendment to go into effect.

The Constitution also includes a second procedure for its amendment, the calling of a new constitutional convention. It has never been used.

Since the ratification of the Bill of Rights, some ten thousand amendments have been proposed, but only seventeen have been adopted. None of those seventeen changed the framers' basic arrangement for making the exercise of political power difficult. Governmental power has remained divided among the three branches of government and the two houses of Congress. Each branch of government maintained the power to check and balance the others. Consensus through compromise remained necessary for change.

Of the seventeen amendments since the Bill of Rights, all but four, thematically, built on the Constitution's promise of a representative democracy. Three of those specifically expanded the right to vote, first to African American men, then to women and finally to young people over seventeen years of age.

Expanding representation beyond those who held power at the time of the Constitution has proved difficult, despite the Constitution's promises of a politically empowered citizenry. It took struggle, and it took time. The amendments broadening political rights "are not just words, but deeds—flesh and blood struggles to redeem America's promise."

SLAVERY, THE COMPROMISE THAT COULD NOT HOLD

The greatest failure of the constitutional system was the American Civil War. In the grand sense, the Constitution's design to force compromise ultimately did not work on an issue that at root revolved around a moral choice with no compromise: Either slave owners had a property right to be protected, or slaves had a human right to be Americans. Both, ultimately, could not be true.

Although many delegates opposed slavery, including the slave owners Washington and Madison, and understood that it would undermine "the very vision of democracy embodied [although not defined] in the United States Constitution," to win support for the Constitution, they did not, at least publically, even suggest its abolition. Moreover, for the new Constitution, the delegates compromised on a number of other issues affecting slavery: Each slave would count as three fifths of a person when determining state population for congressional representation and presidential electors; states could not protect runaway slaves; and Congress could not restrict the trans-Atlantic slave trade until 1808. As Abraham Lincoln would later note, "We had slavery among us. We could not get our Constitution unless we permitted them to remain in slavery, we could not secure the good we did secure if we grasped for more."

Additionally, by creating the Senate as the bulwark of conservatism against tides of public opinion, and giving each state an equal voice, the framers created a base of power that southerners fought ferociously to preserve. When they saw they could preserve this base no longer, they rebelled.

For seventy years, from the enactment of the Constitution to the shelling of Fort Sumter, the history of America is dominated by repeated efforts to create new versions of these compromises that would allow slavery to continue in part of the country. As the country moved west, the question of slavery in the territories and the new states would be continuously debated by Congress. Southerners viewed the outcomes of these debates as critical to their existence. They were protected from all federal antislavery efforts by their voting block in the Senate. New states would mean new senators, and the South was determined to keep its equal share. At first, the matter was settled relatively easily by in effect pairing new slave and new free states. For example, Illinois was admitted as a free state in 1818 and Alabama as a slave state in 1819, giving each side eleven states.

But then, in 1820, Congressman James Tallmadge of New York and a large number of free-state congressman blocked, initially, the admission of Missouri as a slave state. To them, the nation had committed itself to the equality of men under the Declaration of Independence and to a "truly republican government" under the Constitution, and there could be neither as long as there was slavery. In response, southerners went on the attack. Soon-to-be-President Andrew Jackson of Tennessee saw the northern views as nothing short of a "wicked design of demagogues, who talk about humanity, but whose sole object is self aggrandizement regardless of the happiness of the nation."

Thereafter, the admission of new states became an arduous task, requiring a number of very thinly supported, ruggedly fought over compromises for the required congressional approval. From 1820 through Lincoln's election, Maine came in free in 1820; Missouri, slave in 1821; Arkansas, slave in 1836; Michigan, free in 1837; Florida, slave in 1845; Texas, slave in 1845; Iowa, free in 1846; Wisconsin, free in 1848; California, free in 1850 (one senator was proslavery); and Minnesota, free in 1859. Among the most notorious of the compromises was the Fugitive Slave Act of 1850, part of a congressional trade for the admission of California as a free state. This act effectively prevented citizens of northern states from sheltering runaway slaves.

Finally in 1860, with the election of the Republican Abraham Lincoln, the South was no longer willing to stay in the Union. The southern interest in protecting slavery outweighed all others. The Constitutional Conscience of the South failed to rein in southerners' political and economic self-interest. Lincoln said he was willing to compromise. He said he opposed legislation affecting slavery in slave states. His view was that peaceful emancipation would take "a hundred years at the least."

But the slave states determined that they had no future under the constitutional structure. As one southerner proclaimed, "The democratic proclivities of the age pervade our whole country, nothing can arrest our downward tendency to absolute Government." In other words, they understood that the rising demand for abolition of slavery would eventually overwhelm even the powerful checks that the framers had built into the Constitution to slow change. The country was nearing consensus, and their control over the slavery question was slipping.

Here was an irony. Some abolitionists had the same problem

with the Constitution. Like the southerners, they thought its checks and balances worked against their interests, impeded their drive to end slavery. William Lloyd Garrison called it "a covenant with death, and an agreement with hell."

So the Constitution, which depended upon compromise to resolve difficult issues, imploded. The South seceded, and the country went to war. "The system almost died."

Northern victory and the post–Civil War amendments to the Constitution provided a legal end to slavery (Thirteenth Amendment), a promise of equal rights (Fourteenth Amendment) and the vote (Fifteenth Amendment) to former slaves. But in fact this did not really happen—proof positive of the framers' notion that important changes need to be accepted by more than a mere majority. The amendments were effectively imposed by northern Republicans who controlled Congress and ruled the southern slave states through the northern army. They were not supported by most white southerners and many northern Democrats. They were received as the rules of an occupying North. After a brief surge of African American participation in the economic and political life of the South, the door was shut. As the North's energy for and interest in "reconstruction" faded, the former slaves and their families were recaptured in a web of state and local laws and vigilantism (Ku Klux Klan).

The final blow was a political deal to resolve the presidential election of 1876. Neither the winner of the popular vote, Democrat Samuel Tilden, nor the Republican, Rutherford Hayes, had sufficient electoral votes. Congress was required to decide the outcome. In a deal for the withdrawal of northern troops from the South and the appointment of a southern cabinet member, southern Democrats supported the Republican candidate, giving him victory by one vote. He then kept his word. With the removal of northern troops, the southern states fell under the control of the "Redeemers," a group of the Democratic Party that stood for white supremacy. The country as a whole again became more interested in the Union rather than real emancipation.

But the amendments did not disappear. They entered America's Constitutional Conscience. They would serve as a goal and as a standard by which Americans could measure their own conduct and that of their fellow citizens. They would serve as a to-be-fulfilled promise. Yet as Lincoln had predicted, it would take a hundred years of additional struggles for the realization of this constitutional promise.

MARTIN LUTHER KING AND THE
CONSTITUTIONAL CONSCIENCE

Martin Luther King had started speaking. It was August 28, 1963. To his back was the Lincoln Memorial. Before him some 250,000 Americans, black and white, crowded the National Mall eastward to the Washington Monument. Behind the memorial rose the Capitol's dome. These Americans had come to Washington, D.C., to insist that Congress enact an effective civil rights law. As King was soon to say, they had come to the "bank of justice" to cash "a check" that would give them upon demand "the riches of freedom and the security of justice." They had come to insist the Congress pay on the nation's "promissory note . . . that all men . . . would be guaranteed the 'unalienable Rights' of 'Life, Liberty, and the pursuit of Happiness.'"

America was a grim place for many of its African American citizens. Despite the promise of the Civil War amendments to the

Constitution, political and economic discrimination and outright terror kept African Americans as second-class citizens, particularly in the South, but throughout the remainder of the country as well.

Up to this point, the administration of President John F. Kennedy had done little to advance a civil rights agenda. In the first years of his administration, there had been no broad public demand for change, and his 1964 reelection strategy called for southern Democratic support. The "New Frontier," quipped the civil rights leader Clarence Mitchell, "looks like a dude ranch with Senator [James] Eastland [an ardent southern segregationist] as the general manager." But now things were rapidly changing. Discrimination was becoming a more national issue. "Freedom riders" from throughout the country descended on the South to highlight and protest its segregation. And violence against these mostly young people, black and white, was drawing America's attention. The year 1963 had proved particularly violent. That summer, King and the civil rights forces had marched to Birmingham, Alabama, "the most systematically segregated city in the South," for boycotts and sit-ins. And in response, as King had expected, the sheriff overreacted; hosing, beating, setting dogs on and arresting over a thousand demonstrators, many of them children. So harsh was this treatment that some demonstrators broke their vow of nonviolence and showered the police with stones. In response came bombings and then more rock throwing and then more beatings. As many observers recognized at the time, "Non-violence was losing its power as an energizing ideology. A new, more bloody phase of the civil rights movement had begun."

Kennedy had to respond, despite his political reluctance. The brutality was escalating, and it was broadcast by television news throughout the country and world. The question, he announced to the nation, was "whether all Americans are to be afforded equal rights and equal opportunities" to eat "in a restaurant open to the public," to "send [their] children to the best public school available" and to "vote for the public officials who represent [them]"— the very questions the Civil War amendments to the Constitution would seem to have answered but had not. Kennedy announced his support for proposed federal civil rights legislation. Civil rights leaders said the legislation was too weak, and, in any case, southern legislators stalled it.

Against this background, A. Philip Randolph and Bayard Rustin announced a march on Washington for jobs and freedom, a march to pressure Congress to pass a meaningful civil rights law.

Their planned march had not made the Kennedy administration happy. Would it further legislative goals or harden the resistance of powerful southern legislators? What would its effect be on the required Republican Party support? Would violence occur in the nation's capital? What would be its effect on the 1964 elections? But realizing it could not be stopped, the president's advisers entered into a long negotiation with the organizers over the march's tone and logistics. The administration exercised so much control over the logistics of the march that some civil rights leaders balked at their commitment to participate, and Malcolm X named it the "Farce on Washington."

But the day of the march dawned beautiful, and attention was not on the politics or logistics but on the sense of unity and possibility it created.

King was the day's last speaker. The extraordinary gospel singer Mahalia Jackson had just concluded singing the spiritual "I've Been Buked and I've Been Scorned." The towering figures of the civil rights movement had already spoken. But now everyone was waiting to hear from the fiery young minister from Atlanta who had electrified the country that summer by his passion, courage and cunning in Birmingham. He had planned only a short recitation, but as he was finishing, Jackson was heard advising him, "Tell them about your dream, Martin! Tell them about your dream!" And King delivered.

Five score years ago, a great American, in whose symbolic shadow we stand today, signed the Emancipation Proclamation. This momentous decree came as a great beacon light of hope to millions of Negro slaves who had been seared in the flames of withering injustice. It came as a joyous daybreak to end the long night of captivity. But one hundred years later, we must face the tragic fact that the Negro is still not free. I say to you today, my friends, that in spite of the difficulties and frustrations of the moment, I still have a dream. It is a dream deeply rooted in the American dream. I have a dream that one day this nation will rise up and live out the true meaning of its creed: "We hold these truths to be self-evident: that all men are created equal . . ." And if America is to be a great nation this must become true.

King's quote is from the Declaration of Independence. But his appeal was to America's Constitutional Conscience. All Americans knew that African Americans had to be included in the political process. But many had struggled against that. It would limit their power. For real enfranchisement for African Americans would mean opportunities for political and economic power. More competition, less monopoly. But within two years of the march, almost 180 years after the Constitution's enactment and ninety-eight years after the post–Civil War amendments, it would finally be achieved. Congress and President Lyndon Johnson enacted the Civil Rights Act of 1964 and the Voting Rights Act of 1965. The federal government committed itself to the enforcement of both acts.

WOMEN ALSO WIN THE VOTE

Women also had to struggle for their rights, including the right to vote. In the beginning they were often allied with the abolitionists to win enfranchisement. But when African American men were offered the promise of full citizenship, the alliance split.

Women in America, as elsewhere in the world, were essentially without civil or economic rights. "A woman is nobody. A wife is everything," editorialized a Philadelphia newspaper, capturing the predominant sentiment of nineteenth-century Americans (many women included). As a wife or single person, an American woman had few rights. For the most part, as a wife, she could not have her own property, could not enter into a contract, could not keep a salary of her own and could not maintain custody of her children. All her rights depended upon the discretion of her husband. "A married woman has no legal existence; she has no more absolute rights than a slave on a Southern plantation," wrote Elizabeth Cady Stanton in 1850. "Civilly, socially, and religiously, she is what man chooses her to be—nothing more or less—and such is the slave."

The power of the Constitution's message that representation protected liberty was well illustrated by the strategy of women activists. "No country ever has had or ever will have peace until every citizen has a voice in the government," said Stanton, in a pithy adaptation of Madison's theory. "Now let us try universal suffrage. We cannot tell its dangers or delights until we make the experiment."

Under this banner, an alliance between suffragettes and abolitionists was forged. "If that government only is just which governs by the free consents of the governed," argued the former slave and abolitionist Frederick Douglass, "there can be no reason in the world for denying to woman the exercise of the elective franchise." Together they would fight. "For a quarter of a century the two movements, to free the slave and liberate the women, nourished and strengthened one another." Women, for example, provided the grassroots effort necessary to force some reluctant senators to support adoption of the Thirteenth Amendment as it faltered from the resistance of northern Democrats. Four hundred thousand signatures made their petition campaign "the largest in history up to that time."

But this unity, as the framers would have predicted, faltered at the end of the Civil War as the debate began about enfranchising the freed slaves. The suffragists wanted this to be their moment, too.

Legislators were divided on the issue of female suffrage. Even some of those who were committed to it judged that the country was not ready. Many Americans shared the view that "women should not vote because they could not." The "mission" of women, one senator from New Jersey pronounced in an 1866 debate over the franchise in the District of Columbia, "is at home, by their blandishments and their love to assuage the passions of men as they came in from the battle of life, and not by joining in the contest to add fuel to the very flames."

There was a political danger that tying the vote for women to the vote for black men could produce defeat for both. Republicans did not want to lose a political benefit. "Two million newly enfranchised black men offered the party in power the possibility of building a Republican South." Republicans argued that slavery had been the cause of the war and that the North's victory had been greatly aided by the thousands of African American males, freemen and former slaves, who fought in the Union Army.

The Fourteenth Amendment made the issue stark. The first section says that states may not "abridge the privileges or immunities of citizens of the United States" and that "all persons" born or naturalized in the United States "are citizens." Voting would seem to be a privilege of citizenship, women's rights activists argued. But the second section set them straight, describing the right to vote as belonging to "any of the male inhabitants of such state."

How could women support such an amendment? asked Stanton and many other activists. How can you not? asked her longtime ally and friend the abolitionist Wendell Phillips and many other Republicans. "This hour belongs to the negro," he told the Anti-Slavery Society in 1865. "Do you believe the African race is composed entirely of males?" she answered. Stanton and Susan B. Anthony worried that if African American males were assured the vote, the opportunity for women would be lost. "If that word male be inserted as now proposed, it will take us a century to get it out again," Stanton wrote. Actually, it took fifty-five years.

The suffragists lost on the Fourteenth Amendment, but the fight continued into 1869 as Congress debated the Fifteenth Amendment. The Republicans, worried that the prescription for voting in the Fourteenth Amendment was fuzzy, undertook to make it crystal clear through an amendment that expressly barred states from denying citizens the right to vote on the basis of "race, color, or previous condition of servitude." But not gender. In other words, women were left out again. Women activists divided on the issue. Stanton and Anthony adamantly opposed the amendment. "I will cut off this right arm of mine before I will ever work for or demand the ballot for the Negro and not the woman," exclaimed Anthony.

Anthony was passionate about the right to vote. She, like the framers, saw it as a key to freedom. For Anthony, the right to vote would lift the legal burdens that men had placed on women "to protect them." And, since attending a women's rights convention in 1852 in Syracuse, she had committed her life to securing women's suffrage and what she saw as related causes, such as the abolition of slavery. Her life was the relentless pursuit of this goal, through organizing, publishing, writing, speaking and petitioning. She would pursue this goal until her death in 1906, fourteen years before women were enfranchised.

ALL WISE WOMEN WILL OPPOSE THE FIFTEENTH AMENDMENT, blasted a headline of the *Revolution*, a paper Stanton and Anthony coedited. The showdown came in May of 1869 at a convention of the American Equal Rights Association at which Stanton's longtime friend and ally Frederick Douglass rose to challenge her position: "When women, because they are women, are hunted down through the cities of New York and New Orleans; when they are dragged from their houses and hung upon lamp-posts; when their children are torn from their arms, and their brains dashed out upon the pavement . . . then they will have an urgency to obtain the ballot equal to our own."

With this, the matter was settled, at least for then. Many women activists reluctantly supported the Fifteenth Amendment, continuing the fight for their vote separately. In 1869 and 1870, the territories of Wyoming and Utah granted suffrage in state elections to their female citizens, and other territories and states followed suit. But the fight for women to vote in federal elections would continue for another seventy years. Along the way, one woman, Susan B. Anthony, would get to vote in a presidential election, in 1872, although women had not yet received the right to do so.

Susan B. Anthony Is Arrested
for Voting

When Susan B. Anthony entered the parlor of her home in Rochester, New York, to greet the federal deputy marshal, she knew he had come to arrest her. Her crime? As stated in the arrest warrant: "Without having a lawful right to vote in said election district the said Susan B. Anthony, being then and there a person of the female sex . . . did knowingly, wrongfully and unlawfully vote." On November 5, 1872, she had entered the polling place in Rochester's Eighth Ward, convinced the inspectors of her right to vote (she had convinced them of her right to register several days earlier) and cast her ballot for the Republican Ulysses S. Grant and the rest of the Republican ticket, whom she judged were most sympathetic to women's rights. "Well I have been & gone & done it!!—positively voted the Republican ticket," she would write her friend and ally Elizabeth Cady Stanton.

Anthony believed she did have a lawful right to vote. She and many others found it in the recently ratified Fourteenth Amendment. The magistrate hearing her case did not agree. After her arrest, he required the posting of bail, which Anthony refused to do. So she was held. This was a part of her strategy, not a sign of her poverty. Anthony had plenty of money available to her to secure her freedom. Rather, she wanted to be held so she could bring her case directly to the Supreme Court under the rules of habeas corpus. This would allow a national test of the question of whether the Fourteenth Amendment gave women the right to vote. But her lawyer, Henry Selden, a former judge on New York's highest court and supporter of women's suffrage, posted bond for her without her approval. In a triumph of gallantry over political stratagem, he would later explain, "I could not see a lady I respected put in jail."

But despite her anger over her lawyer's act, she used her case to publicize the issue of women's suffrage. In her writing and speaking she would ask the simple question of whether an American should be arrested for voting in a presidential election. Anthony brought all the strands of thinking from the revolutionary era together. She offered arguments from the Declaration of Independence, the Constitution and the writings of Thomas Paine and James Madison, asking her audience to see the denial of suffrage as slavery. She was speaking for history but also to influence potential jurors. "The only alleged ground of illegality of the defendant's vote is that she is a woman," her defense argued.

There is evidence her campaign was working. First prosecutors moved the case to find a less influenced jury pool. Then, when the trial was held, Justice Ward Hunt, in a very unusual and probably unconstitutional move, refused to let the jury decide the case, finding her guilty himself. Depriving the jury of the opportunity to decide Anthony's case again underscores the extent to which those with power are unwilling to share it. A jury of "one's peers" is another important representative institution with which government power is shared. No other country gives as much power to juries. Before the Revolution, juries were often a way for colonists to subvert the edicts of the Crown. And after the Revolution, juries could effectively render unpopular laws null, as, for example, some northern juries did with laws demanding the payment of debt or later the return of fugitive slaves.

Justice Hunt, newly appointed to the Supreme Court, no doubt was well acquainted with this history. So he intervened before this jury could act and ruled on his own that Anthony was guilty. Perhaps he sensed that her defense would prevail even with an all-male jury. In fact, one juror was reported to say, "Could I have spoken, I should have answered 'not guilty' and the men in the jury box would have sustained me."

Having imposed a verdict, the judge then imposed a fine of one hundred dollars on Anthony, only to further rule, "The Court will not order you committed until the fine is paid." A fine, as the Court no doubt understood, she would never pay so she would never be committed to jail.

Anthony continued her crusade for suffrage. "If it is a mere question of who got the best of it," an upstate newspaper editorialized, "Miss Anthony is still ahead; she has voted and the American Constitution has survived the shock. Fining her one hundred dollars does not rule out the facts that fourteen women voted, and went home, and the world jogged on as before."

But the Constitution was designed so that a mere shock would not lead to a change in the Constitution. It would take much more. Suffrage was spreading at the state level. But the Congress failed around forty times to pass an amendment giving women the vote. The framers expected people to operate in their own self-interest. And what subject could possibly generate more self-interest than this one? The opponents all argued that suffrage would add an "unbearable burden on women, whose place was in the home," or set men against women. Many actually believed this. But also hidden behind these arguments were a variety of broad and specific fears that enfranchising women would dilute men's power.

Southern Democrats did not want to add to the number of

black voters. There were many economic interests who were afraid that politically empowered women might support progressive reforms such as workplace protections and child labor laws, which would undermine profitability. The brewers worried that women would tilt the balance for temperance. The animus produced by all of these self-interests would require an enormous effort to overcome. Through various tactics—from grassroots organizing to Capitol Hill lobbying, from marches to silent pickets, from protests to alliance building, women pushed the suffrage agenda.

Finally, in 1919 Congress, in a very close vote, approved and submitted to the states the Nineteenth Amendment. The battle then raged state by state. In 1920, Tennessee became the thirty-sixth and last state necessary for ratification. The amendment was approved by one vote in the Tennessee legislature, when its youngest member, Harry Burns, switched sides after receiving a pro-amendment telegram from his mother. Burns was then reportedly chased from the Capitol by an angry mob.

So on the vote of the swift-footed Burns, the country officially completed a task set in motion 131 years earlier. The framers had argued in 1787 that broader representation would make a stronger, freer country and produce better decisions. But only in 1920 did the country finally complete the essence of this challenge. In one act, the nation enfranchised more voters than at any other time in its history. Struggles over the vote would continue, of course. The enfranchisement of African Americans was official but not yet real, and would not be for another forty years. Younger people, who were dying for the country in its wars, would eventually be allowed to vote too as a result of the pain of Vietnam.

But this moment when women were admitted to the vote was the moment the last philosophical divide was crossed. The country had recognized constitutionally that a country built on the participation of its citizens needed to allow all its citizens to participate.

Did the enfranchisement of women change the nature of government? That is a subject of endless and continuing debate. At first, women were more likely than men to vote Republican, the party more favorable to their enfranchisement. In 1928, political analysts said Herbert Hoover, a defender of Prohibition, was helped into office by women voters. What is clear is that less than a generation after women were given the vote, the nature of the federal government would be radically altered. Perhaps the participation of women played a role. Clearly, the crises of the Great Depression and World War II did.

The 1920 presidential election was the first in which women voted. Warren G. Harding and Calvin Coolidge, the Republicans, defeated James Cox and Franklin D. Roosevelt by a landslide. At a time of strikes and terrorism (the worst attack on Wall Street until 9/11), Harding promised a return to normalcy.

But Roosevelt would be back. In 1932, he would defeat Herbert Hoover, whose scruples against big government restrained his actions against the Depression. The stage was being set for both the nation's greatest success and for its current challenge.

Part Three

THE CHALLENGE

If we forget what we did, we won't know who we are. I'm warning of an eradication of the American memory that could result, ultimately, in an erosion of the American spirit.

—RONALD REAGAN, 1989

6

A MANDATE FOR VIGOROUS ACTION

> *You cannot extend the mastery of government over the daily life of a people without somewhere making it master of people's souls and thoughts.*
>
> —HERBERT HOOVER, 1932

> *Ours has become—as it continues to be, and should remain—a society of large expectations. Government helped to generate these expectations. It undertook to meet them.*
>
> —RICHARD NIXON, 1970

FROM 1789 TO the start of the twentieth century, American government changed in many ways within the constitutional system. Sometimes, as with the invention of an independent judiciary, the change occurred with no rewording of the Constitution. At other times, as with the enfranchisement of African Americans and women, a long and painful struggle was required to amend the Constitution. Yet none of this changed a basic truth about America in its first 140 years: The federal government played a small role in our lives.

That was about to change to an extraordinary degree. The Great Depression brought on a constitutional crisis much more menacing than most Americans in our time truly understand. From economic disintegration, authoritarian governments were rising around the world. Some Americans thought the same changes were needed in the United States. For years after, Eleanor Roosevelt remembered the chill she felt at her husband's first inaugural when he said he might have to assume extraordinary powers and received his strongest ovation.

The question was whether or not America's Constitution and the Constitutional Conscience we had created around it would be supple enough to accommodate the needs of a nation in crisis. Roosevelt rallied the country to answer yes and set in motion a period of remarkable change. For close to forty years, starting with Roosevelt's inaugural promise of economic security and lasting into Nixon's support for the environment, the federal government grew enormously in both size and power. A broad consensus in the country supported this greater federal government involvement in our lives. That consensus brought with it a subtle, but very significant, change in our expectations of government. The framers had given us a system whose primary purpose was to resolve our conflicts and then stay out of the way of our activities. What we created in the twentieth century was a massive administrative state that we expected would directly solve our problems. So long as we agreed in a broad way which problems we wanted solved and how we wanted them solved, this worked well enough. But by the 1970s, that broad agreement was disintegrating. "There is no consensus," the historian Henry Steele Commager wrote in 1974. "There is less harmony in our society, to my mind, than at any time, say, since

Reconstruction." We were left with high expectations for what government could do and little agreement about what government should do. With so many interests pushing the government in different directions, it could do little or nothing. This is exactly what the framers designed the system to do when consensus was lacking. We coined a phrase to describe this result: *governmental gridlock*.

A DIM BODY

Except in times of war, American government from 1787 through the election of FDR in 1932 had played little role in the lives of most Americans, particularly when measured against today's standards. It managed the postal system, established some roads and other internal improvements, enforced a few criminal laws and collected some taxes. There was little government bureaucracy. There were few or no safety nets, little protection for women, minorities, workers or consumers. Things began to change in the late 1800s and then in the era of Theodore Roosevelt, although not nearly as fast as proponents wanted.

Twice during this era the Constitution was amended in a way it had never been amended before, to expand the federal role in a policy area—the first to allow taxation of income (1913) and the second to bar distribution of alcohol (1920).

Even so, by the early 1920s the federal government remained such a "distant, dim, and motionless body in the political firmament" that Republican president Coolidge could with some truth observe that "if the Federal Government should go out of existence, the common run of people would not detect a difference in the affairs of their daily life for a considerable length of time."

Thomas Jefferson had described the government's purpose as solely to "restrain men from injuring one another," leaving them "otherwise free to regulate their own pursuits of industry and improvement." Jefferson was a profound romantic. He needed Madison, Hamilton and others to tether him to the reality of the world. Yet his portrait of minimalist government was not far off, and it captured something about the limited expectations citizens held of their federal government for most of the country's first century or more. Americans did not ask for much. If they had a problem, their first instinct was not to petition the federal government for relief. They shared Jefferson's romanticized vision of self-reliant Americans who could in a land of abundance house and feed themselves and could, if things really became difficult, move west.

Jefferson viewed America as an Eden.

Kindly separated by nature and a wide ocean from the exterminating havoc of one quarter of the globe; too high-minded to endure the degradations of the others; possessing a chosen country, with room enough for our descendants to the thousandth and thousandth generation; entertaining a due sense of our equal right to the use of our own faculties, to the acquisitions of our own industry, to honor and confidence from our fellow-citizens, resulting not from birth, but from our actions and their sense of them; enlightened by a benign religion, professed, indeed, and practiced in various forms, yet all of them inculcating honesty, truth, temperance, gratitude, and the love of man; acknowledging and adoring an overruling Providence, which by all its dispensations proves that it delights in the happiness of man here and his greater happiness hereafter—with all these

blessings, what more is necessary to make us a happy and a pros-
perous people?

ANOTHER NEW WORLD

Things were never, of course, so idyllic. But by the beginning of
the twentieth century, America had become a far different country.
Settlement and industrialization had dramatically changed its landscape and its social organization. As President Franklin Delano
Roosevelt observed, "The age of machinery, of railroads; of steam
and electricity; the telegraph and the radio; mass production, mass
distribution—all of these combined to bring forward a new civilization and with it a new problem for those who sought to remain
free."

The new civilization was one of cities and factories. The new
problem was whether America's constitutional democracy, established in an agricultural America, could function in an industrial-
ized, urbanized one. America had been built on the notion of the
"free, self-reliant, unencumbered" pioneer, who was able to carve a
life for himself and his family from a country of "virtually unlim-
ited" resources with "room and wealth for all." But as Americans
rushed from their farms and rural community life for this new
modern pot of gold, they left behind their independence and self-
reliance. In this new America, you could not go it alone, as much as
you might want to. Americans raised on a somewhat overstated vision of self-reliance were feeling and actually becoming much
more dependent on large industrial enterprises for their well-
being.

To protect themselves, Americans began to organize. Americans had always been joiners of a myriad of religious, social and political clubs, but now their focus was on "groupings which centered around economic interests—labor unions, industrial combines, farmers' organizations, occupations associations." They organized because they understood that through numbers they could exercise political power in America's representative democracy and through political power they could demand laws that would accomplish their goals. "Self-reliance gave way to 'social justice through community action.' " Through groups, Americans would amplify their individual voices and then turn to the political processes and their government to demand "position and power in society."

For the early part of the twentieth century, change was evolutionary.

The government's role in regulating business expanded, through, for example, the antitrust laws. But World War I and subsequent national prosperity tamped Americans' enthusiasm for change.

Then the bottom fell out of the economy.

The Great Depression came as an enormous shock to America's political sense of itself. A nation built on a belief that anyone could rise to be anything was suddenly "bursting with class conflict." As the noted psychiatrist Erik Erikson would reflect, "Here was a great and wealthy country having undergone a traumatic economic depression which, as I can now see, must have seemed to paralyze that very self-made identity and put into question its eternal renewal."

When President-elect Franklin Delano Roosevelt checked in to the Mayflower Hotel in Washington, D.C., the day before his inauguration, the sign on the counter said, DUE TO UNSETTLED BANKING CONDITIONS THROUGHOUT THE COUNTRY, CHECKS ON OUT-OF

TOWN BANKS CANNOT BE ACCEPTED. Eleanor Roosevelt was concerned they would not be able to pay their bills.

Roosevelt had won against President Herbert Hoover in a landslide vote. Indeed, so strong was the vote that the Democrats had also taken control of Congress. Four years earlier, Hoover and his pro-business Republican Party had beaten the Democrats with an even larger landslide vote. But in those four years the country had come undone.

In fact Americans were in a panic, feeling both hopeless and useless. In the land of opportunity and plenty, there was little of either. "The fog of despair hung over the land," wrote the historian Arthur Schlesinger Jr. The economy was paralyzed. "The Country was dying by inches," Roosevelt would later say.

The stock market crash of 1929 had just been the first symptom of the economic plague that hit the country. By 1932, many millions were unemployed, one out of every four, and many millions more were in need. Breadlines were prevalent and long, as were lines at garbage dumps, where many Americans foraged for their food. Writing in his diary in December of 1932, Rex Tugwell, a member of Roosevelt's Brain Trust, said, "No one can live and work in New York this winter without a profound sense of uneasiness. Never, in modern time, I should think, has there been so widespread unemployment and such moving distress from sheer hunger and cold."

Banks were closed; schools were closed; factories were closed; offices were closed. And the ties that connected the society were unwinding. In a famous incident General Douglas MacArthur had used the army, with bayonets and tear gas, to rout thousands of unemployed World War I veterans, the "bonus army," who with their families had come to Washington to lobby Congress for the earlier payment of a promised future bonus. The nationally syndicated columnist Thomas L. Stokes expressed his despair: "The United States Army turned on American citizens—just fellows like myself down on their luck, dispirited, hopeless."

Through most of the country's history, the Constitution's promise of liberty had been closely intertwined with the promise of economic success. But now that success was in tatters. The American dream was becoming a nightmare. And from this nightmare a constitutional crisis was growing. According to Arthur Schlesinger Jr., "The American experiment in self-government was now facing what was, excepting the Civil War, its greatest test."

For example, reminiscent of Shays's Rebellion, farmers in many parts of the country were turning to violence to stop the shipment of produce to market. Their hope was that a reduction of supply would raise prices that were well below what it was costing to produce the crops. Others wanted help from their state legislatures. "If we don't get beneficial service from the Legislature, 200,000 of us are coming to Lincoln [Nebraska] and we'll tear that new State Capitol to pieces," a southern planter told the Senate. "Unless something is done for the American farmer we will have revolution in the countryside within less than twelve months."

Congressman Hamilton Fish Jr. saw the nation's economic chaos as an emerging threat to the Constitution. He warned his colleagues in the House of Representatives in 1932, "If we don't give [security] under the existing system, the people will change the system." Even moral leaders seemed to despair. They wondered whether the nation's elite, who even during the economic crisis remained rich and powerful, would give up some power for reform of the system. "There is nothing in history to support the thesis that a dominant class ever yields its position or its privileges in society because its rule has been convicted of ineptness or injustices," lamented the important American theologian Reinhold Niebuhr.

Some Americans were beginning to think, and say, that America's constitutional democracy could no longer work. They worried that our constitutional form of government could not bring either order or change to the country. Much in the way that members of the Constitutional Convention bruited about restoring a king, there were those who talked about undoing the Constitution. As Washington had worried back then, talking can proceed to doing.

The influential journalist Henry Hazlitt suggested replacing Congress with a "directorate of twelve men." Others proposed an even more draconian and direct response, vesting a leader "with dictatorial powers." "I don't often envy other countries their governments," said Republican senator David Reed of Pennsylvania, "but if this country ever needed a Mussolini, it needs one now." The magazine *Barron's* called for a "genial and lighthearted dictator." Walter Lippmann, perhaps the country's most influential journalist, advised Roosevelt: "The situation is critical, Franklin. You may have no alternative but to assume dictatorial powers."

Several times in Americans history the country has faced a crisis with two roads out. One road was to strengthen the democratic system to preserve it. The other road was to abandon a democratic union because other goals seemed more urgent. This was exactly the choice the framers faced when they invented the more powerful central government under the Constitution to replace the Articles of Confederation. It was the choice Lincoln faced when he decided the Union would be preserved at gunpoint. Now it was Franklin D. Roosevelt's choice.

In his First Inaugural Address, Roosevelt asked a desperate country to be patient with the Constitution. Action was needed, he said, but such action was "feasible under the form of government which we have inherited from our ancestors." With one hundred thousand before him around the Capitol steps and millions gathered around their radios, Roosevelt reassured the country that even the "extraordinary needs" of the nation had been met in the past, and could be met now, "by changes in emphasis and arrangement" in the Constitution "without loss of essential form. That is why our Constitutional system has proved itself the most superbly enduring political mechanism the modern world has produced. It has met every stress of vast expansion of territory, of foreign wars, of bitter internal strife, of world relations."

The Scary Thought of a Stronger Government

President Roosevelt, as former New York governor Mario Cuomo used to say, rose from his wheelchair to lift a nation from its knees. The fact that he needed to use a portion of his First Inaugural Address to reaffirm the value of the Constitution captures how perilous a political moment this was. Part of the purpose of Roosevelt's embrace of the Constitution was to send a message of reassurance that he was not seeking to become a dictator. But he was also entering a second debate going on at that time, in many ways even more interesting in the context of our story about the country's relationship to the Constitution. It was a reprise of the debate between 1776 and 1787.

Roosevelt didn't want dictatorial powers, certainly not permanently. But he did want to vastly expand the reach and authority of the federal government to address the emergency. To some Americans, that was profoundly scary, and it revived the debate over limits to federal power that tore at the country between 1776 and 1787. Did America need a stronger national government to solve its problems? Or would relying on the public virtue of the people be enough?

Across the political divide from Roosevelt were Americans who agreed the crisis of economic collapse had to be addressed. But like Tom Paine and Patrick Henry in the revolutionary era, they saw concentrating power in the federal government as a needless threat to personal liberty even in—no, especially in—a time of crisis.

This strain of thinking was summed up by Herbert Hoover, who was president when the markets crashed: "You cannot extend the mastery of government over the daily life of a people without somewhere making it master of people's souls and thoughts." These thoughts echoed those Patrick Henry had expressed in his great speech to the Virginia convention, where he pleaded with Americans to think about liberty before economic growth and prosperity.

There were those after the crash who fought federal intervention. "Stick it out," thought many conservatives and, of course, many who would be unfavorably affected by regulation. Anything else, they would argue, would "overburden the shoulders of government and industry" and push the country "towards the Socialistic goal, the abolition of private property." Like the plague it was, they argued, the bad time would pass. And when it did, American freedom would still be protected.

President Hoover believed the federal government had an important role. Were it not for the market crash, poor Herbert Hoover might be well remembered. He was a pragmatic figure and a truly excellent manager. He was a hero of the relief efforts after World War I. He was a supporter of business but an enlightened one. In the practices of banks and other financial institutions, he saw predatory self-interest without regard for the common good of the nation. But like the revolutionary leaders of 1776, and unlike the framers of the Constitution, Hoover believed in a uniquely American form of public virtue, through which Americans could restrain self-interest for the common good. Government's job was "to articulate and organize the aspiration of these better selves and to provide the information for them to come together." Government should forge volunteerism to meet the Depression crisis. Anything else would result in "tyranny and the corruption of America's unique political soul."

But Roosevelt, like Madison, found a reliance on virtue inadequate to the crisis. Like the framers, he viewed America in chaos. Unchecked, this chaos would slide toward despotism. A reliance on virtue would not be enough. States, as they had been in the years leading up to the ratification of the Constitution, were again seen as the culprits. "To the New Dealers, the states were weak and ineffectual, unable to protect rights or deal with serious social problems." Often they were dominated by "well organized private groups." Domination in this case was not that of majority factions controlling the political process, but of what Roosevelt would later call "a new despotism," a "new industrial dictatorship" protected by government. "A small group had concentrated into their own hands an almost complete control over other people's property, other people's money, other people's labor, other people's lives. For too many of us life was no longer free; liberty no longer real; men could no longer follow the pursuit of happiness."

To respond, Roosevelt introduced a new definition of liberty and with it a radical new role for the federal government. The protection of Americans' liberty required the "opportunity to make a living—a living decent according to the standard of the time, a living which gives man not only enough to live by, but something to live for." For Americans to have that opportunity, the federal government would now be intimately and immediately involved with the lives of its citizens and strongly led by the president. "We do not distrust the future of essential democracy," FDR maintained. "The people of the United States have not failed. In their need they have registered a mandate that they want direct, vigorous action. They have asked for discipline and direction under leadership. They have made me the present instrument of their wishes. In the spirit of the gift I take it."

The New Presidency, Vigorous Action and Consensus

In common, Americans wanted "vigorous action" from their government. They wanted their president to fix things. This role for the president was new for America. Long seen as focused on foreign affairs or war, the role of the president had been limited in domestic affairs. There was relatively little to do there, and Congress dominated the efforts. But this was a matter of history, not law.

Although the framers properly worried about the determination of an executive to aggregate power (as they worried about that inevitable tendency in every official), they limited the executive's capacity to achieve such through both separation of powers and, ultimately, the electoral process. But nothing in the Constitution constrained the president from aggressively asserting himself into domestic policy making. A forceful president was possible from the beginning of the Republic. "Energy in the Executive is a leading character in the definition of good government," wrote Hamilton, and most of the founders no doubt agreed. As President Woodrow Wilson had rightly observed, "the President [was] at liberty both in law and conscience to be as big a man as he can."

In fact, the Constitution provides opportunities for a president who wants to be, in Wilson's words, a "big man." The design of Congress tends toward policy-making "inertia," as the representatives of multitudes of different interests argue over their relative values. For the legislative ball to roll, it usually needs a big push, which the president is well positioned to give.

The president is the voice of the nation, an increasingly important notion as that voice became magnified by broadcasting. He (with the vice president) is the only official who is elected by all Americans. Each year the president is constitutionally obligated to report to the nation on the state of the Union, and thus only the president is officially charged with measuring and reporting on the nation's needs. And through the veto power, he also can stop legislation he judges unsatisfactory.

These powers, in the context of the Depression and later World War II, allowed FDR to become the domestically forceful president he was. And his successes would not be lost on future candidates. From that moment on, candidates for president would campaign as domestic leaders, who, if elected, would make the everyday lives of Americans better. The job now included setting and pursuing a national agenda for Americans and their Congress to consider. The task also included managing a vast government, created by these new programs, which intersected everywhere with the lives of its citizens.

Roosevelt did not simply take these powers, nor was the

Constitution amended to create them. Roosevelt persuaded the country, the Congress and the courts to accede to them. The members of Roosevelt's administration understood this critical element of American governance well. They saw their leadership task as winning broad support for their programs. "The New Dealers sought to effect a truce similar to that of wartime, when class and sectional animosities abated and the claims of partisan or private economic animosities were sacrificed to the demands of the national unity."

This is an essential point. A number of Roosevelt's successors have complained that they could not get Congress to do what they wanted. Of course not. The president cannot change the law himself. Making laws is the task assigned to Congress. Indeed, the framers envisioned Congress as the primary branch of government and expected the president to keep an eye on it. It is the members of Congress, at least a majority of each house, who must accept the need for change. This requires that the members of Congress be convinced that proposed changes are necessary both substantively and politically. If either the president or the Congress fails to assert its role, the system doesn't work.

This requirement of consensus if there is to be change is central to our society. Majority rule of 50 percent plus 1 is not the goal the framers established for American democracy. As designed, America's representative government is intended to embed our factionalism in our government, particularly in its two legislative houses. That is the essence of American representation. As long as there are many and opposing voices, Congress cannot act. That is why compromise is so critical to progress. The idea, again, is to protect Americans' freedom by limiting even a majority faction from imposing its interests on others. Change only occurs when members of each house of Congress and the president can agree on the precise change, or when each house of Congress can override a presidential veto.

Roosevelt did not win every battle. He famously lost an effort to expand the Supreme Court so it would be more accepting of his efforts (which it ultimately became without enlargement.) But over time and overall, he was successful. With bipartisan support, every aspect of the economy came, at least temporarily, under some form of regulation. Millions of Americans were put to work directly by the federal government in programs such as the Civilian Conservation Corps and the Works Projects Administration. Permanent security nets such as Social Security insurance, federal deposit insurance, workers' compensation, disability insurance and unemployment insurance were all commenced. Finally, Americans successfully demanded limits on a vast array of business practices. Child labor, work hours, minimum wages, the right to organize, banking and security industry practices, the sale of foods and pharmaceuticals and many more subjects were addressed. And from these large governmental programs, democratically approved, the government itself grew enormously.

The growth in government continued even as the Depression waned. World War II thrust America, and the American president, into a leadership role in the world. At the same time, the large new domestic programs Americans had demanded required proper administration and enforcement. Who was going to implement these extensive new programs? Who was going to determine which Americans were actually eligible and which were not? Who was going to ensure that those who attempted to defraud the government were caught? Between 1930 and 1949, the federal expenditures and number of federal employees rose dramatically. Many of today's well-known agencies emerged or were greatly empowered.

Among them were the Social Security Administration, the Securities and Exchange Commission, the Federal Reserve Board, the Federal Trade Commission, the National Labor Relations Board and the Food and Drug Administration. With them came what we now call the American Administrative State, the mass of congressionally created agencies within the executive branch of government that details and enforces programs enacted by Congress.

But perhaps the most important political legacy of the Roosevelt era was the attitude of Americans as they entered the postwar era. The crises of depression and war were behind them, but Americans maintained large expectations about government's capacity to resolve their problems. "The Great Depression and, on its heels, World War II, followed by the cold war, dramatically raised Americans' expectation of their government and especially of their presidents." Under Presidents Harry Truman, Dwight Eisenhower, John Kennedy, and Lyndon Johnson, bipartisan coalitions of Americans supported programs for veterans, the poor, the elderly, racial minorities and women, federal aid for education, immigration reform and social insurance for the elderly and poor.

In the mid-1960s, some thirty years after Roosevelt took office, the New Deal consensus began to unravel. The country was increasingly divided. The Civil Rights Act of 1964 and the Voting Rights Act of 1965 created a racial schism in the electorate that Republicans used to propel their rise in the South.

Discord was everywhere. Not just as a result of the war in Vietnam but from the breakup of the consensus of Americans of all stripes on which the country's progress had been based for the last forty years. "The American home was divided," President Johnson had proclaimed in announcing his decision not to seek reelection in 1968. The year 1968 is well recorded as one of the most discordant in our history. Toward its end, after a year of assassinations, protests and riots, Richard Nixon was elected president.

Nixon is most remembered for his foreign policy prowess and the Watergate scandal. But he played another important, but less remarked on, role. He was the transitional president from the Roosevelt age of expanded expectations and large consensus to the very different era of expanded expectations and an elusive consensus.

Because even as Nixon, the ever sharp politician, seized the divisions in the country to secure his election, he was also the last president to defend the large expectations Americans had of their federal government—and to expand its role into yet another territory: protection of the environment. Through the enactment of the Clean Air Act of 1970, the creation of the Environmental Protection Agency in 1970 and the passage of the Clean Water Act of 1972, American government entered even more prominently into the nooks and crannies of Americans' lives.

A REPUBLICAN PRESIDENT
EXPANDS THE GOVERNMENT

Watergate had not yet befallen Nixon when he delivered his second State of the Union address. His first year had not been easy. His divisive campaign had succeeded, and he was now president, but his efforts did nothing to change Congress. It continued under Democratic control and was hostile toward him. The country was at war in Vietnam. Despite Nixon's strong interest and long experience in foreign policy, his campaign's "secret plan" to end the war in Vietnam had produced no evident results. Nixon had no plan for reuniting Americans. In fact, his southern electoral strategy aimed at winning southern Democrats by criticizing the growth of government and promising to reduce the reach of the federal government.

Additionally, Nixon had little real interest in domestic policy. "All you need is a competent cabinet to run the country at home," he would say. His attention was on world affairs—"the great questions that concern world leaders at summit conferences," he would label them. And there were many to be discussed: ending the war, détente with the USSR, opening relations with China. But things were not yet going well on any of these fronts. Perhaps that is what changed his focus from the "summits," where he sought his greatness, to "the foothills," where he knew Americans lived. "It is time," he said in his second State of the Union address, "for all of us to concern ourselves with the way real people live in real life."

And with that "discovery" of this evident political point, he set aside his announced commitment to state and local rights and embraced the environmental revolution and a new expanded role for the federal government.

> Ours has become—as it continues to be, and should remain—a society of large expectations. Government helped to generate these expectations. It undertook to meet them . . .
>
> In the next 10 years we shall increase our wealth by 50 percent. The profound question is: Does this mean we will be 50 percent richer in a real sense, 50 percent better off, 50 percent happier?
>
> Or does it mean that in the year 1980 the President standing in this place will look back on a decade in which 70 percent of our people lived in metropolitan areas choked by traffic, suffocated by smog, poisoned by water, deafened by noise . . .
>
> These are not the great questions that concern world leaders at summit conferences.

Restoring nature to its natural state is a cause beyond party and beyond factions. It has become a common cause of all the people of this country. It is a cause of particular concern to young Americans, because they more than we will reap the grim consequences of our failure to act on programs which are needed now if we are to prevent disaster later.

LARGE EXPECTATION, NO CONSENSUS

As we look back from our own age of political strife and factionalism—a factionalism Nixon himself played a role in propelling—there is something almost poignant in Nixon's second State of the Union message. Ask Americans today what they most long for from their politics, and many will say words to the effect of "a cause beyond party and beyond faction . . . a common cause of all the people." But at the level at which government operates, creating actual rights and obligations, such common cause is hard to find. While Americans may hope for a unified America, they fight over what should be common. During the forty-year consensus between FDR and Nixon, hopes were fulfilled because individual Americans demanded similar things from their government. Nixon's environmental push was the last hurrah of this era.

Much like the country itself, Nixon went in both directions at once. He ushered in one more major expansion of federal power, while warning that the government was "becoming increasingly unable" to satisfy Americans' expectations. On this point he was unquestionably right and foreshadowed the struggle to come. Nixon tried to lower these expectations: "It's time to have power go back from Washington to the states and to the cities of this country all over America."

But as Nixon's expanded environmental policy illustrated, Americans were themselves of two minds. They were not opposed to an assertive federal government in areas where they wanted something done.

The problem now was that the consensus for change that had steered American politics for almost forty years had shattered. The sense of American unity which had allowed the country to act broadly against the Depression through the New Deal, against the Axis in World War II, against the Communists in the cold war and even against poverty and racism through the Great Society could not last forever. Americans' shared view of the common good had finally worn out.

What was left was a political stew of high expectations and divergent demands. Many American political leaders have "learned to their dismay that while people might claim to despise government, they also developed ever higher expectations from it." Indeed, the demands took on new forms. The New Deal and World War II created a much broader sense of what the government was capable of. By the 1960s and 1970s, what emerged was a much deeper sense among many Americans of what they were entitled to. John F. Kennedy could feel this coming as early as 1961 when he pleaded with Americans, "Ask not what your country can do for you—ask what you can do for your country."

But within a decade America was in the full flower (flower children were no doubt among the many instigators) of what historians now describe as "the rights revolution."

The Rights Revolution

Rights, what the framers would have called liberties, have always been an essential part of the American political tapestry. The right to participate in government was summed up in the revolutionary-era bumper sticker NO TAXATION WITHOUT REPRESENTATION. The right to pursue one's own interests was essential to the Constitution—indeed it was the energy the framers were harnessing in their complicated system of government, a system designed to allow action while preventing majority tyranny. And, of course, that government would not have been established at all were it not for the promise of a bill of rights intended to protect certain individual rights against any government actions.

From the Bill of Rights onward, Americans have amended the Constitution to expand the political rights of more and more citizens. These are civic rights. They include the rights to free speech, to vote, to a free press, to free worship, to trial by jury, to freedom from unreasonable searches and seizures. Through them, Americans are assured the opportunity to participate in the political process and freedom from arbitrary governmental action. The emphasis throughout these provisions is on keeping government out of the lives of Americans and giving Americans a voice in that government.

The Depression produced a new notion of rights. Economic rights, or what FDR was in 1944 to call a "second Bill of Rights," "under which a new basis of security and prosperity can be established for all—regardless of station, race, or creed." Among these were the right to a job with a living wage, the right to protection "from the economic fears of old age and sickness," the right to medical care, the right to a home and the right to a good education.

Under FDR, working Americans were guaranteed minimum wages, maximum daily and weekly hours, unemployment compensation and a pension. Modest bank accounts were insured, and their investments were also protected to some degree from both downward business cycles and business skullduggery. And from these programs grew Johnson's Great Society, which promised civil rights and various benefits for the poor and elderly. None of these changes became part of the written Constitution, but the general principles behind them entered the Constitutional Conscience. Americans accepted that maintaining the Republic now required the fundamentals of these programs, although they argued over the details.

But by the mid-1960s, groups of Americans began to push for a new level of rights, rights which reflected their particular group interests. Perhaps this was predictable. The government had proven itself responsive to the large demands of Americans for several decades, and there was no reason now to expect otherwise, or at least not to demand.

From the civil rights movement flowed movements to protect the rights of the poor, Hispanics, Native Americans, women, the elderly, the disabled and defendants (and it has continued through today with the addition of crime victims, unborn children, gays, lesbians and transsexuals). Fueling this rights explosion, at least in the early 1970s, were federal courts, which, with unclear authority, made a number of decisions, for example, on forced busing and affirmative action, that actively pitted whites and blacks against each other. These decisions also thrust the federal courts into the political vortex, leading many Americans to complain about activist courts and the Senate to become far more partisan in its confirmation process.

The framers of course expected factionalism, even tribalism. But their system envisioned factions fighting over interests that could be compromised through the process of government. Philosophically, the new language of rights demanded that the government fulfill obligations that could not be compromised.

An enormous crisis was developing. Roosevelt's addition of economic rights had become part of a national consensus, but the demand for something beyond that triggered a fierce backlash.

To many Americans, the focus of various groups on their own agendas and the preoccupations of many individuals with themselves seemed out of control, selfish, indulgent and threatening. Particularly unsettling were the claims of some groups that they were entitled to special treatment, affirmative action of one kind or another. The idea, for example, that one employee might be promoted over another on the basis of race alone simply seemed outrageous and un-American to a wide swath of Americans. The Constitutional Conscience spoke for equality of opportunity, not group-based advantages. Americans were fine with a "Social Gospel," in which opportunities would be shared, but balked at anything much beyond that. "Americans were much less sympathetic when people demanded the 'right' to social equality or special entitlements for groups. That was taking the Rights Revolution too far." The American political culture, a reflection, of course, of the larger society, was going from the spirit of we to a culture of me (or, sometimes, us, as groups vied for advantage).

Politicians seized on these divides, these "wedge issues," and became part of the problem. Nixon showed the way. He called on the "silent" or "forgotten" majority to support him. They were in his words "the non demonstrators," of every color, age and nationality. "They work in American factories, they run American businesses. They serve in government; they provide most of the soldiers who die to keep it free. They give drive to the spirit of America. They give lift to the American dream. They give steel to the backbone of America." And although this rhetoric served Nixon's southern strategy to pick up southern voters repelled by the Civil

Rights Act of 1964 and the Voting Rights Act of 1965 and also his regional strategy to isolate the Northeast, there was power in what he was saying for many Americans. The backlash was not simply a refusal to share rights with others; it was a reaction against what many Americans saw as a tearing apart of the American way, however they defined it. That is why the picture of a student desecrating an American flag resulted in such angry reactions. As the prize-winning historian James T. Patterson wrote: "The backlash represented considerably more than white racism, which polls suggested was less intense than in the past. It also affirmed the behaviors and the moral standards of traditional ways. It exposed a fragmentation of society and culture that seemed if anything to grow in the next thirty years."

The point for our story is not which side of this divide you find yourself on. The point is that there was a deep divide. The framers had built a system to force antagonistic factions to the middle, where they would compromise to get action.

From the 1930s to the 1960s, this system had worked. The political consensus under which American government expanded from the election of President Roosevelt to the resignation of Richard Nixon created, even in its declining days, a sense that American government could successfully address any problem. But the essential ingredient is that there had to be a consensus on the problem and a willingness to compromise to win support for solutions. But by the time Jimmy Carter came to office, it was clear such consensus was out of reach, at least out of his reach. The expectation the framers had of "mutual concessions and sacrifices . . . mutual forbearance and conciliation" had been replaced by a nation of citizens unforgiving of a government that was not fulfilling their demands. As James Patterson put it, "Conditioned to expect progress, they [Americans] were impatient, and they resisted leaders who asked them to sacrifice."

The leaders, in turn, looked for someone to blame (certainly not themselves). In the 1960s, the notion that government was the problem was heard mostly from the political fringes. "We wanted to create a situation in which . . . the federal government . . . would self-destruct," said Jerry Rubin, a leader of one group of demonstrators at the Democratic convention in 1968.

But by the time of the Carter administration, the notion that something was wrong in the government could be heard from the White House itself. In 1979, President Carter complained that what he viewed as his "balanced" legislative agenda was being stymied.

What you see too often in Washington and elsewhere around the country is a system of government that seems incapable of action. You see a Congress twisted and pulled in every direction by hundreds of well-financed and powerful special interests. You see every extreme position defended to the last vote, almost to the last breath by one unyielding group or another. You often see a balanced and a fair approach that demands sacrifice, a little sacrifice from everyone, abandoned like an orphan without support and without friends.

How much of this gridlock was the result of an unyielding Congress? How much was a president's inability to rally consensus on how to solve the nation's emerging energy crisis? And how much were these politicians unyielding because the public was demanding, unyielding and deeply divided?

Historians are still debating these questions. But it is clear the country wanted change. A new leader, Ronald Reagan, strong and articulate, would soon be brought to power by this discontent and division in the country. A lapsed New Dealer himself, he would try to rekindle a sense of common cause and a spirit, like Tom Paine, that it was morning in America again. About the gridlock in Washington, he would go one step further than Carter had, and place the blame squarely on the government itself.

7

GOVERNMENT IS NOT THE SOLUTION, GOVERNMENT IS THE PROBLEM

*The separation of powers between the legislative and ex-
ecutive branches, whatever its merits in 1793, has become
a structure that almost guarantees stalemates today.*
    —LLOYD CUTLER, WHITE HOUSE COUNSEL, 1980

BY THE TIME Ronald Reagan was elected president in 1980,
a serious rebellion was under way against the complicated system the framers had designed to manage America's democracy.
Acts of rebellion could be found from left to right in the political
spectrum, and in the highest reaches of society, including in the
White House itself. Some acts of rebellion were highly intellectual.
Some were fervently political. A few were just plain criminal. The
rebels included a California opponent of the New Deal consensus,
a Democratic White House counsel and a marine colonel who
only later would emerge as a conservative spokesman. Their back-
grounds were diverse. What they shared was a frustration that the
system was blocking them from achieving what they believed was

best for the country. This was happening, they concluded, because the system had fallen into the hands of "special interests" that pursued their own interests, not the country's best interests.

The framers worried about special interests, too. They called them factions. The suggestion that factions or individuals would confuse their own goals with the general interest of the country would hardly have surprised the framers. They designed the constitutional system precisely to absorb that kind of self-interested drive. What probably would have worried the framers is that all three of these rebels believed that the way to solve the problem of factions, and achieve their aims, was to abandon the constitutional system by going around it, dismantling it entirely or simply disobeying its decisions.

By the end of the 1970s, frustration with government was rampant. The government seemed better at producing strife than at finding solutions to the tangle of inflation, unemployment and social fragmentation that plagued the Carter administration. "Our political institutions do not match the scales of economic and social reality," complained the liberal sociologist Daniel Bell. "The national state has become too small for the big problems of life and too big for the small problems."

This disillusionment bubbled over in many places. In 1978, a conservative activist named Howard Jarvis revived a tool from the Progressive Era of the early twentieth century, known as initiative and referendum, and used it to go around the deliberations of the California legislature and restrict that state's ability to raise taxes. In 1980, the counsel to President Jimmy Carter, Lloyd Cutler, said directly that the system Madison and his colleagues had invented not quite two hundred years before was outmoded and should be replaced. And in 1984, the marine colonel Oliver North, sworn to uphold the Constitution, simply disobeyed the explicit orders of the Congress and ran a private little war from the White House.

For many Americans, Ronald Reagan came to embody the widespread discontent toward government. A "revolution" against big government came to bear his name. As he took office, Reagan sounded as if Tom Paine had returned to help craft his inaugural address with its call for simpler government resting directly on the people. "In the present crisis, government is not the solution to our problem," Reagan proclaimed. "Government is the problem."

Reagan in many ways was like Paine. He was a great communicator of his idealism, a great optimist about the potential of Americans. He, like Paine, could speak simply and powerfully to and for the discontentment of Americans.

The attack on government had already been heard from the White House under Reagan's predecessor, Jimmy Carter. Carter had described the country's divisions as "wounds" from the 1960s that were "still very deep. They have never healed." In Carter's view, these divisions had frustrated his legislative efforts. Even with a Congress controlled by his own party, Carter had failed to build a consensus for needed energy and economic policy. This failure he blamed on the selfishness of members of Congress and the "self-indulgence" of the American people. The framers might have advised Carter to get over his shock at discovering the "sinfulness" of self-interest. But they would have agreed with his analysis of human nature, if perhaps not his naive hope that Americans could be lectured into being more virtuous.

Ronald Reagan, harking back to Paine, took the other course offered by American political history, embracing the ideas of 1776 rather than 1787. He shared Carter's belief that the government was paralyzed by special interests. But he expressed none of

Carter's skepticism about the virtue of Americans. It was not the competing claims of self-interested Americans that paralyzed the government. It was the government itself. Get the government out of the way, and "we the people this breed called Americans . . . can and will resolve the problems that confront us." Get government off their backs, Paine had said, and Americans would have a blank slate to write upon.

Reagan's optimistic message was well received. He legitimized the frustrations felt by millions of Americans, while restoring a sense of confidence. Perhaps his message to Americans that they were not at fault for the country's obvious fault lines was a needed part of that restoration. Reagan remains one of our most influential twentieth-century presidents. But as we look back, it is also easy to see how the Reagan era, and his message that government was the problem, accelerated the crumbling of our Constitutional Conscience that has become so apparent in the last few years.

Reagan coaxed the country out of what Carter had called its malaise. But he was not able to forge a new consensus to replace the one that had driven the country from FDR almost to Nixon. Indeed, one of Reagan's great strengths was his pragmatism. He held his beliefs strongly. But in the best American tradition, he valued progress more than ideological purity or coherence. He cut taxes a lot, then raised them a bit. He could not end most social programs, but then again after four decades of growth he did not add new ones either. Reagan worked with the Democrats. His friendship with that quintessential Democrat Tip O'Neill, Speaker of the House, is often cited as the last hurrah of a bygone bipartisan era. As one historian wrote, "While fond of damning big government . . . he recognized that liberal interest groups had effective lobbies on the Hill, that major New Deal–Great Society social programs . . . were here to stay, and that rights consciousness had become a powerful political source."

Reagan won victories. After four decades of New Deal liberalism, he revived conservatism as a plausible political alternative in national politics. But by the end of his presidency, the country remained politically divided. And across that divide the strife worsened. As the differences deepened, the confidence in the constitutional system designed to channel our political differences continued to erode. A *Time* magazine cover provocatively asked, IS GOVERNMENT DEAD? and followed with this unsettling observation: "After almost nine years of the Reagan Revolution, Americans may wonder whether the Government—from Congress to the White House, from the State Department to the Office of Management and Budget—can govern at all anymore."

Reagan's statement that America's problem was the government was politically, and rhetorically, powerful. But it probably had an unintended consequence. It took Americans off the hook. They were not asked to take responsibility for their own divisions and factionalism. The system created to force them to resolve differences or face paralysis was now redefined as the source of the paralysis.

Over the next twenty years, this rejection of the value of the institutions began to pervade the institutions themselves. The Congress became a pitch for partisan warfare. As the liberal consensus of the New Deal crumbled, many on the left became more fervent and moralistic in pursuit of their claims. On the right, Reagan, who had been a leader of conservative clarity and political flexibility, was replaced by politicians who revered his clarity and forgot his flexibility. The framers' notion that conciliation and compromise were essential values was replaced with a winner-take-all fever. A Republican president had been driven from office (albeit by bipartisan consensus), so Republicans impeached (but did not convict) a Democratic president. In 2007, the former majority leader of the House of Representatives, Tom DeLay, the driving figure behind the impeachment of Bill Clinton, summed up the political approach that now dominated Washington: "No retreat. No surrender."

Tom DeLay's approach to government is an illustration of how the mood of the 1970s and 1980s—disaffection with government—came home to roost in our own time as disrespect for the institutions of government. The most significant impact of this attitude has been the decline of Congress as a coequal branch of government. The framers saw Congress and the presidency as essential checks on each other (and the House and Senate as checks on each other, too!). The balance was essential. But in recent years the institutional role of Congress has deteriorated to the point where two of the nation's leading experts on Congress, Thomas E. Mann and Norman J. Ornstein, have called it the "broken branch." In President Clinton's second term, the Republicans in Congress set out not so much to check the president as to destroy him. Then, after President George W. Bush's excruciatingly thin victory (perhaps because of it), the Republicans in Congress effectively adopted Lloyd Cutler's call for a parliamentary system, one in which the legislature follows the instructions of the executive. They did not amend the Constitution. They simply became the president's loyal lieutenants. "The institutional rivalry designed by the framers gave way to a relationship in which Congress assumed a position subordinate to the executive. Party trumped institution." There is no better example of the decline of our Constitutional Conscience.

Reagan's attack on government did not create all of this, of course. He was a reflection of the times, but as president his voice was more important than all others and through it he gave encouragement to the growing national attitude that government itself was broken.

The decline of respect for institutions was widespread in the country when Reagan took office, and began with Vietnam and Watergate. The governmental leaders of our time grew up amid the strife and cynicism of Vietnam and Watergate. It is easy to see where they developed the attitude that the institutions of government—and the process of government—were tools to an end rather than responsibilities to be safeguarded. They brought these attitudes with them from the society. Tom DeLay was inspired to enter politics by Ronald Reagan. But Reagan's attack on government was tempered by his faith in America, the hard-won faith of the Depression and world war generations. On the other hand, DeLay's attitudes toward the constitutional system combined the antigovernment message of the Reagan era with the cynicism of the Vietnam and Watergate eras.

THE "PEOPLE" REBEL

As with so many ideas in American politics, the antigovernment sentiment grew outside of Washington. Indeed, as with Reagan himself, the notion that government was the problem came out of the West.

One of its prime expressions in the late 1970s was the initiative movement, and one of its prime spokesmen was Howard Jarvis.

Howard Jarvis was interested in a revolution, a tax revolution. For years this Californian had watched as the state legislature took no action on what he considered to be suffocatingly high property taxes. "We're mad as hell" was Jarvis's reported message in a *Time* magazine cover story dated June 19, 1978. And from that anger grew Jarvis's and his allies' determination to do something.

The California Constitution provided the opportunity. During the Progressive Era, Californians and the citizens of a number of other states added an initiative and referendum process to their constitution that allowed citizens to amend both their state constitutions and state laws directly. All it took was a petition drive to secure a minimum number of signatures of support for a question to be put on a ballot for voter consideration. There would be no governmental interference.

The Progressives themselves had come to realize that the reality of this direct democracy was a lot less than the promise. The initiative system fell into disuse but remained on the books. The frustrations of the 1970s led to its rediscovery. In California, as elsewhere in the country, people were deeply divided over what they wanted their government to do, so it did little. On Jarvis's particular issue, high tax levels generally and property taxes specifically, the California legislature could not act without a consensus. And while there might have been a consensus on cutting taxes, Californians had supported the establishment of the many services the state provided, and there was no agreement now on which ones ought to be reduced.

Jarvis cut this knot. Through an initiative he separated the integrally related issues of taxing and spending. He asked Californians if they wanted to reduce taxes. On June 6, 1978, they overwhelmingly voted yes on Proposition 13, under which there would be a limitation on their property taxes and on the legislature's capacity to increase state revenues of any sort by requiring a two-thirds vote of each house. The legislators were left holding the bag. They had to decide what programs should be eliminated without the necessary revenues.

Many applauded this action. California governor Jerry Brown, chastened by his opposition to Proposition 13, called it "the strongest expression of the democratic process in a decade." From this vote grew a movement of initiatives in the twenty or so states where they were available. People were being put back into politics, supporters said. But it was more radical. The essential elements of the framers' version of democracy—struggle, debate, compromise—were stripped away from government decision making by "minimizing, even spurning, the role of the representative intermediaries that stood between the public and its government—parties, legislators, private interests, ultimately politics [which is after all the art of compromising] itself."

Over the next years, citizens in various states would cast their votes with varying outcomes on such controversial topics as voters' rights, auto insurance rates, gay rights, immigrant rights, abortion rights, taxpayers' rights, minority rights, housing rights, language rights, victims' rights and the rights of the terminally ill.

Direct democracy, as initiatives are called, can be, as Jerry Brown said, a strong expression of public sentiment. But it is certainly not the process invented by the framers or envisioned by the Constitution. Indeed, initiatives represent the very antithesis of the representative, deliberative process the framers invented to stabilize democracy. Through initiatives, a tyranny of the majority is possible, even a tyranny of the minority. Every state legislature (and both houses of Congress) require at least a majority of all legislators to enact a law. But states do not require that a majority of all registered voters support an initiative for it to pass. In fact, a minority of voters can change the law. Proposition 13 is such a case. The proposition won in a landslide among those who voted. But even so, fewer than 50 percent of California's registered voters cast a yes vote for the proposition. Thus a minority of registered Californians decided to reduce tax burdens and limit the capacity of the government to increase its future revenues.

It was appealingly easy to adopt this initiative. There was none of the scrutiny of normal legislative process nor the need for coalition building and compromise. No committee of one legislative house and then of the second could block its path to a vote. No requirement that a bill pass two separate legislative houses stood in the way. No executive stood waiving a veto pen. No colleagues were hovering around demanding compromise for support. No lobbyists were demanding changes. No time-consuming hearings from which concerns of the public or experts had to be addressed and weighed. No long public debates in which legislators had to explain why they favored or disfavored the issue. No arcane procedural rules blocked a vote in either a committee or legislative house. No worries that a wrong step might anger constituents. No competition among this idea and the thousands of other ideas wanting legislative attention. In short, the initiative did not have to pass through any of the screens that in the legislature protect against the tyranny of the majority or even the minority and require deliberation and consensus.

The reformers who introduced the process of initiative and referendum to America did not favor tyranny. They thought that American government—particularly state government—had become corrupt, which for them meant that it worked against the "people's" interests. Through initiatives, these reformers wanted "the restoration of the classic republican constituency," the simple government of Tom Paine. They "would put Madison aside." And putting "Madison aside" meant that these reformers would replace Madison's and other framers' realistic view of human nature with the idealistic one envisioned by America's revolutionary leaders in 1776. John Q. Public, the Progressives called him, a man who thought for himself, who "would study the issues and think them through," a man who had the time, intellect and curiosity to inform "himself in ample detail about the many issues that he would have to pass on," a man who "could master their intricacies sufficiently to pass intelligent judgment."

But soon the reformers realized the weakness of their view. They could not push Madison aside. Just as the generation of the Revolution was forced to reevaluate its view of human nature in the face of real conduct, the reformers of the early twentieth century realized human nature was not as they had hoped (but rather as Madison had understood). Using initiatives and referendums to resolve society's major conflicts was asking voters to be something they were not, wrote the journalist Walter Lippmann: "In ordinary circumstances voters cannot be expected to transcend their particular, localized and self-regarding opinions. As well expect men laboring in the valley to see the land as from a mountain top. In their circumstances, which as private persons they cannot readily surmount, the voters are most likely to suppose that whatever seems obviously good to them must be good for the country, and good in the sight of God."

Instead of the people speaking through initiatives, the reformers found the results disappointing, as the historian Richard Hofstadter explained: "Small and highly organized groups with plenty of funds and skillful publicity" made "use of these devices," and then faced with "an array of technical questions, often phrased in legal language, the voters shrank from the responsibilities the new system attempted to put upon them."

Just as the Progressives needed to relearn the political lesson the framers learned between 1776 and 1787, so by the 1970s the lesson of the Progressive Era had been forgotten. Again frustrated by the workings of government, Howard Jarvis and other citizens revived the initiative process. Again, the motivation was to make government respond. Again, as the journalist David Broder recorded, the outcome was at best flawed: "Government by initiative is not only a radical departure from the Constitution's system of checks and balances, it is also a big business, in which lawyers and campaign consultants and signature-gathering firms and other players sell their services to affluent interest groups or millionaire do-gooders with private policy and political agendas . . . These players . . . have learned that the initiative is a far more efficient way of achieving their ends than the cumbersome process of supporting candidates for public office and then lobbying them to pass or sign the measures they seek."

Howard Jarvis saw initiatives as the means of getting what he had failed to persuade the state legislature to do: cut taxes. Through the initiative process he could provide a means for citizens to vote on an isolated issue without being held responsible for the larger consequences of their vote, in this case the impact of the cuts on the services funded by them. Additionally, the initiative process is stripped of any deliberative characteristics. In the darkness of the voting booth, a voter can vote his or her self-interest without worrying about being held accountable for a greater good. And these voting decisions are "typically the result of snap judgments based upon superficial emotional appeals broadcast on television." Of course, such television campaigns can cost many millions of dollars.

The point is not whether Jarvis was right about tax levels in California. Clearly, many Californians thought so, and their government was not addressing their concerns. The point for our story is that the initiative movement is one important example of how Americans by the late 1970s were pulling away from an allegiance to the constitutional process the framers had devised to balance competing interests. There are other, even more explicit, examples.

INSIDERS REBEL

The supporters of the initiative movement were so determined to win that they ignored the lessons of half a century earlier. No one could accuse Lloyd Cutler of forgetting American political history. By 1980, he felt the Constitution had outlived its usefulness. Cutler was the consummate Washington insider. "A commanding presence among the capital's power elite for decades and at home in the highest levels of industry, government and politics," wrote one reporter. A graduate of Yale and Yale Law School, Cutler had apprenticed for a major New York law firm, moved to Washington, D.C., served the government in a number of roles, including in army intelligence, and started one of the nations largest law firms. In 1980, he was just ending his services as counsel to President Jimmy Carter.

The Carter administration had experienced great frustration over the refusal of a democratic Congress to submit to the president's views on how to resolve the energy crisis and economic stagnation. No matter the efforts he exerted, Carter could not persuade his fellow Democrats of the wisdom of his proposals. In truth he was not a good politician. As he observed, Congress was "twisted and pulled in every direction by hundreds of well-financed and powerful special interests." But it was his job to forge a consensus from these competing interests.

Cutler saw Carter's inability to build a consensus for his programs as a failure of the system, not a failure of his president. A president elected by all the people should have the support of Congress, Cutler reasoned. So in 1980 he wrote in the influential magazine *Foreign Affairs*: "The separation of powers between the legislative and executive branches, whatever its merits in 1793, has become a structure that almost guarantees stalemates today. As we wonder why we are having such a difficult time making decisions we all know must be made, and projecting our power and leadership we should reflect on whether this is one big reason."

And for this reason Cutler went on to call for a form of government in which the president would have far more control over Congress.

Lloyd Cutler's profound criticism of the American form of government seems startling at first. If a man so steeped in the American constitutional tradition and so advantaged by it was now so willing to overthrow it, there must have been something truly wrong with the system. But here was a man committed to the vision of his leader and clear in his own mind of that vision's public virtue. Hence its rejection by Congress had to be wrong, the work of "special interests." Just the kind of narrow motivation the framers built the system to guard against.

One analyst of the Reagan era, John Ehrman, identifies Cutler's proposal as an example of a frustration among liberal intellectuals, who for forty years had been at the heart of the American consensus. With the end of that consensus, they felt isolated. So "they began by deciding that America's ruling institutions needed a complete overhaul, one borrowing from foreign models." Cutler proposed an English-style Parliament. Ezra Vogel, a Harvard sociologist, urged the country to adopt a Japanese approach to solving problems "through study and consensus rather than American Style competition."

These proposals ignored the intrinsically homegrown nature of American democracy, as if something else could be grafted on our roots. But there was more: "a desire to avoid politics, either by placing authority in the hands of technocrats or by reducing the power of the president's opponents." This spared the liberals "from having to explain how their ideas would work, gain popular support, and be put into action." Ehrman's critique of the liberals is a mirror image of the critique others offered of the conservatives who were pushing the initiative movement at the same time.

Thus on the right, through initiatives and referendum, and on the left, through proposals for institutional overhaul, efforts were under way to escape the complicated demands and constraints of the democratic process the framers had developed. When Ronald Reagan said government was the problem, many Americans agreed, although they came to different solutions. One of them, a marine colonel, decided that if Congress rejected his view of what was good for the country, he would just take matters into his own hands.

Unlike Lloyd Cutler, marine colonel Oliver North did not want to discuss what was wrong with American government. He wanted to act. And, with others, he determined that, for the good of America, its Constitution and laws needed to be ignored. North, a graduate of the Navel Academy and a decorated officer in the Vietnam War, was in 1984 on assignment to the White House and the National Security Council, the executive branch agency charged with managing national security policy.

His National Security Council assignment was to aid the Nicaraguan Contras in their insurgency against the left-wing, oppressive, anti-American Sandinista government of Nicaragua, which several years earlier had toppled the right-wing, oppressive, pro-American Somoza government. But North had a problem. After the CIA had carried out some acts of sabotage in support of the Contras' efforts, Congress, under its constitutionally granted authority to control the expenditures of federal money, with the reluctant approval of President Ronald Reagan, had enacted a statute that prohibited any funds from being expended to support "directly or indirectly . . . any military or paramilitary operations in Nicaragua."

In short, Congress was now blocking his mission. North and his supervisor, John M. Poindexter, the national security adviser, decided that it was in America's best interest for them to disobey this law. North's job, in his view, was to help the "freedom fighters," as he was to call them, and no act of Congress would stop him.

Like the best of American entrepreneurs, he had a big view of things. In the White House basement, he established "the Enterprise." Through it, he brought substantial resources to the Contras. "The Enterprise, functioning largely at North's direction, had its own airplanes, pilots, airfield, operatives, ship, secure communications devices and secret Swiss bank accounts. For sixteen months, it served as the secret arm of the NSC staff, carrying out with private and nonappropriated money, and without the accountability or restrictions imposed by law on the CIA, a covert Contra aid program that Congress thought it had prohibited."

Then the Enterprise, literally, came crashing down. In 1986, Nicaraguan soldiers shot down one of the Enterprise's cargo planes and with it the Enterprise itself. Within a year congressional investigations began, as did one by a White House–appointed special prosecutor. North was fired. And finally in 1988, he was indicted and resigned from the marines. He was convicted on a number of counts, but ultimately his conviction was overturned on a technicality.

North's determination to fulfill his mission was in one sense quintessentially American. He had a job to do, and he wanted to get it done. He thought what he wanted was right for everyone. This is the American spirit that settled and populated the country and drove many of America's great successes. It is also the part of the American character about which the framers were most worried. Self-interest and self-regard (thinking that one's interest is the public interest) would lead to conflict and to tyranny. For this reason, the Constitution separates governmental power and protects individual rights against arbitrary governmental action.

In this sense, North was unremarkable. His overzealous exercise of his power was the kind of problem the framers anticipated. Certainly, the president's, his commander in chief's, proclamation that "government is the problem" gave North no incentive to obey the law. But what is remarkable in this tale, and what connects it directly to today, was the response of some members of Congress. The investigatory committees found wrongdoing on the part of North and others in the White House. But several members of the committee filed a dissenting report that provided a radical justification for North's behavior, one that set the table for a larger struggle in our time over America's constitutional design. "The Chief Executive will on occasion feel duty bound to assert monarchical notions of prerogative that will permit him to exceed the laws."

The guiding hand of that minority report was Congressman, now Vice President, Dick Cheney.

The effort by President George W. Bush and Vice President Dick Cheney to strengthen the presidency is sometimes characterized as Hamiltonian. Philosophically, that is pretty accurate. But historically, it leaves out something crucial. The convention in Philadelphia embraced Hamilton's view of human nature. But the delegates rejected his ideas for a monarchical presidency.

Howard Jarvis, Lloyd Cutler and Oliver North are representative of a long history of struggles for power in America. We have retold their stories because each is an illustration of, and provides an insight into, a loss of faith in government institutions that became widespread in the late 1970s and 1980s. At the heart of this disaffection was an attitude common to all three: a disregard for the Constitutional Conscience. To Jarvis, Cutler and North, the outcome was more important than the process (which was not giving them what they wanted). Opposing views were obstacles to be defeated, not ideas to be incorporated. Conciliation was weakness, rather than flexibility.

We linger on this period in the 1970s and 1980s because we believe these attitudes have only gained strength in the years since then. In his insightful book on the Reagan era, John Ehrman describes two virtually simultaneous political actions that illustrate the importance of constitutional principles and what happens when they weaken. You can't conduct controlled scientific experiments in politics of course. But these two moments were about as close as you can come. One was the effort, known as Gramm-Rudman, to create an automatic way to control the federal deficit. The other was the tax reform legislation of 1986.

In the mid-1980s, politicians were worried about the federal deficit and about the danger that voters would punish them for it. But there was no consensus on the steps to take to curb it: raise taxes, cut defense spending, cut social spending. So they adopted Gramm-Rudman, what Ehrman called "one of the most disgraceful and irresponsible laws ever passed." The law gave to a non-elected official the power to simply cut the budget if the deficits didn't shrink. This was enacted without any legislative process. No hearings. No committee debate or vote. "Congress and the White House abandoned their political responsibilities for making fiscal decisions, and rushed instead to hand power to automatic, technical mechanisms," wrote Ehrman. "This is hardly how republican institutions are intended to function."

But during virtually the same period, Congress also enacted a tax reform measure that made substantial strides toward a simpler and fairer tax code. The measure demonstrated that "when politicians acted seriously, the political system was able to deal with complex issues quite well." But this accomplishment was not the product of public virtue. "None of those involved in the process rose above party or personal interests." The parties advocated their positions as hard as they could and then, recognizing that a winner-take-all attitude would fail, compromised. Tax reform was the system working just as the framers had designed it to. "In contrast, Gramm-Rudman was the product of panic and a desire to circumvent politics."

We wish we could report that the spirit of the tax reform bill of 1986 had triumphed over the cynicism of Gramm-Rudman. But sadly the opposite seems to be true. Respect for the constitutional process and contempt for it seemed to pass each other like ships in the night that year on Capitol Hill. Disrespect became increasingly the norm in our time.

Look, for one example, at what is happening now to the initiative movement that Howard Jarvis launched in California thirty years ago. Jarvis was focused on the state level. But as the initiative movement gathered strength in other states after passage of Proposition 13, David Broder observed: "I do not think it will be long before the converging forces of technology and public opinion coalesce in a political movement for a national initiative—to allow the public to substitute the simplicity of majority rule by referendum for what must seem to many frustrated Americans the arcane, ineffective, out-of-date model of the Constitution."

There is a reason why other political reporters admire Broder so much. He is nothing if not prescient. The technological capacity now exists through the Internet to hold referendums across the whole country. In 2006, former U.S. senator Mike Gravel announced his candidacy for president on a platform primarily dedicated to creating national direct democracy that would go around the Congress. The National Initiative, he called it.

Mike Gravel is the embodiment of how far we have drifted from our constitutional moorings. Ornstein and Mann point out how much attitudes have changed in the Congress since Senator John F. Kennedy was elected president: "Senators were intensely loyal to the Senate as an institution; they identified first as senators rather than as partisans or through their ideology, and they were fiercely protective of their prerogatives vis-a-vis the President or the House of Representatives." That was in 1960. Now a former senator is campaigning to give voters a tool to go around the Senate and the House. If this were an isolated case, it might not matter. The nation has always had, and benefited from, gadflies.

But there are many connections between the antigovernment attitudes that flowered in the 1970s and 1980s and the governmental problems we are having now—problems we believe are directly the result of our drift away from the principles that the Constitution was built on.

Many current and recent members of Congress share former senator Gravel's lack of institutional commitment. Presumably they have brought this "lack of institutional identity" with them from the larger society. They do not understand or they choose to ignore their constitutional obligations. Wrote Mann and Ornstein about the Republicans who controlled Congress from 1993 to 2006: "Members of the majority party, including the leaders of Congress, see themselves as field lieutenants in the president's army far more than they do as members of a separate and independent branch of government." The result, according to them, has been a series of governmental failures—from the management of Hurricane Katrina to the prosecution of the war in Iraq—that might have been prevented or mitigated if the Congress had exercised greater oversight and forced more debate.

Two foreign policy experts, Stefan Halper and Jonathan Clarke, cite the run-up to the Iraq war as a quintessential breakdown of the roles of Congress and the media. "Those institutions that could have challenged the scare scenarios governing the nation's perception of the terror challenge and Saddam Hussein failed to do so," they wrote. In an almost plaintive appeal to revive our Constitutional Conscience, they titled their new book *The Silence of the Rational Center.*

But this institutional deterioration did not begin with President Bush. Looking back into President Clinton's administration, we find another example of how the indifference to institutional responsibility, by both the president and the Congress, may well have cost the nation dearly in executing the constitutional requirement to "provide for the common defense."

President Clinton was a very smart and agile leader. He often saw issues before others did. One of those issues was terrorism. He understood the gathering threat and talked about it. During Clinton's tenure there were three major terrorist attacks on American lives and property. First, terrorists drove a truck bomb into the basement of the World Trade Center in New York, killing six. Then two American embassies in east Africa were attacked, and hundreds died. Finally, terrorists blew open an American warship at dock, killing seventeen sailors. Clinton understood the challenge, but he and the Congress failed to muster an effective response.

Why? Clearly their minds were elsewhere. Clinton was enmeshed in an impeachment crisis that could be described as either epic or comic opera. Certainly, Clinton brought the crisis on himself by showing first contempt for his office and then for the authorities that he lied to. But the Republicans who controlled the House of Representatives were no better. Mann and Ornstein point out that when the Democrats investigated Richard Nixon in 1974, they insisted that every action of the House be by consensus or at least bipartisan. In further evidence of the decline of our Constitutional Conscience from then until now, the Republicans said they would handle Clinton's impeachment the same way and then did not. They impeached Clinton by party line votes, knowing there was little chance the Senate would convict him and force him from office.

The failure of the House to pull back from the precipice spoke volumes about the bitter polarization that had come to shape life in the Washington community. Impeachment was just another weapon in the partisan wars, a further escalation of the criminalization of political differences. Activists in the party base would be courted, not ordinary citizens. James Madison would be turned on his head: Rather than the mob whose passions had to be cooled by their more deliberate leaders, the public struggled to contain the sectarian passions of their representatives in Washington.

The problem was not the institutional structure but the attitudes of the men and women who had come to populate it. Clinton survived and finished his term. But a terrible sense of what might have been hangs over that period. Clinton, a border-state moderate, left office having "failed to rebuild the political center." Partisanship would only deepen, "and both the presidency and the Congress were diminished as the central institutions of American democracy."

But perhaps, if this is possible, the missed opportunities are even more horrible than all that. During this period, when the nation's leaders were using Madison's instruments of government to wage partisan war, a group of young men with a profoundly different view of how society should be organized slipped into the country and began learning to fly passenger airplanes, but not to land them. Neither the Congress nor the president set the needed priorities, although most Americans could not see this until September 11, 2001.

Ronald Reagan's large footprint on American politics is complex. So it is with the question of our Constitutional Conscience. Reagan's own intellectual journey is fascinating. He came to office amid a rebellion against government and embraced it. He had since the 1960s crusaded against bloat in government and what he saw as needless expansion. But by the time he took office, this strand of thought had become intertwined with attacks not just on the size of government but on the process of government as well. Certainly, Proposition 13 represented both. The framers had no consensus view on the proper size of government, only that it was something for the society to work out through the process they created. From FDR to Johnson, and in a sense even Nixon, there was a consensus among Americans that expanding government would fulfill their desires. But when that consensus collapsed, and nothing replaced it, political warfare ensued. Howard Jarvis, Lloyd Cutler and Oliver North all attacked the process. So did Reagan himself, some of the time.

These attacks took root among American people whose understanding of their Constitution was growing thin. A survey during 1988, Reagan's final year in office, found that civic knowledge had declined since 1976. A 1976 survey had "found that civic competence diminished markedly from 1969 to 1976." The trend was unmistakable and has continued. Without this knowledge, it is very hard for Americans to meaningfully measure the conduct of their leaders and their government against the standards set by the Constitution and its principles.

Civic illiteracy erodes our American unity. It is our commitment to and understanding of the Constitution that makes us Americans, as much as anything else. Without knowledge of our Constitution and its context, without a sense of the Constitutional Conscience, we are losing the thread of what makes us Americans, what holds us together. In the words of Professor Michael Sandel, there is "a growing danger that individually and collectively we will find ourselves slipping into a fragmented, storyless condition." And in this condition, "there is no continuity between present and past, and therefore no responsibility, and therefore no possibility for acting together to govern ourselves."

President Reagan himself expressed this point clearly on leaving office. "I am warning of an eradication of the American memory that could result, ultimately, in an erosion of the American spirit." American memory is at the heart of our Constitutional Conscience. That conscience, that sense of the Constitution and its principles, is, as Senator Lowell Weicker said soon after Reagan took office, "what holds us all together." Without it, our country becomes different, less appealing. Reagan worried about this as he left office. We worry about it now.

Conclusion

WE

*A Constitution which . . . has brought such a happy
order out of so gloomy a chaos.*
—JAMES MADISON, 1831

*People revere the Constitution yet know so little about
it—and that goes for some of my fellow senators.*
—SENATOR ROBERT BYRD, 2005

WE LIVE IN a remarkable political age. More people than
ever before in history, possibly a majority of all the people
on earth, live under governments that could reasonably be described as democracies. The enormity of this can only be grasped
by going back, as we have in this book, to that moment in the late
1700s when democracy as we now know it barely existed in the
world. Indeed, the word *democracy* was essentially an insult, a syn-
onym for *mob rule*. Yes, there were places where the king had ceded
some measure of power to aristocracies or even to semirepresenta-
tive parliaments. There were also commercial cities in Europe that
had allowed considerable popular participation in decision making.

But nowhere was there anything like what a group of men, desperately trying to save their fledgling country, invented in Philadelphia in the summer of 1787. They wrote "a Constitution which . . . has brought such a happy order out of so gloomy a chaos," James Madison said of his handiwork many years later. They wrote a Constitution that invented a new kind of representative government. It ushered in what we can now see as the Age of Democracy in which "representative government bottomed on the principle of popular sovereignty . . . has become the political norm." In a recent book on the rise of democracy, the British scholar John Dunn finds Madison's pride understandable given the far-reaching effects of his invention: "It secured the new Republic extremely effectively, and, as we now know, for a very long time. In doing so, it turned the United States into the most politically definite, the best consolidated and the most politically self-confident society on earth. It also, over time . . . opened the way for it to become overwhelmingly the most powerful state in human history."

Quite an impressive summer's work.

But where are we in the life span of this invention? The American experiment has now lasted longer than any democracy in history. (Athens, for example, lasted only around 170 years as a democracy.) It has also spawned and inspired many others to pursue democracy. After much spillage of words and blood across the twentieth century, there is no longer even a serious intellectual challenger to representative democracy as the best and most legitimate way to organize government. What a long way we have come from 1787! "The United States is now the oldest enduring republic in world history, with a set of political institutions and traditions that have stood the test of time," wrote the historian Joseph J. Ellis.

The framers would have been stunned by this success. They

knew the lessons of history were against them. They had learned from experience that individuals set free pursued their own interests. Large numbers of individuals pursuing their own interests led to chaos. Chaos invited dictators, homegrown or external, to intervene to restore order, snuffing out the very liberty people had fought to establish. They understood this cycle from their reading and, more, from the first eleven years of their own nation, which by 1787 seemed to them to be descending into the gloomy chaos Madison wrote of later.

That is why they saw democracy as "fragile."

Fragile because the framers had come to understand that in pursuit of their self-interests, Americans, like everyone else, would be willing to trample the "democracy" of others thus endangering their own.

Fragile because it was dependent on the broad participation of Americans in the nation's political processes.

Fragile because it was dependent on the willingness of Americans to acquiesce to the results of such a process.

Fragile because of the Constitution's delicate arrangement of checks and balances.

Fragile because it was a system for institutionalizing compromise. There would always be citizens searching for a more perfect system, some system that promised more wealth, or more security, or more equality, or a more glorious future, or just more of whatever it is they particularly wanted.

That was the challenge the framers confronted in 1787. People wanted what they wanted for themselves. The framers' solution, wonderfully modern and, in 1787, totally original, was to adopt a more realistic view of people and adapt their design for government to that view. They enlisted vice "on the side of virtue." They set out to prove how a representative democracy could operate without special public virtue, how "an avaricious society can form a government able to defend itself against the avarice of its members." In other words, this was not a government as good as its people. It was a government designed to produce results better than the desires of each individual person! And that is how the people ensured their own liberty. Out of many, one—*e pluribus unum*.

To accept democracy as it emerged from Philadelphia meant to accept, as Franklin said, that this was no perfect system, just the closest to perfection a human design could come.

The framers worried that their new democracy would last only a few years. But amazingly it succeeded. Two hundred and twenty years later, the many offshoots of modern representative democracy have triumphed around the world. How ironic, then, that its original American version, with its complicated checks and balances, faces meaningful challenge in the place where it was born.

This is not the first such challenge in American history, of course, and we hope not the last. It won't be if we face it, as previous generations faced their constitutional challenges. The challenge takes new forms each time. But at heart the issue is always the same: We want what we want, and we are convinced that the system that is stopping us is wrong, flawed, broken or outmoded.

This is the essence of our present challenge. The bond between government and governed has become strained. Americans are deeply frustrated with the workings of their government. They see it as unresponsive, unrepresentative, ineffective, crippling. Can you imagine even a handful of Americans acknowledging today that the purpose of their government is to produce results better than the desires of the people as individuals? Not likely.

We Americans love the framers. We consume books about them and revere their words. But we have lost our connection to what they actually invented and how that invention over time created in us what we have come to call a Constitutional Conscience. We have lost the narrative thread that connects us to the story of our constitutional democracy. That story tells us two things. First, how the framers learned a series of lessons between 1776 and 1787 and used these lessons to craft our government, the blueprint for which became the Constitution. And second, how we, the people, created a Constitutional Conscience from the essential meaning of that Constitution—its freedoms and its processes and tradeoffs—and guided by these principles were then able to adapt time and again through our history to an evolving America.

This narrative thread is vital to us. It is the story that makes us Americans, ties us to our government and ties our government to us. Without it we have begun, without being totally conscious of what we are doing, to drift away from our constitutional system. We are drifting away because our knowledge of our system has grown thin. From the 1960s onward, according to Derek Bok, civic education has been declining and by the 1980s had nearly vanished. "It is striking how little energy is devoted to trying to engage citizens more actively in the affairs of government. Civic education in the public schools has been almost totally eclipsed by a preoccupation with preparing the workforce of a global economy. Most universities no longer treat the preparation of citizens as an explicit goal of their curriculum."

Reports have documented this steady decline in civic understanding. In 1998, the Department of Education found that 75 percent of high school seniors were "not proficient in civics; one third lacked even a basic comprehension of how the government operates, while only 9 percent could give two reasons why citizens should participate in the democratic process." A report in 2002 concluded "that the nation's citizenry is woefully under-educated about the fundamentals of our American Democracy."

This lack of connection is producing a dangerous spiral of frustration and disenchantment. On the one hand, Americans take the existence of our democracy for granted, while, on the other hand, being frustrated with its workings. This produces a dangerous spiral of frustration and disenchantment. Observes Bok: "Americans have expectations for politics and the political process that are often unrealistic. Convinced that presidents can often accomplish more than is humanly possible, that legislators should be able to arrive at sensible decisions without prolonged disagreement or controversy, and that politicians should refrain from pandering to the voters yet still reflect the views of their constituents, the public seems fated to endure repeated disappointment over the government and those who run it."

Some Americans respond to this disappointment by demanding changes in the system, others by distancing themselves from the system, which leaves those who stay engaged more powerful to push for the agenda they want.

Those demands for change come in two basic forms, although proponents of each argue that their proposals would make the system more democratic by shifting power. There are the Lloyd Cutlers, Oliver Norths and Dick Cheneys who want to shift more power to the president so he can either force the rest of the government to respond or just act without being fettered by the process. And there are others who want to shift more power directly to citizens so they can force the government to respond, or simply go around the process. That they want such changes is within their rights. But any meaningful argument for them must occur in the context of the lessons the framers learned long ago. Without this context, we risk making changes that dismantle what has been proven right about our system and even endanger the freedoms it was built to guarantee.

It might be helpful to restate those lessons, in a simple form that everyone can paste on their refrigerator.

The framers boiled their experience down to a Constitution. We have boiled their experience down to these five lessons.

1. Everyone is selfish. This is not to say that people cannot act well or perform acts of great nobility. But essentially people act to achieve their own self-interest, particularly at the level at which government operates: regulating conduct and redistributing wealth. People are, however, willing to trade one benefit for another and sometimes even sacrifice a narrow interest for a broader one that they feel will ultimately do them more good. The government's job is to find those areas of common ground. That is where we can build a common good.

2. Government is the steam valve of society. It funnels and relieves the pressures that build from competing interests.

3. Political process is more important than product. Consensus around a flawed plan can still produce great progress. (The Constitution itself is the best example.) But a "perfect plan" without consensus will only produce conflict and deadlock. (The Clinton health care debacle is one example.) Respect for the system is thus a vital prerequisite for progress. When respect is in such short supply, it is no surprise that progress is, as well.

4. The strength of consensus is directly related to the breadth of representation and the depth of deliberation. A sound-bite society where civic education has vanished has little basis for forging strong consensus.

5. Every interest is a special one. The founders would no doubt be amazed by the scale and power of modern corporations and trade unions. But they would have no difficulty at all with the idea that everyone has wants and desires and that these drive their views and their allegiances to groups and factions. To them, the only meaningful definition of the *common good* would be the agreement that emerged from an inclusive political and legislative process to resolve competing (special) interests.

Our world is very different from that of the framers. People have powers now they could not have dreamed of then. Information, the lifeblood of democracy, moved then at the speed of sail. It moves now at the speed of light.

But there is no evidence that people have changed. Therefore, we see no reason to abandon the lessons the framers formed about people or the system they built from those lessons. Indeed, some of the changes, most particularly the speed with which society can now move, only reinforce the need for care in our political deliberations and for the speed bumps in the process that prevent us from rushing to judgment. That is what the framers built for us.

Recent experience reminds us that we make mistakes as a country when we move away from how our system was built to work. When people say now they wish the Congress and the media had done more to question the march to war in Iraq, they are saying, too, that they wish the leaders of Congress and of the press had done more to assert their authority, and fulfill their responsibilities, under, respectively, Article 1 and the First Amendment to the Constitution. Even many proponents of the war concede now that the checks and balances did not work well. We believe this failure was due to the weakening of our sense of constitutional roles, of our Constitutional Conscience.

We as Americans need to continue to remind ourselves of the framers' concern that democracy was fragile.

So far, unlike in the past, no one is openly arguing for an abandonment of democracy. Indeed, what many Americans think we need is what they see as more democracy. Both the proponents of strengthened presidential power and the proponents of direct democracy argue that their proposals would make the system more representative of the general public: the president as the only nationally elected official, and direct democracy as the only means to involve Americans more directly in the decision-making processes. Either way, the argument is for a more direct engagement and less entanglement in Washington process. We understand those feelings. They rise historically from a treasured strain of American belief running back to, at least, Tom Paine, the Declaration of Independence and the Articles of Confederation.

But we must not forget the warning of the framers that the most likely undoing of democracy would be in the name of more democracy.

That thought is why we wrote this book. We wanted to pick up the dropped narrative thread of the American democratic story, to remind ourselves that the democratic thinking of 1776 is only the first half of our legacy. The second half was born of Madison and his colleagues in 1787. The framers in 1787 saw liberty and direct democracy as inadequate on their own to ensure the very democracy they purported to further. For in the real world in which government works, this directly democratic perspective translates into one group getting its way over the interest of other groups or one branch, whether a powerful legislature or monarchical president, getting too much power over everyone else.

The framers' ideas transformed the thirst for liberty into a real nation. Madison and his colleagues invented a form of government whose purpose, as the historian Gordon Wood summed it up, was not to transcend our differences but to reconcile them.

Americans' current frustration and anger with their government is sapping their commitment to the principles that have made the country work. Rather than drift away from the Constitution, we should renew our connection to it. We should remember that consultation and process and debate are good things, even when they slow and complicate decisions. Most of all, we should remind each other that compromise is a show of strength, not weakness. Reaffirming these constitutional principles will actually address our frustration better than inventing something different, or more accurately, returning to what did not work between 1776 and 1787.

People say that what they want is compromise and consensus. The framers believed in that. It is why the most important and radical word in the Constitution was the first word, *We*. The government was the people and is the people. The power of each branch of government is a grant from the people, and each branch to one degree or another is accountable to them. Nothing like this had ever been created before. One British political leader, comparing the evolution of Britain's unwritten constitution to the seemingly overnight drafting of the U.S. Constitution, called the latter "the most wonderful work ever struck off at a given time by the brain and purpose of man."

But Americans in practice, in the grind of life, are no longer seeing it this way. For one thing, they do not connect their desire for consensus with the Constitution's governmental design. For another, they routinely, and predictably, define the consensus they want as the achievement of their own goals, not something larger. Americans' demands on government are today broad and deeply diverse. And when they are in an uncompromising mood, when they are divided fifty-fifty, red from blue, their representative government reflects this division, and it stalls.

The problem is not that government is unrepresentative. The problem, if you want to call it that, is that the government is very representative. The message we are hearing is that our government does not work. The message we should be hearing is that our government is a reflection of our own divisions. What we need is not a new system of government. We need a renewed willingness to work out our differences and find compromises, consensus and that other now-popular phrase, common ground.

The purpose of American-style democracy is not to guarantee each of us what we want individually. It is to give each of us as large an opportunity as possible to pursue what we want within the limits the Constitution and our Constitutional Conscience impose on us. This tension between individual liberty and community restraint has over time produced a great deal of good for a great many people and worked better than any alternative yet tried. It is still the best system for our sprawling, complicated nation.

To say that ours is the best system is not to say that it is a perfect system. It is not and never will be perfect. It can't be. It is composed of we, the people, with all our flaws. That is the point. We make it work. Our drive. Our demands. Our participation! In 1888, the poet and editor James Russell Lowell remarked on the "splended complacency" he found among his fellow Americans who were "neglectful" of their "political duties." He traced this neglect back to a widespread but mistaken belief that the framers of the Constitution had "invented a machine that would go of itself." Lowell said he admired the ability of Americans to let "confidence in our luck" and "absorption with material interests" subsume attention to the state of our democracy.

But Lowell's warning was plain.

In the midst of the rising tide of antigovernment sentiment of the 1980s, Professor Michael Kammen thought this message was so important that he used Lowell's phrase, a machine that would go of itself, as the title of his book on the Constitution and constitutionalism. A hundred years apart, the poet and the professor were trying to send us the same warning. Our system is not a machine that will go of itself. The evidence for this is all around us now. As we have drifted from constitutional principles in recent years, our system is working less well. But these problems are not about the design of the system; they are problems in the system and in the weakening of the Constitutional Conscience of its participants. That is a crucial distinction. The problems are directly related to the weak connection between the public and our leaders and the principles of the Constitution.

These problems have been building for years. By the end of the 1980s, politicians in Washington were in open despair that the political system was unable to deal with the problems facing the country.

The political deterioration has grown steadily worse. Not surprisingly, since it is our most representative branch of government, the dysfunction is most visible in the Congress. In a nation of citizens so lacking in an understanding of our system, it is hardly surprising that, increasingly, the men and women they send to Washington don't make an adherence to constitutional principles an important part of their daily work. "People revere the Constitution yet know so little about it—and that goes for some of my fellow senators," said the Senate's top institutionalist, Robert Byrd of West Virginia.

The framers counted on a balance of power between Congress and the president. They were, critically, intended to watch each other. But, as we explored in chapter 7, in the last few years, Congress has wavered in the exercise of its constitutional duty.

The weakness of the legislature throws off the whole design of the system. The strong reassertions of presidential prerogatives would not have surprised the framers. They would have expected this, although some may have been surprised at the degree. "You must . . . oblige [the government] to control itself," Madison wrote. The American system counts on each branch asserting its authority, just as it counts on each individual to press his or her wishes. Balance is essential to the framers' design, but to find the right balance each participant has to push and pull. The danger comes when one branch pushes and the other folds.

When then-Representative Dick Cheney defended Oliver North's crimes as an expression of the president's all but stated "monarchial" authority, he was expressing a very narrow minority view in Congress. But then that minority became the majority, controlled Congress, and Cheney became the vice president. Under his leadership, the "monarchical executive argument" was then "deployed."

The imbalance we refer to here is far more than the common instinct of members of Congress trying to protect a president of the same party. To some extent, this will always happen. But American history is marked with examples of members of Congress of each party asserting their institutional, constitutional role and challenging a president of their own party. Senator Harry S. Truman investigated President Roosevelt's administration, and Senator Lyndon B. Johnson investigated president Truman's administration. It was a Republican senator, Howard Baker, whose incessant questions crystallized the belief that a Republican president knew more about Watergate than he had told. And it was a Democratic senator, Daniel Patrick Moynihan, who blocked the Democratic president and his wife from their plan to overhaul American health care. Moynihan's critique was a classic defense of constitutional process. The Clintons drafted their plan, Moynihan complained, behind closed doors and failed to consult the Congress or build a consensus. And a few Republican legislators had begun challenging President George W. Bush's Iraq policy by the end of 2006.

But over the last few years on Capitol Hill, the Republican leadership seemed to disown the institutional role in the constitutional design. These leaders were intelligent, educated men. One was a former high school teacher and the other a doctor. Presumably they had the basic schooling we all get (or should get) on the constitutional design. Yet they determined that the best interest of the country required them to set aside constitutional roles and follow presidential directives. Without amending the Constitution, both Senator Bill Frist and Speaker Dennis Hastert effectively gave President Bush the parliamentary type of system that Lloyd Cutler had so desperately wanted for President Carter. They operated as the president's floor leaders in the Congress, rather than as his separate and coequal partners in government.

Congress of course is not a piece of machinery. It is 535 individual members. They are the ones who decide how assertive to be. The single most important factor in that decision is the question of how assertive American voters expect them to be. Senator Frist and Speaker Hastert followed their path because it was easy, because they did not feel political pressure to assert their institutional roles under the Constitution. We can blame the voters for not pressuring the leaders. Or we can blame the leaders for not leading the citizens. Both are true. If two of the top elected figures in the country have such little regard for the institutional obligations handed down to them, how can we expect ordinary Americans to pay attention to the Constitution? Yet it is also hard to ask politicians to exercise institutional responsibilities that we give them no credit for exercising.

Both sides of the problem are an outgrowth of how far we have fallen away from an intimate knowledge of or connection to our Constitutional Conscience. We judge our politicians heavily by what we want and how well they deliver. We measure them in the present tense alone. We don't praise honest men and women for taking clear stands on constitutional principle or exercising those institutional responsibilities. We want to know what they have done for us lately; not what they have done to faithfully exercise the responsibilities given them by the Constitution. And how could it be otherwise, for we have little idea what those responsibilities are. The *New York Times* columnist David Brooks makes this point vividly: "In short, our democracy, at least as it has evolved, takes individuals who are reasonable in private and it churns them through a public process that is almost tailor-made to undermine their virtues. The process of perpetually kissing up to the voters destroys the leadership qualities the voters are looking for in the first place: tranquillity of spirit, independence of mind and a sensitivity to the contours and complexity of reality."

The 2006 election sent a message to the incumbents in Congress. In very much the way the Federalists were tossed out in

1800, after President Adams failed to stop a Federalist Congress from plunging forward with the reviled Sedition Act, the Republicans were tossed out of Congress in 2006 for failing to check a Republican president's plunge into an unpopular war. Elections, as vital as they are, are in effect a last resort—the voters passing judgment after the fact. The system was designed to produce better results before the fact, when it is allowed to work. Whether you in the end supported or opposed American entry into Iraq, that decision, and more particularly the decision of the president and Congress, would have been stronger and more effective if it had been subject to more oversight in Congress and more debate in public. Perhaps you think the more effective policy would have been to stay out of war. Or perhaps you wish the war and its aftermath had been more effectively executed. As it turned out, Congress did not watch over the president, and the country got neither peace nor effective war. In both 1800 and 2006, the election produced dramatic shifts because classic checks and balances had failed and thus produced policies that angered the voters. The election results were a punishment. But punishment by itself did not correct the more basic reasons the system of checks and balances failed.

The downward spiral will continue unless we get to the root of the problem. And what is the root of the problem? All of us, Americans, and each of us. A public opinion survey once asked Americans to "suppose the President and Congress have to violate a Constitutional principle to pass an important law the public wanted. Would you support them in this action?" Only 49 percent of the public said no. The other half were a mix of yes (22 percent) and undecided or neither (29 percent). Even on a simple statement of a bedrock principle of our system, we are divided. That is a shaky foundation on which to rest the most important government on earth.

Why does our constitutional commitment seem so thin? At one level, we have come to mistake longevity for permanence. We take for granted the existence of what not so long ago was remarkable and revolutionary. We assume that because we have been a free and successful democracy for our lifetimes and our parents' and grandparents' lifetimes that we will remain such for our children's and our children's children's lifetimes, too. That alone would be worrisome. When citizens take their democracy for granted, they undermine its most basic tenet. Democracy dissolves without the commitment to it of its citizens. That loss of commitment is what the framers most feared.

In our own time, the historian Sean Wilentz put it this way: "Democracy is never a gift bestowed by benevolent, far seeing rulers who seek to reinforce their own legitimacy. It must always be fought for, by political coalitions that cut across distinctions of wealth, power, and interest. It succeeds and survives only when it is rooted in the lives and expectations of its citizens and continually reinvigorated in each generation. Democratic successes are never irreversible."

But instead of reinvigorating our representative government, current generations are disparaging it. We are not fighting for it. Instead, we as a people are frustrated with the day-to-day workings of government and restlessly search for some "fix" for the system.

Perhaps our confidence in the permanence of our democracy has left us feeling free to attack its workings. To a point, that is healthy. The system was built for robust debate, and it has survived a great deal of it. But robust debate requires engagement and information. It requires the debaters to have some context, some sense of shared ground.

Where do we find that common ground? By looking behind

the trouble signs. We said that taking our democracy for granted while also being frustrated with our government seems almost contradictory. We said "almost" because in fact we believe they rise from the same source.

Americans don't know their own government anymore. They don't know their own history. We take our democracy for granted because we don't understand how hard it was to build it, how much courage (not just on the battlefield) it took to preserve it, and how close it came to failure on several occasions from the Alien and Sedition Acts, through the Civil War to the Great Depression. And we are frustrated with how it works today because no one is explaining that how it works (most of the time) is how the framers, benefiting from the real-life experience of the early nation, designed it to work. Defending the system is not a politically popular thing to do. And in our hurry-up society, no one wants to sit still long enough to hear explanations of the system, let alone defenses. This is frightening. The framers expected flaws to emerge in their design. They expected fixes to be needed.

What is dangerous now is that the debate over the system has lost the context of how the system got to be what it is. In an environment where citizens do not particularly understand the system's basic design, many of the fixes are actually challenges to the overall design. Madison and his colleagues envisioned the Senate, with its members chosen for longer terms from entire states, as a balance and a check to the House, with its larger membership with shorter terms from narrower constituencies. Together they would check the president, with a term halfway between that in the House and that in the Senate. Yet today former senator Gravel is running for president on the express platform of creating a national system of referendum to circumvent the Congress. His campaign is welcome to the extent that it encourages a debate that teaches Americans about the design of the Constitution. Americans are free to change that design. But they should understand what they are doing and what they are abandoning if they do.

We hope the result will be an embrace of improvements, rather than a dismantling of constitutional principles. But if only 49 percent of the country is willing to speak up for a fundamental constitutional principle, we are perilously close to undoing the system itself. The wrong crisis at the wrong moment could push us over the edge before we realize what we have done. Indeed, all that protects us in this situation is the framers' prescience in creating a system where a majority of one is not enough to make radical changes. But then of course we become frustrated that we can't get the change we want, and the spiral starts all over again.

Thomas Jefferson said that the tree of liberty needs to be refreshed from time to time with the blood of patriots and tyrants. What a wonderful bit of Jeffersonian poetry. But we think something less dramatic, but perhaps harder in its own way, is needed right now. We as Americans need to tend our own garden. We need to renew not just our faith in but our understanding of the system the framers gave us. That understanding requires more than some sound bites about liberty and freedom. We need to embrace that our liberty and freedom flow directly from less glamorous but still vital ideas, such as compromise, and checks and balances, and representation and process. A dash of humility would not hurt either.

Two of our most important modern presidents, Franklin Roosevelt and Ronald Reagan, each saw the importance of renewing our understanding of American constitutional government.

Roosevelt became president in the middle of the worst crisis of American democracy since the Civil War. The link between the American political system and its economic success had snapped. Around the world, dictatorships of the left and the right were on the rise. There were people who came to FDR—serious, important people—to advise him that he might have to take authoritarian powers himself. Looking back, we came much closer than many people realize to the loss of our democracy. But we did not lose it, thanks to the resolve of FDR and the strength in the American people of what we have come to describe as our Constitutional Conscience. Four years later, Roosevelt, in his first fireside chat of his second term as president, said he hoped the American people had reread their Constitution in the last few weeks. "Like the Bible," he said, "it ought to be read again and again." Ironically, Roosevelt made this remark in a speech in which he argued for a plan to weaken the Supreme Court and strengthen the power of the presidency and the Congress by putting more of his appointees on the Court. It is a testament to the strength of our Constitutional Conscience that Roosevelt's way of arguing for this plan was to present it as a defense of the Constitution, not an infringement of it. The system stopped him anyway, and even without these expanded powers he guided the country out of the Depression. The Court-packing plan he outlined in that fireside chat has vanished into history. It turns out that the more important notion of that speech was Roosevelt's insistence that we reconnect with the Constitution regularly.

Half a century later, Ronald Reagan was saying farewell after eight years as president. He had come to office in the midst of a crisis of confidence. Watergate, stagflation, the Iran hostage crisis, the residue of the 1960s had combined to shake Americans' faith in their country. Reagan had worked with considerable success to re-build that faith. As he said farewell, he took pride in that accom-plishment. But he recognized that the job was only partly done: "This national feeling is good, but it won't count for much and it won't last unless it is grounded in thoughtfulness and knowledge. An informed patriotism is what we want. And are we doing a good enough job teaching our children what America is and what she represents in the long history of the world? Those of us who are over thirty five or so years of age grew up in a different America. We were taught, very directly, what it means to be an American. And we absorbed, almost in the air, a love of country and an ap-preciation of its institutions."

But as America prepared to enter the 1990s, Reagan warned, the fashion had changed. "Younger parents aren't sure that an unam-bivalent appreciation of America is the right thing to teach mod-ern children. And as for those who create the popular culture, well-grounded patriotism is no longer the style. Our spirit is back, but we haven't reinstitutionalized it."

Roosevelt and Reagan are the touchstone presidents of the American Century. In some ways they could not represent more different political moments. The first brought a powerful central-ized federal government into our domestic lives. The other drew the line to limit it. Yet across the half century that separated them, they each affirmed the centrality of connecting Americans to their democratic heritage.

"So we've got to teach history based not on what's in fashion but what's important," said Reagan. He concluded: "If we forget what we did, we won't know who we are. Let's start with some ba-sics: more attention to American history and a greater emphasis on civic ritual."

We agree. Indeed, we think we owe it to the framers and all suc-
ceeding Americans who have struggled for the Constitution to renew our connection to our own history. But even more, we owe it
to the future, which will be shaped by our actions.

There is a strong sense that we have become selfish and self-
involved as a people. It is hard to say whether we are more self-
interested than Americans at the time the Constitution was written.
It was written because the framers thought we were very selfish, and
they decided they could not fight human nature, only harness it.
That was the genius of their system. It accepted us for who we are
and yet still offered the optimistic vision that we could, as a nation,
compromise our differences to agree to do great things.

We are all for ideas to make us less selfish or self-interested. But
we are with the framers in doubting that human nature can be fundamentally changed.

They were right that our more selfish impulses can be chan-
neled. Americans throughout their history have understood that it
was in their own interest, ultimately, to preserve this system that
balanced everyone's demands. That understanding is what we
mean by our Constitutional Conscience. It is what Sean Wilentz is
talking about when he describes coalitions that cut across lines of
wealth, power and interest. It is noble to try to make people different. We admire those who try. But politics is the art of the possible.
The framers made it possible for us to live together in liberty and
community. The 220-year history of our Constitution is a history
of Americans repeatedly rekindling their belief that their own interests are served by this system that grants extensive liberty in exchange for a willingness to compromise and tolerate differences.
We Americans need to rekindle that belief once more.

If this book has one message, it is that there is nothing about our past success that guarantees our future success. Each generation must do that for itself. Nevertheless, this is a hopeful message, because we are not alone in our struggle. We have been given a great gift and with it a great responsibility. We are the inheritors of the longest democratic tradition in the world. We still hold in great respect the men who began that tradition and the men and women who carried it forth and bequeathed it to us. That respect is a resource for us now. The struggles we are having, the frustrations we are feeling, are exactly the struggles and frustrations the framers anticipated when they designed our democracy. We can lean on them and their experience. By reaching backward to them and their ideas, we can move forward.

THE CONSTITUTION OF THE UNITED STATES OF AMERICA

WE THE PEOPLE of the United States, in Order to form a more perfect Union, establish Justice, insure domestic Tranquility, provide for the common defence, promote the general Welfare, and secure the Blessings of Liberty to ourselves and our Posterity, do ordain and establish this Constitution for the United States of America.

Article I

SECTION 1

All legislative Powers herein granted shall be vested in a Congress of the United States, which shall consist of a Senate and House of Representatives.

SECTION 2

The House of Representatives shall be composed of Members chosen every second Year by the People of the several States, and the electors in each State shall have the qualifications requisite for electors of the most numerous branch of the State legislature.

No Person shall be a Representative who shall not have attained to the Age of twenty five Years, and been seven Years a citizen of the United States, and who shall not, when elected, be an Inhabitant of that State in which he shall be chosen. Representatives and direct Taxes shall be apportioned among the several States which may be included within this Union, according to their respective Numbers, which shall be determined by adding to the whole number of free Persons, including those bound to Service for a Term of Years, and excluding Indians not taxed, three fifths of all other Persons. The actual Enumeration shall be made within three Years after the first Meeting of the Congress of the United States, and within every subsequent Term of ten Years, in such Manner as they shall by law Direct. The number of Representatives shall not exceed one for every thirty Thousand, but each State shall have at least one Representative; and until such enumeration shall be made, the State of New Hampshire shall be entitled to chuse three, Massachusetts eight, Rhode Island and Providence Plantations one, Connecticut five, New York six, New Jersey four, Pennsylvania eight, Delaware one, Maryland six, Virginia ten, North Carolina five, South Carolina five, and Georgia three.

When vacancies happen in the Representation from any State, the Executive Authority thereof shall issue Writs of Election to fill such Vacancies.

The House of Representatives shall chuse their Speaker and other Officers; and shall have the sole Power of Impeachment.

The Senate of the United States shall be composed of two Senators from each State, chosen by the legislature thereof, for six Years; and each Senator shall have one Vote.

Immediately after they shall be assembled in Consequence of the first Election, they shall be divided as equally as may be into three Classes. The Seats of the Senators of the first Class shall be vacated at the expiration of the second Year, of the second Class at the expiration of the fourth Year, and of the third Class at the expiration of the sixth Year, so that one third may be chosen every second Year; and if vacancies happen by Resignation, or otherwise, during the recess of the Legislature of any State, the Executive thereof may make temporary Appointments until the next meeting of the Legislature, which shall then fill such Vacancies.

No person shall be a Senator who shall not have attained to the Age of thirty Years, and been nine Years a Citizen of the United States, and who shall not, when elected, be an Inhabitant of that State for which he shall be chosen.

The Vice-President of the United States shall be President of the Senate, but shall have no Vote, unless they be equally divided.

The Senate shall choose their other Officers, and also a President pro tempore, in the Absence of the Vice-President, or when he shall exercise the Office of President of the United States.

The Senate shall have the sole Power to try all Impeachments.

When sitting for that Purpose, they shall be on Oath or Affirmation.

When the President of the United States is tried, the Chief Justice shall preside: And no Person shall be convicted without the Concurrence of two thirds of the Members present.

Judgment in cases of Impeachment shall not extend further than to removal from Office, and disqualification to hold and enjoy any Office of honor, Trust or Profit under the United States: but the Party convicted shall nevertheless be liable and subject to Indictment, Trial, Judgment and Punishment, according to Law.

SECTION 4

The Times, Places and Manner of holding Elections for Senators and Representatives, shall be prescribed in each State by the Legislature thereof; but the Congress may at any time by Law make or alter such Regulations, except as to the Places of chusing Senators.

The Congress shall assemble at least once in every Year, and such Meeting shall be on the first Monday in December, unless they shall by law appoint a different Day.

SECTION 5

Each House shall be the Judge of the Elections, Returns and Qualifications of its own Members, and a Majority of each shall constitute a Quorum to do Business; but a smaller Number may adjourn from day to day, and may be authorized to compel the Attendance of absent Members, in such Manner, and under such Penalties as each House may provide.

Each house may determine the Rules of its Proceedings, punish its Members for disorderly Behavior, and, with the Concurrence of two-thirds, expel a Member.

Each house shall keep a Journal of its Proceedings, and from time to time publish the same, excepting such Parts as may in their Judgment require Secrecy; and the Yeas and Nays of the Members of either House on any question shall, at the Desire of one fifth of those Present, be entered on the Journal.

Neither House, during the Session of Congress, shall, without the Consent of the other, adjourn for more than three days, nor to any other Place than that in which the two Houses shall be sitting.

SECTION 6

The Senators and Representatives shall receive a Compensation for their Services, to be ascertained by Law, and paid out of the Treasury of the United States. They shall in all Cases, except Treason, Felony and Breach of the Peace, be privileged from Arrest during their Attendance at the Session of their respective Houses, and in going to and returning from the same; and for any Speech or Debate in either House, they shall not be questioned in any other Place.

No Senator or Representative shall, during the Time for which he was elected, be appointed to any civil Office under the authority of the United States, which shall have been created, or the Emoluments whereof shall have been increased during such time; and no Person holding any Office under the United States, shall be a Member of either House during his Continuance in Office.

SECTION 7

All Bills for raising Revenue shall originate in the House of Representatives; but the Senate may propose or concur with Amendments as on other Bills.

Every Bill which shall have passed the House of Representatives and the Senate, shall, before it become a Law, be presented to the President of the United States; If he approve he shall sign it, but if not he shall return it, with his Objections to that House in which it shall have originated, who shall enter the Objections at large on their Journal, and proceed to reconsider it.

If after such Reconsideration two thirds of that house shall agree to pass the Bill, it shall be sent, together with the Objections, to the other House, by which it shall likewise be reconsidered, and if approved by two thirds of that House, it shall become a law. But in all such Cases the Votes of both Houses shall be determined by Yeas and Nays, and the Names of the Persons voting for and against the Bill shall be entered on the Journal of each House respectively. If any Bill shall not be returned by the President within ten Days (Sundays excepted) after it shall have been presented to him, the Same shall be a Law, in like Manner as if he had signed it, unless the Congress by their Adjournment prevent its Return, in which case it shall not be a Law.

Every Order, Resolution, or Vote to which the Concurrence of the Senate and House of Representatives may be necessary (except on a question of Adjournment) shall be presented to the President of the United States; and before the Same shall take Effect, shall be approved by him, or being disapproved by him, shall be repassed by two thirds of the Senate and House of Representatives, according to the Rules and Limitations prescribed in the Case of a Bill.

SECTION 8

The Congress shall have Power to lay and collect Taxes, Duties, Imposts and Excises, to pay the Debts and provide for the common Defence and general Welfare of the United States; but all Duties, Imposts and Excises shall be uniform throughout the United States;

To borrow Money on the credit of the United States; To regulate Commerce with foreign Nations, and among the several States, and with the Indian Tribes; To establish an uniform Rule of Naturalization, and uniform Laws on the subject of Bankruptcies throughout the United States;

To coin Money, regulate the Value thereof, and of foreign Coin, and fix the Standard of Weights and Measures; To provide for the Punishment of counterfeiting the Securities and current Coin of the United States;

To establish Post Offices and Post Roads;

To promote the Progress of Science and useful Arts, by securing for limited Times to Authors and Inventors the exclusive Right to their respective Writings and Discoveries;

To constitute Tribunals inferior to the supreme Court;

To define and punish Piracies and Felonies committed on the high Seas, and Offenses against the Law of Nations;

To declare War, grant Letters of Marque and Reprisal, and make Rules concerning Captures on Land and Water;

To raise and support Armies, but no Appropriation of Money to that Use shall be for a longer term than two Years;

To provide and maintain a Navy;

To make Rules for the Government and Regulation of the land and naval Forces;

To provide for calling forth the Militia to execute the Laws of the Union, suppress Insurrections and repel Invasions;

To provide for organizing, arming, and disciplining the Militia, and for governing such Part of them as may be employed in the Service of the United States, reserving to the States respectively, the Appointment of the Officers, and the Authority of training the militia according to the discipline prescribed by Congress;

To exercise exclusive Legislation in all Cases whatsoever, over such District (not exceeding ten Miles square) as may, by Cession of particular States, and the Acceptance of Congress, become the Seat of the Government of the United States, and to exercise like Authority over all Places purchased by the Consent of the Legislature of the State in which the Same shall be, for the Erection of Forts, Magazines, Arsenals, Dockyards, and other needful Buildings;—And

To make all Laws which shall be necessary and proper for carrying into Execution the foregoing Powers, and all other Powers vested by this Constitution in the Government of the United States, or in any Department or Officer thereof.

SECTION 9

The Migration or Importation of such Persons as any of the States now existing shall think proper to admit, shall not be prohibited by the Congress prior to the Year one thousand eight hundred and eight, but a Tax or Duty may be imposed on such Importation, not exceeding ten dollars for each Person.

The Privilege of the Writ of Habeas Corpus shall not be suspended, unless when in Cases of Rebellion or Invasion the public Safety may require it.

No Bill of Attainder or ex post facto Law shall be passed.

No Capitation, or other direct, Tax shall be laid, unless in Proportion to the Census or Enumeration herein before directed to be taken.

No Tax or Duty shall be laid on Articles exported from any State.

No Preference shall be given by any Regulation of Commerce or Revenue to the Ports of one State over those of another: nor shall Vessels bound to, or from, one State, be obliged to enter, clear, or pay Duties in another.

No Money shall be drawn from the Treasury, but in Consequence of Appropriations made by Law; and a regular Statement and Account of the Receipts and Expenditures of all public Money shall be published from time to time.

No Title of Nobility shall be granted by the United States; and no Person holding any Office of Profit or Trust under them, shall, without the Consent of the Congress, accept of any present, Emolument, Office, or Title, of any kind whatever, from any King, Prince, or foreign State.

No State shall enter into any Treaty, Alliance, or Confederation; grant Letters of Marque and Reprisal; coin Money; emit Bills of Credit; make any Thing but gold and silver Coin a Tender in Payment of Debts; pass any Bill of Attainder, ex post facto Law, or Law impairing the Obligation of Contracts, or grant any Title of Nobility.

No State shall, without the Consent of the Congress, lay any Imposts or Duties on Imports or Exports, except what may be absolutely necessary for executing it's inspection Laws: and the net Produce of all Duties and Imposts, laid by any State on Imports or Exports, shall be for the Use of the Treasury of the United States; and all such Laws shall be subject to the Revision and Controul of the Congress.

No State shall, without the Consent of Congress, lay any Duty of Tonnage, keep Troops, or Ships of War in time of Peace, enter into any Agreement or Compact with another State, or with a foreign Power, or engage in War, unless actually invaded, or in such imminent Danger as will not admit of delay.

Article II

SECTION I

The executive Power shall be vested in a President of the United States of America. He shall hold his Office during the

Term of four Years, and, together with the Vice President chosen for the same Term, be elected, as follows:

Each State shall appoint, in such Manner as the Legislature thereof may direct, a Number of Electors, equal to the whole Number of Senators and Representatives to which the State may be entitled in the Congress: but no Senator or Representative, or Person holding an Office of Trust or Profit under the United States, shall be appointed an Elector.

The Electors shall meet in their respective States, and vote by Ballot for two Persons, of whom one at least shall not be an Inhabitant of the same State with themselves. And they shall make a List of all the Persons voted for, and of the Number of Votes for each; which List they shall sign and certify, and transmit sealed to the Seat of the Government of the United States, directed to the President of the Senate. The President of the Senate shall, in the Presence of the Senate and House of Representatives, open all the Certificates, and the Votes shall then be counted.

The Person having the greatest Number of Votes shall be the President, if such Number be a Majority of the whole Number of Electors appointed; and if there be more than one who have such Majority, and have an equal Number of votes, then the House of Representatives shall immediately chuse by Ballot one of them for President; and if no Person have a Majority, then from the five highest on the List the said House shall in like Manner chuse the President. But in chusing the President, the Votes shall be taken by States, the Representation from each State having one Vote; a Quorum for this Purpose shall consist of a Member or Members from two thirds of the States, and a Majority of all the States shall be necessary to a Choice. In every Case, after the Choice of the President, the Person having the greatest Number of Votes of the

Electors shall be the Vice President. But if there should remain two or more who have equal Votes, the Senate shall chuse from them by Ballot the Vice President.

The Congress may determine the Time of chusing the Electors, and the Day on which they shall give their Votes; which Day shall be the same throughout the United States.

No Person except a natural born Citizen, or a Citizen of the United States, at the time of the Adoption of this Constitution, shall be eligible to the Office of President; neither shall any Person be eligible to that Office who shall not have attained to the Age of thirty five Years, and been fourteen Years a Resident within the United States. In Case of the Removal of the President from Office, or of his Death, Resignation, or Inability to discharge the Powers and Duties of the said Office, the Same shall devolve on the Vice President, and the Congress may by Law provide for the Case of Removal, Death, Resignation or Inability, both of the President and Vice President, declaring what Officer shall then act as President, and such Officer shall act accordingly, until the Disability be removed, or a President shall be elected.

The President shall, at stated Times, receive for his Services, a Compensation, which shall neither be increased nor diminished during the Period for which he shall have been elected, and he shall not receive within that Period any other Emolument from the United States, or any of them.

Before he enter on the Execution of his Office, he shall take the following Oath or Affirmation:—"I do solemnly swear (or affirm) that I will faithfully execute the Office of President of the United States, and will to the best of my Ability, preserve, protect and defend the Constitution of the United States."

The President shall be Commander in Chief of the Army and Navy of the United States, and of the Militia of the several States, when called into the actual Service of the United States; he may require the Opinion, in writing, of the principal Officer in each of the executive Departments, upon any Subject relating to the Duties of their respective Offices, and he shall have Power to grant Reprieves and Pardons for Offenses against the United States, except in Cases of impeachment.

He shall have Power, by and with the Advice and Consent of the Senate, to make Treaties, provided two thirds of the Senators present concur; and he shall nominate, and by and with the Advice and Consent of the Senate, shall appoint Ambassadors, other public Ministers and Consuls, Judges of the supreme Court, and all other Officers of the United States, whose Appointments are not herein otherwise provided for, and which shall be established by Law: but the Congress may by Law vest the Appointment of such inferior Officers, as they think proper, in the President alone, in the Courts of Law, or in the Heads of Departments.

The President shall have Power to fill up all Vacancies that may happen during the Recess of the Senate, by granting Commissions which shall expire at the End of their next session.

SECTION 3

He shall from time to time give to the Congress Information of the State of the Union, and recommend to their Consideration such Measures as he shall judge necessary and expedient; he may, on extraordinary Occasions, convene both Houses, or either of them, and in Case of Disagreement between them, with Respect to the Time of Adjournment, he may adjourn them to such Time as he shall think proper; he shall receive Ambassadors and other public Ministers; he shall take Care that the Laws be faithfully executed, and shall Commission all the Officers of the United States.

SECTION 4

The President, Vice President and all civil Officers of the United States, shall be removed from Office on Impeachment for, and Conviction of, Treason, Bribery, or other high Crimes and Misdemeanors.

Article III

SECTION I

The judicial Power of the United States, shall be vested in one supreme Court, and in such inferior Courts as the Congress may from time to time ordain and establish. The Judges, both of the supreme and inferior Courts, shall hold their Offices during good behavior, and shall, at stated Times, receive for their Services, a Compensation, which shall not be diminished during their Continuance in Office.

SECTION 2

The judicial Power shall extend to all Cases, in Law and Equity, arising under this Constitution, the Laws of the United States, and Treaties made, or which shall be made, under their Authority; — to all Cases affecting Ambassadors, other public Ministers and Consuls; —to all Cases of admiralty and maritime Jurisdiction; — to Controversies to which the United States shall be a Party; —to Controversies between two or more States; —between a State and Citizens of another State; —between Citizens of different States; — between Citizens of the same State claiming Lands under Grants of different States, and between a State, or the Citizens thereof, and foreign States, Citizens or Subjects.

In all cases affecting Ambassadors, other public Ministers and Consuls, and those in which a State shall be Party, the supreme Court shall have original Jurisdiction. In all the other Cases before mentioned, the supreme Court shall have appellate Jurisdiction, both as to Law and Fact, with such Exceptions, and under such Regulations as the Congress shall make.

The Trial of all Crimes, except in Cases of Impeachment, shall be by Jury; and such Trial shall be held in the State where the said Crimes shall have been committed; but when not committed within any State, the Trial shall be at such Place or Places as the Congress may by Law have directed.

SECTION 3

Treason against the United States, shall consist only in levying War against them, or in adhering to their Enemies, giving them Aid and Comfort. No Person shall be convicted of Treason unless on the Testimony of two Witnesses to the same overt Act, or on Confession in open Court.

The Congress shall have power to declare the punishment of Treason, but no Attainder of Treason shall work Corruption of Blood, or Forfeiture except during the Life of the Person attainted.

Article IV

SECTION 1

Full Faith and Credit shall be given in each State to the public Acts, Records, and judicial Proceedings of every other State.

And the Congress may by general Laws prescribe the Manner in which such Acts, Records, and Proceedings shall be proved, and the Effect thereof.

SECTION 2

The Citizens of each State shall be entitled to all Privileges and Immunities of Citizens in the several States.

A Person charged in any State with Treason, Felony, or other Crime, who shall flee from Justice, and be found in another State, shall on Demand of the executive Authority of the State from which he fled, be delivered up, to be removed to the State having Jurisdiction of the Crime.

No person held to Service or Labor in one State, under the Laws thereof, escaping into another, shall, in Consequence of any Law or Regulation therein, be discharged from such Service or Labor, but shall be delivered up on Claim of the Party to whom such Service or Labor may be due.

SECTION 3

New States may be admitted by the Congress into this Union; but no new States shall be formed or erected within the Jurisdiction of any other State; nor any State be formed by the Junction of two or more States, or Parts of States, without the Consent of the Legislatures of the States concerned as well as of the Congress.

The Congress shall have Power to dispose of and make all needful Rules and Regulations respecting the Territory or other Property belonging to the United States; and nothing in this Constitution shall be so construed as to Prejudice any Claims of the United States, or of any particular State.

The United States shall guarantee to every State in this Union a Republican Form of Government, and shall protect each of them against Invasion; and on Application of the Legislature, or of the Executive (when the Legislature cannot be convened) against domestic Violence.

Article V

The Congress, whenever two thirds of both Houses shall deem it necessary, shall propose Amendments to this Constitution, or, on the Application of the Legislatures of two thirds of the several States, shall call a Convention for proposing Amendments, which, in either Case, shall be valid to all Intents and Purposes, as Part of this Constitution, when ratified by the Legislatures of three fourths of the several States, or by Conventions in three fourths thereof, as the one or the other Mode of Ratification may be proposed by the Congress; Provided that no Amendment which may be made prior to the Year one thousand eight hundred and eight shall in any Manner affect the first and fourth Clauses in the ninth Section of the first Article; and that no State, without its Consent, shall be deprived of its equal Suffrage in the Senate.

Article VI

All Debts contracted and Engagements entered into, before the Adoption of this Constitution, shall be as valid against the United States under this Constitution, as under the Confederation. This Constitution, and the Laws of the United States which shall be made in Pursuance thereof; and all Treaties made, or which shall be made, under the Authority of the United States, shall be the supreme Law of the Land; and the Judges in every State shall be bound thereby, any Thing in the Constitution or Laws of any State to the Contrary notwithstanding.

The Senators and Representatives before mentioned, and the Members of the several State Legislatures, and all executive and judicial Officers, both of the United States and of the several States, shall be bound by Oath or Affirmation, to support this Constitution; but no religious Test shall ever be required as a Qualification to any Office or public Trust under the United States.

Article VII

The Ratification of the Conventions of nine States, shall be sufficient for the Establishment of this Constitution between the States so ratifying the Same.

Amendment I

Congress shall make no law respecting an establishment of religion, or prohibiting the free exercise thereof; or abridging the freedom of speech, or of the press; or the right of the people peaceably to assemble, and to petition the Government for a redress of grievances.

Amendment II

A well regulated Militia, being necessary to the security of a free State, the right of the people to keep and bear Arms, shall not be infringed.

Amendment III

No Soldier shall, in time of peace be quartered in any house, without the consent of the Owner, nor in time of war, but in a manner to be prescribed by law.

Amendment IV

The right of the people to be secure in their persons, houses, papers, and effects, against unreasonable searches and seizures, shall not be violated, and no Warrants shall issue, but upon probable cause, supported by Oath or affirmation, and particularly describing the place to be searched, and the persons or things to be seized.

Amendment V

No person shall be held to answer for a capital, or otherwise infamous crime, unless on a presentment or indictment of a Grand Jury, except in cases arising in the land or naval forces, or in the Militia, when in actual service in time of War or public danger; nor shall any person be subject for the same offense to be twice put in jeopardy of life or limb; nor shall be compelled in any criminal case to be a witness against himself, nor be deprived of life, liberty, or property, without due process of law; nor shall private property be taken for public use, without just compensation.

Amendment VI

In all criminal prosecutions, the accused shall enjoy the right to a speedy and public trial, by an impartial jury of the State and district wherein the crime shall have been committed, which district shall have been previously ascertained by law, and to be informed of the nature and cause of the accusation; to be confronted with the witnesses against him; to have compulsory process for obtaining witnesses in his favor, and to have the Assistance of Counsel for his defence.

Amendment VII

In Suits at common law, where the value in controversy shall exceed twenty dollars, the right of trial by jury shall be preserved, and no fact tried by a jury shall be otherwise re-examined in any Court of the United States, than according to the rules of the common law.

Amendment VIII

Excessive bail shall not be required, nor excessive fines imposed, nor cruel and unusual punishments inflicted.

Amendment IX

The enumeration in the Constitution, of certain rights, shall not be construed to deny or disparage others retained by the people.

Amendment X

The powers not delegated to the United States by the Constitution, nor prohibited by it to the States, are reserved to the States respectively, or to the people.

Amendment XI

The Judicial power of the United States shall not be construed to extend to any suit in law or equity, commenced or prosecuted against one of the United States by Citizens of another State, or by Citizens or Subjects of any Foreign State.

Amendment XII

The Electors shall meet in their respective states, and vote by ballot for President and Vice-President, one of whom, at least, shall not be an inhabitant of the same state with themselves; they shall name in their ballots the person voted for as President, and in distinct ballots the person voted for as Vice-President, and they shall make distinct lists of all persons voted for as President, and of all persons voted for as Vice-President and of the number of votes for each, which lists they shall sign and certify, and transmit sealed to the seat of the government of the United States, directed to the President of the Senate; The President of the Senate shall, in the presence of the Senate and House of Representatives, open all the certificates and the votes shall then be counted; The person having the greatest Number of votes for President, shall be the President, if such number be a majority of the whole number of Electors appointed; and if no person have such majority, then from the persons having the highest numbers not exceeding three on the list of those voted for as President, the House of Representatives shall choose immediately, by ballot, the President. But in choosing the President, the votes shall be taken by states, the representation from each state having one vote; a quorum for this purpose shall consist of a member or members from two-thirds of the states, and a majority of all the states shall be necessary to a choice. And if the House of Representatives shall not choose a President whenever the right of choice shall devolve upon them, before the fourth day of March next following, then the Vice-President shall act as President, as in the case of the death or other constitutional disability of the President. The person having the greatest number of votes as Vice-President, shall be the Vice-President, if such number be a majority of the whole number of Electors appointed, and if no person have a majority, then from the two highest numbers on the list, the Senate shall choose the Vice-President; a quorum for the purpose shall consist of two-thirds of the whole number of Senators, and a majority of the whole number shall be necessary to a choice. But no person constitutionally ineligible to the office of President shall be eligible to that of Vice-President of the United States.

Amendment XIII

1. Neither slavery nor involuntary servitude, except as a punishment for crime whereof the party shall have been duly convicted, shall exist within the United States, or any place subject to their jurisdiction.
2. Congress shall have power to enforce this article by appropriate legislation.

Amendment XIV

1. All persons born or naturalized in the United States, and subject to the jurisdiction thereof, are citizens of the United States and of the State wherein they reside. No

State shall make or enforce any law which shall abridge the privileges or immunities of citizens of the United States; nor shall any State deprive any person of life, liberty, or property, without due process of law; nor deny to any person within its jurisdiction the equal protection of the laws.

2. Representatives shall be apportioned among the several States according to their respective numbers, counting the whole number of persons in each State, excluding Indians not taxed. But when the right to vote at any election for the choice of electors for President and Vice-President of the United States, Representatives in Congress, the Executive and Judicial officers of a State, or the members of the Legislature thereof, is denied to any of the male inhabitants of such State, being twenty-one years of age, and citizens of the United States, or in any way abridged, except for participation in rebellion, or other crime, the basis of representation therein shall be reduced in the proportion which the number of such male citizens shall bear to the whole number of male citizens twenty-one years of age in such State.

3. No person shall be a Senator or Representative in Congress, or elector of President and Vice-President, or hold any office, civil or military, under the United States, or under any State, who, having previously taken an oath, as a member of Congress, or as an officer of the United States, or as a member of any State legislature, or as an executive or judicial officer of any State, to support the Constitution of the United States, shall have engaged in

insurrection or rebellion against the same, or given aid or comfort to the enemies thereof. But Congress may by a vote of two-thirds of each House, remove such disability.

4. The validity of the public debt of the United States, authorized by law, including debts incurred for payment of pensions and bounties for services in suppressing insurrection or rebellion, shall not be questioned. But neither the United States nor any State shall assume or pay any debt or obligation incurred in aid of insurrection or rebellion against the United States, or any claim for the loss or emancipation of any slave; but all such debts, obligations and claims shall be held illegal and void.

5. The Congress shall have power to enforce, by appropriate legislation, the provisions of this article.

Amendment XV

1. The right of citizens of the United States to vote shall not be denied or abridged by the United States or by any State on account of race, color, or previous condition of servitude.

2. The Congress shall have power to enforce this article by appropriate legislation.

Amendment XVI

The Congress shall have power to lay and collect taxes on incomes, from whatever source derived, without apportionment among the several States, and without regard to any census or enumeration.

Amendment XVII

The Senate of the United States shall be composed of two Senators from each State, elected by the people thereof, for six years; and each Senator shall have one vote. The electors in each State shall have the qualifications requisite for electors of the most numerous branch of the State legislatures.

When vacancies happen in the representation of any State in the Senate, the executive authority of such State shall issue writs of election to fill such vacancies: Provided, That the legislature of any State may empower the executive thereof to make temporary appointments until the people fill the vacancies by election as the legislature may direct.

This amendment shall not be so construed as to affect the election or term of any Senator chosen before it becomes valid as part of the Constitution.

Amendment XVIII

1. After one year from the ratification of this article the manufacture, sale, or transportation of intoxicating liquors within, the importation thereof into, or the exportation thereof from the United States and all territory subject to the jurisdiction thereof for beverage purposes is hereby prohibited.
2. The Congress and the several States shall have concurrent power to enforce this article by appropriate legislation.
3. This article shall be inoperative unless it shall have been ratified as an amendment to the Constitution by the legislatures of the several States, as provided in the Constitution,

within seven years from the date of the submission hereof to the States by the Congress.

Amendment XIX

The right of citizens of the United States to vote shall not be denied or abridged by the United States or by any State on account of sex.

Congress shall have power to enforce this article by appropriate legislation.

Amendment XX

1. The terms of the President and Vice President shall end at noon on the 20th day of January, and the terms of Senators and Representatives at noon on the 3d day of January, of the years in which such terms would have ended if this article had not been ratified; and the terms of their successors shall then begin.
2. The Congress shall assemble at least once in every year, and such meeting shall begin at noon on the 3d day of January, unless they shall by law appoint a different day.
3. If, at the time fixed for the beginning of the term of the President, the President elect shall have died, the Vice President elect shall become President. If a President shall not have been chosen before the time fixed for the beginning of his term, or if the President elect shall have failed to qualify, then the Vice President elect shall act as President until a President shall have qualified; and the Congress may by law provide for the case wherein neither a

President elect nor a Vice President elect shall have qualified, declaring who shall then act as President, or the
manner in which one who is to act shall be selected, and
such person shall act accordingly until a President or Vice
President shall have qualified.

4. The Congress may by law provide for the case of the death
of any of the persons from whom the House of Representatives may choose a President whenever the right of
choice shall have devolved upon them, and for the case of
the death of any of the persons from whom the Senate may
choose a Vice President whenever the right of choice shall
have devolved upon them.

5. Sections 1 and 2 shall take effect on the 15th day of October following the ratification of this article.

6. This article shall be inoperative unless it shall have been
ratified as an amendment to the Constitution by the legislatures of three-fourths of the several States within seven
years from the date of its submission.

Amendment XXI

1. The eighteenth article of amendment to the Constitution
of the United States is hereby repealed.

2. The transportation or importation into any State, Territory, or possession of the United States for delivery or use
therein of intoxicating liquors, in violation of the laws
thereof, is hereby prohibited.

3. The article shall be inoperative unless it shall have been
ratified as an amendment to the Constitution by conventions in the several States, as provided in the Constitution,

within seven years from the date of the submission hereof
to the States by the Congress.

Amendment XXII

1. No person shall be elected to the office of the President
   more than twice, and no person who has held the office of
   President, or acted as President, for more than two years of
   a term to which some other person was elected President
   shall be elected to the office of the President more than
   once. But this Article shall not apply to any person holding
   the office of President, when this Article was proposed by
   the Congress, and shall not prevent any person who may
   be holding the office of President, or acting as President,
   during the term within which this Article becomes operative from holding the office of President or acting as President during the remainder of such term.

2. This article shall be inoperative unless it shall have been
   ratified as an amendment to the Constitution by the legislatures of three-fourths of the several States within seven
   years from the date of its submission to the States by the
   Congress.

Amendment XXIII

1. The District constituting the seat of Government of the
   United States shall appoint in such manner as the Congress may direct: A number of electors of President and
   Vice President equal to the whole number of Senators
   and Representatives in Congress to which the District

would be entitled if it were a State, but in no event more than the least populous State; they shall be in addition to those appointed by the States, but they shall be considered, for the purposes of the election of President and Vice President, to be electors appointed by a State; and they shall meet in the District and perform such duties as provided by the twelfth article of amendment.

2. The Congress shall have power to enforce this article by appropriate legislation.

Amendment XXIV

1. The right of citizens of the United States to vote in any primary or other election for President or Vice President, for electors for President or Vice President, or for Senator or Representative in Congress, shall not be denied or abridged by the United States or any State by reason of failure to pay any poll tax or other tax.

2. The Congress shall have power to enforce this article by appropriate legislation.

Amendment XXV

1. In case of the removal of the President from office or of his death or resignation, the Vice President shall become President.

2. Whenever there is a vacancy in the office of the Vice President, the President shall nominate a Vice President who shall take office upon confirmation by a majority vote of both Houses of Congress.

3. Whenever the President transmits to the President pro tempore of the Senate and the Speaker of the House of Representatives his written declaration that he is unable to discharge the powers and duties of his office, and until he transmits to them a written declaration to the contrary, such powers and duties shall be discharged by the Vice President as Acting President.

4. Whenever the Vice President and a majority of either the principal officers of the executive departments or of such other body as Congress may by law provide, transmit to the President pro tempore of the Senate and the Speaker of the House of Representatives their written declaration that the President is unable to discharge the powers and duties of his office, the Vice President shall immediately assume the powers and duties of the office as Acting President.

Thereafter, when the President transmits to the President pro tempore of the Senate and the Speaker of the House of Representatives his written declaration that no inability exists, he shall resume the powers and duties of his office unless the Vice President and a majority of either the principal officers of the executive department or of such other body as Congress may by law provide, transmit within four days to the President pro tempore of the Senate and the Speaker of the House of Representatives their written declaration that the President is unable to discharge the powers and duties of his office. Thereupon Congress shall decide the issue, assembling within forty eight hours for that purpose if not in session. If the Congress, within twenty one days after receipt of the latter written declaration, or, if Congress is not in session, within twenty one days after Congress is required to assemble, determines by two thirds vote of both Houses that the President is unable to discharge the powers and duties of his office, the Vice President shall continue to discharge the same as Acting President; otherwise, the President shall resume the powers and duties of his office.

Amendment XXVI

1. The right of citizens of the United States, who are eighteen years of age or older, to vote shall not be denied or abridged by the United States or by any State on account of age.
2. The Congress shall have power to enforce this article by appropriate legislation.

Amendment XXVII

No law, varying the compensation for the services of the Senators and Representatives, shall take effect, until an election of Representatives shall have intervened.

ACKNOWLEDGMENTS

The ideas in this book began as a conversation close to thirty years ago in Albany, New York. One of us was a young legislative counsel and the other a young journalist. There is no place where American politics, with all its strengths and weaknesses, lies closer to the surface than in a state legislature. We would circle each other carefully in those days, the journalist trying to get the news, the counsel wanting to spin the news. Even as friendly adversaries, we shared a fascination with (and a respect for) how government worked. Each of us moved on from Albany to other roles, engaged with or observing politics at the city, state and federal level. As we became friends, the conversation deepened and our shared concern about the deterioration of the political system increased. Ultimately, our obsession became a family affair. Over those many years at our many get-togethers in Robbins Rest, Red Rock, Fairfield, Washington and New York, we would return to the topic, joined by our insightful wives, Joyce and Geraldine, and more and more by our children and stepchildren, Adam, Josh, Ben and, as she got older and ever more articulate, Louisa. Finally, a couple of years ago while walking, carefully, in a cow pasture in upstate New York, we decided the conversation needed to be broadened. Hence, this book.

Along this thirty-year path, our understanding of American government and politics has been deepened and enriched by conversations with many people. We could never name them all, but among those we feel a particular intellectual debt to are: Jill Abramson, Burt Agata, Johnny Apple, Dean Baquet, Joel Benenson, Rick Berke, Michael Beschloss, Shelly Binn, Gloria Borgia, Gerald Boyd, David Broder, John Broder, Ron Brownstein, Elisabeth Bumiller, Karen Burstein, Hugh Carey, Bob Caro, Jim Carville, Bill Clinton, Adam Clymer, Tony Coelho, Charlie Cook, Les Crystal, Mario Cuomo, Al D'Amato, Michael DelGuidice, E. J. Dionne, Bob Dole, Dick Donelli, Maureen Dowd, Gretchen Dykstra, Tom Edsall, Janet Elder, Steve Engleberg, Stanley Fink, Tom Foley, Ed Fouhy, Max Frankel, Kathy Frankovic, Tom Friedman, Ester Fuchs, Jim Gaines, Newt Gingrich, Peter Goldmark, Al Gore, Linda Greenhouse, Mark Halperin, Melinda Henneberger, Harold Ickes, the Reverend Jesse Jackson, Kathy Jameison, Mike Kagay, Al Kaplan, Bill Keller, Mike Kelly, Ed Koch, Andy Kohut, Betsy Kolbert, Bill Kovach, Brian Lamb and his quintessentially American audience, Jim Lehrer, Joe Lelyveld, Tom Mann, Mary Matalin, Frank Mauro, John McCain, Doyle Mc-Manus, Bob Michel, Ab Mikva, Arnie Miller, Gifford Miller, David Milrod, Alison Mitchell, Lance Morgan, Eva Moskowitz, Adam Nagourney, Rob Newman, Peggy Noonan, Fred Ohrenstein, Mike O'Neill, Norm Ornstein, Kevin Phillips, Joyce Purnick, Howell Raines, Carmi Rapport, Dick Ravitch, Anne Reingold, Cokie Roberts, Steve Roberts, the Reverend Pat Robertson, David Rosenbaum, Michael Rosenbaum, A. M. Rosenthal, Andy Rosenthal, Stu Rothenberg, Tim Russert, Bill Safire, David Sanger, Eric Schmertz, Fritz Schwarz, Tom Schwarz, Mark Shields, Robin Sproul, Leslie Stahl, Robin Toner, Marcel Vanooyen, Michael Waldman, Jake Weisberg, Steve Weissman and Mort Zuckerman.

Our parents, Susan and Irwin Oreskes and Louise and Jesse Lane, taught us what it meant to be, and what it took to be, Americans.

This is a work of applied history. It explores current challenges through the lessons of history. We learned these lesson from our own reading of many historical texts and, importantly, from the works of a number of fine academics, most of whom are listed in our bibliography. In particular we were influenced by Gordon Wood's incisive studies of the revolutionary period, Michael Kammen's study of the Constitution in American culture and John Dunn's views on the history of democracy. To them we owe a special debt that we repay by urging our fellow Americans to read their works, too.

We also happily acknowledge many who contributed specifically to this effort. Karen Burstein helped work through many problems, and Fritz Schwarz read an entire draft and sharpened our thinking. The Hofstra University School of Law was especially generous in its support of this project. The Brennan Center of Justice at New York University Law School provided a rich environment in which to discuss many of this book's ideas. Our agent, David Black, like us, was not always sure what we were doing, but pushed on anyway. Our editor, Kathy Belden, took our swirl of ideas and got us to make a book. Kevin Shelton of Hofstra kept finding the unfindable. A number of Hofstra Law students participated in this effort. Ella Govshtein and Josh Wolf performed yeoman service in putting together the bibliography and notes and along with Mimi Alinikoff provided valuable research. These students along with another, Gariel Nahoum, all then proofed the text one last time. A special law school seminar focused on the book, and it was greatly improved by the comments of Scott Buszko, Chad Fisher, Alexander Gallin, Nick Garaufis, Robert Henry, Michael Kauke, Dustin Owens, Michael Smith, Frederick Trelfa, and Michael Ushkow. Geraldine Baum read our early proposals and kept saying, "This is not a book," until she forced us to make it one. Joyce Talmadge read every word, many times, and provided keen perspectives all along the way.

One of the major themes of this book is that we have a constitutional responsibility to fulfill, each in our own way. Arthur Sulzberger and Michael Golden run a company that lives up to the meaning of that responsibility every day. The men and women of the *International Herald Tribune*, led by managing editor Alison Smale, are an inspiration in their devotion to spreading one of America's great creations, nonpartisan journalism, around the world. Sarah Alexander and Isabelle Aubree made it possible for Mike to do his day job while completing this book.

If the ideas in this book have any merit, the credit goes to all those who helped us along the way. Mistakes, distortions, blind spots and biases are very much our own (and, by the way, different between us). Our only defense is that we are just what the framers expected us to be—human.

ABBREVIATIONS AND BIBLIOGRAPHY

Adams McCullough, David. *John Adams.* New York: Simon and Schuster, 2001.

Adler Adler, Stephen J. *The Jury: Trial and Error in the American Courtroom.* New York: Times Books, 1994.

Amar Amar, Akhil Reed. *America's Constitution: A Biography.* New York: Random House, 2005.

Anthony I Anthony, Susan B. *An Account of the Proceedings on the Trial of Susan B. Anthony, on the Charge of Illegal Voting, at the Presidential Election in Nov., 1872, and on the Trial of Beverly W. Jones, Edwin T. Marsh, and William B. Hall, the Inspectors of Election by Whom Her Vote Was Received.* Rochester: Daily Democrat and Chronicle Book Print, 1874.

Anthony II Anthony, Susan B., Elizabeth Cady Stanton, and Ida H. Harper. *The History of Woman Suffrage.* Vol. 1. New York: Fowler and Wells, 1881.

Bailyn I Bailyn, Bernard. *To Begin the World Anew: The Genius and Ambiguities of the American Founders.* New York: Knopf, 2003.

Bailyn II Bailyn, Bernard. *The Debate on the Constitution: Federalist and Antifederalist Speeches, Articles, and Letters During the Struggle over Ratification.* Part 1, *September 1787 to February 1788.* New York: Literary Classics of the United States, 1993.

Bailyn III Bailyn, Bernard. *The Debate on the Constitution: Federalist and Antifederalist Speeches, Articles, and Letters During the Struggle over Ratification.* Part 2, *January 1788 to August 1788.* New York: Literary Classics of the United States, 1993.

Bailyn IV Bailyn, Bernard. *The Ideological Origins of the American Revolution.* Cambridge: Belknap Press, 1967.

Baldwin Baldwin, Neil. *The American Revelation: Ten Ideals that Shaped Our Country from the Puritans to the Cold War.* New York: St. Martin's Press, 2005.

Bates Bates, Katharine Lee. *America the Beautiful: And Other Poems.* New York: Little, Brown, 2004.

Bennett Bennett, William J. *America the Last Best Hope.* Vol. 1, *From the Age of Discovery to a World at War.* Nashville: Thomas Nelson, 2006.

Berkin Berkin, Carol. *A Brilliant Solution: Inventing the American Constitution.* Orlando: Harcourt, 2003.

Bok Bok, Derek Curtis. *The Trouble with Government.* Cambridge: Harvard University Press, 2001.

Bowen Bowen, Dinker Katherine. *Miracle at Philadelphia: The Story of the Constitutional Convention, May to September 1787.* New York: Little, Brown, 1986.

Brant Brant, Irving. *James Madison: Father of the Constitution, 1787–1800.* New York: Bobbs-Merrill, 1950.

Broder Broder, David S. *Democracy Derailed: Initiative Campaigns and the Power of Money.* New York: Harcourt, 2000.

Burns Burns, James MacGregor, and Susan Dunn. *The Three Roosevelts: Patrician Leaders Who Transformed America.* New York: Atlantic Monthly Press, 2001.

Centinel "Centinel No. 1." *Independent Gazetteer.* October 5, 1787. The Constitution Society. http://www.constitution.org/afp/centino1.htm (accessed April 7, 2007).

Chernow Chernow, Ron. *Alexander Hamilton.* New York: Penguin Books, 2004.

Contra U.S. House Select Committee to Investigate Covert Arms Transactions with Iran and U.S. Senate Select Committee on Secret Military Assistance to Iran and the Nicaraguan Opposition. *Report of the Congressional Committees Investigating the Iran-Contra Affair: With Supplemental, Minority, and Additional Views.* Washington, D.C.: U.S. Government Printing Office, 1987.

Cornell Cornell, Saul. *Anti-Federalism and the Dissenting Tradition in America, 1788–1828.* Chapel Hill: University of North Carolina Press, 1999.

Corwin Corwin, Edward S. *The Doctrine of Judicial Review: Its Legal and Historical Basis and Other Essays.* London: Oxford University Press, 1914.

CQ Doherty, Carroll J., and Jeffrey L. Katz. "Firebrand GOP Class of '94 Warms to Life on the Inside." *Congressional Quarterly Weekly Report* 56, no. 4 (January 24, 1998).

DeLay DeLay, Tom, and Stephen Mansfield. *No Retreat, No Surrender: One American's Fight*. New York: Sentinel, 2007.

DI The Declaration of Independence. 1776.

DMC "The Address and Reasons of Dissent of the Minority of the Convention of Pennsylvania to Their Constituents." The Constitution Society. http://www.constitution.org/afp/penn_min.htm (accessed April 7, 2007).

DTDA De Tocqueville, Alexis. *Democracy in America*. Vol. 1. Henry Reeve Translation. 1899.

Dunn Dunn, John. *Setting the People Free: The Story of Democracy*. London: Atlantic Books, 2005.

East East, Robert A. *John Quincy Adams, the Critical Years: 1785–1794*. New York: Bookman Associates, 1962.

Ehrman Ehrman, John. *The Eighties: America in the Age of Reagan*. London: Yale University Press, 2005.

Elkins Elkins, Stanley, and Eric McKitrick. *The Age of Federalism: The Early American Republic, 1788–1800*. Oxford and New York: Oxford University Press, 1993.

Elliot I Elliot, Jonathan, ed. *The Debates in the Several State Conventions on the Adoption of the Federal Constitution, as Recommended by the General Convention in Philadelphia, in 1787*. Vol. 1. Buffalo: William S. Hein, 1996.

Elliot II Elliot, Jonathan, ed. *The Debates in the Several State Conventions on the Adoption of the Federal Constitution, as Recommended by the General Convention in Philadelphia, in 1787*. Vol. 2. Buffalo: William S. Hein, 1996.

Elliot III Elliot, Jonathan, ed. *The Debates in the Several State Conventions on the Adoption of the Federal Constitution, as Recommended by the General Convention in Philadelphia, in 1787*. Vol. 3. Buffalo: William S. Hein, 1996.

Elliot IV Elliot, Jonathan, ed. *The Debates in the Several State Conventions on the Adoption of the Federal Constitution, as Recommended by the General Convention in Philadelphia, in 1787*. Vol. 4. Buffalo: William S. Hein, 1996.

Elliot V Elliot, Jonathan, ed. *The Debates in the Several State Conventions on the Adoption of the Federal Constitution, as Recommended by the General Convention in Philadelphia, in 1787*. Vol. 5. Buffalo: William S. Hein, 1996.

Ellis Ellis, Joseph J. *Founding Brothers: The Revolutionary Generation*. New York: Knopf, 2000.

FA Cutler, Lloyd N. "To Form a Government." *Foreign Affairs*, Fall 1980.

Farkas Farkas, Steve, Jean Johnson, and Ann Duffett. *Knowing it by Heart: Americans Consider the Constitution and its Meaning*. Philadelphia: National Constitution Center, 2002.

Farrand I Farrand, Max, ed. *The Records of the Federal Convention of 1787.* Vol. 1. New Haven and London: Yale University Press, 1966.

Farrand II Farrand, Max, ed. *The Records of the Federal Convention of 1787.* Vol. 2. New Haven and London: Yale University Press, 1966.

Farrand III Farrand, Max, ed. *The Records of the Federal Convention of 1787.* Vol. 3. New Haven and London: Yale University Press, 1966.

FC Roosevelt, Franklin Delano. "Address of the President Delivered by Radio from the White House." May 7, 1933. http://www.mhric.org/fdr/chat9.html (accessed April 30, 2007).

FDRA I Roosevelt, Franklin Delano. "First Inaugural Address." March 4, 1933. http://www.yale.edu/lawweb/avalon/presiden/inaug/froos1.htm (accessed April 15, 2007).

FDRA II Roosevelt, Franklin Delano. "State of the Union Message to Congress." January 11, 1944. http://www.presidency.ucsb.edu/ws/index.php?pid=16518 (accessed April 30, 2007).

Federalist 1 Hamilton, Alexander. *Federalist No. 1.*

Federalist 6 Hamilton, Alexander. *Federalist No. 6.*

Federalist 10 Madison, James. *Federalist No. 10.*

Federalist 14 Madison, James. *Federalist No. 14.*

Federalist 16 Madison, James. *Federalist No. 16.*

Federalist 21 Hamilton, Alexander. *Federalist No. 21.*

Federalist 39 Madison, James. *Federalist No. 39.*

Federalist 44 Madison, James. *Federalist No. 44.*

Federalist 51 Madison, James. *Federalist No. 51.*

Federalist 55 Madison, James. *Federalist No. 55.*

Federalist 63 Madison, James. *Federalist No. 63.*

Federalist 68 Hamilton, Alexander. *Federalist No. 68.*

Federalist 70 Hamilton, Alexander. *Federalist No. 70.*

Federalist 71 Hamilton, Alexander. *Federalist No. 71.*

Federalist 78 Hamilton, Alexander. *Federalist No. 78.*

Ferling Ferling, John. *A Leap in the Dark: The Struggle to Create the American Republic.* Oxford: Oxford University Press, 2003.

Fiske Fiske, John. *The Critical Period of American History, 1783 to 1789.* Boston and New York: Houghton Mifflin, 1897.

Flexner Flexner, Eleanor, and Ellen Fitzpatrick. *Century of Struggle: The Woman's Rights Movement in the United States.* Cambridge: Harvard University Press, 1996.

Friedman Friedman, Lawrence Meir. *A History of American Law.* New York: Simon and Schuster, 1973.

Frohnmayer Frohnmayer, David. "The New Tribalism: Will Special Interest Politics Tear Oregon Apart?" *Old Oregon,* Autumn 1992.

GFA Ford, Gerald R. "On Taking the Oath of the U.S. Presidency." August 9, 1974. http://www.americanrhetoric.com/speeches/geraldfordpresidentialoath.html (accessed April 15, 2007).

GWFA Washington, George. "Farewell Address." 1796. http://www.yale.edu/lawweb/avalon/washing.htm (accessed April 15, 2007).

Halper Halper, Stefan A., and Jonathan Clarke. *The Silence of the Rational Center: Why American Foreign Policy Is Failing.* New York: Basic Books, 2007.

Hand Hand, Learned. *The Spirit of Liberty: Papers and Addresses of Learned Hand.* Edited by Irving Dillard. New York: Legal Classics Library, 1989.

Hofstadter I Hofstadter, Richard. *The Age of Reform: From Bryan to F.D.R.* New York: Vintage Books, 1955.

Hofstadter II Hofstadter, Richard. *Ten Major Issues in American Politics.* New York: Oxford University Press, 1968.

JFKA Kennedy, John F. "Inaugural Address." January 20, 1961. http://www.yale.edu/lawweb/avalon/presiden/inaug/kennedy.htm (accessed May 2, 2007).

Johnson Johnson, Kimberly S. *Governing the American State: Congress and the New Federalism, 1877–1929.* Princeton: Princeton University Press, 2007.

Kammen Kammen, Michael. *A Machine That Would Go of Itself: The Constitution in American Culture.* New York: Knopf, 1986.

Kennedy Kennedy, David M. *Freedom from Fear: The American People in Depression and War, 1929–1945.* New York: Oxford University Press, 1999.

Ketcham Ketcham, Ralph. *James Madison.* Charlottesville and London: University of Virginia Press, 1971.

Koch Koch, Adrienne, comp. *Notes of Debates in the Federal Convention of 1787.* New York: Norton, 1966.

KR "Kentucky Resolution." 1799. http://www.yale.edu/lawweb/avalon/ken res.htm (accessed April 15, 2007).

KY Ketchum, Richard M. *Victory at Yorktown: The Campaign That Won the Revolution.* New York: Holt, 2004.

L-I Dickinson, John. *Letters from a Farmer in Pennsylvania: Letter I.* 1787.

L-X Dickinson, John. *Letters from a Farmer in Pennsylvania: Letter X.* 1787.

L-XII Dickinson, John. *Letters from a Farmer in Pennsylvania: Letter XII.* 1787.

Labunski Labunski, Richard. *James Madison and the Struggle for the Bill of Rights.* New York: Oxford University Press, 2006.

Leuchtenburg Leuchtenburg, William E. *Franklin D. Roosevelt and the New Deal: 1932–1940.* New York: Harper and Row, 1963.

LFD Franklin, Benjamin. Letter to Du Pont De Nemours, June 9, 1788.

LHM Hamilton, Alexander. Letter to Gouverneur Morris, May 19, 1777.

Linder Linder, Douglas. *The Trial of Susan B. Anthony for Illegal Voting.* http://www.law.umkc.edu/faculty/projects/ftrials/anthony/sbahome.html (accessed April 23, 2007).

Lippmann Lippmann, Walter J. *Essays in the Public Philosophy.* Boston: Little, Brown, 1955.

LJM Jefferson, Thomas. Letter to James Madison, March 15, 1779.

LMJ I Madison, James. Letter to Thomas Jefferson, February 19, 1788.

LMJ II Madison, James. Letter to Thomas Jefferson, October 17, 1788.

LMW I Madison, James. Letter to George Washington, December 7, 1786.

LMW II Madison, James. Letter to George Washington, April 16, 1787.

LNS Nixon, Richard. Letter to Judge John Sirica, July 26, 1973.

LWJ Washington, George. Letter to John Jay, August 15, 1786.

LWL Washington, George. Letter to Lafayette, February 7, 1788.

LWTJ Jefferson, Thomas. *The Life and Writings of Thomas Jefferson: Including All of His Important Utterances on Public Questions, Compiled From State Papers and From His Private Correspondence.* Edited by Samuel E. Forman. Indianapolis: Bowen-Merrill, 1900.

LWTP Paine, Thomas. *The Life and Major Writings of Thomas Paine.* Collected, edited and annotated by Philip S. Foner. Secaucus: Citadel Press, 1974.

Madison Madison, James. *Letters and Other Writings of James Madison, Published by Order of Congress.* Vol. 4. Edited by Philip R. Fendall. Philadelphia: Lippincott, 1865.

Mann Mann, Thomas E., and Norman J. Ornstein. *The Broken Branch: How Congress Is Failing America and How to Get It Back on Track.* New York: Oxford University Press, 2006.

Marone I Marone, James A. *The Democratic Wish: Popular Participation and the Limits of Democratic Government.* New Haven: Yale University Press, 1998.

Marone II Marone, James A. *Hellfire Nation: The Politics of Sin in American History.* New Haven: Yale University Press, 2004.

Martin Martin, Joseph Plumb. *A Narrative of a Revolutionary Soldier.* Edited by Thomas Fleming. New York: Signet Classics, 2001.

Mayer Mayer, Henry. *A Son of Thunder: Patrick Henry and the American Republic.* New York: Grove Press, 1991.

Middlekauff Middlekauff, Robert. *The Glorious Cause: The American Revolution, 1763–1789.* New York: Oxford University Press, 1982.

Miller Miller, John C. *Crisis in Freedom: The Alien and Sedition Acts, the Stirring Events of the Days When Hard-pressed Federalists Made Political Use of Our Undeclared War With France.* Boston: Little, Brown, 1951.

Montesquieu Montesquieu. *The Spirit of Laws.* Edited by David Wallace Carrithers. Berkeley: University of California Press, 1977.

Morgan Morgan, Edmund S. *The Birth of the Republic, 1763–1789.* Chicago: University of Chicago Press, 1977.

NDFC Madison, James. *Notes of Debates in the Federal Convention of 1787.* New York: Norton, 1987.

NYT I Brooks, David. "Private Virtue, Public Vice." *New York Times,* February 8, 2007.

NYT II Dillon, Sam. "From Yale to Cosmetology School, Americans Brush Up on History and Government." *New York Times,* September 16, 2005.

Pamphlets Ford, Paul Leicester, ed. *Pamphlets on the Constitution of the United States: Published During Its Discussion by the People, 1787–1788.* New York: Lenox Hill, 1971.

Patterson I Patterson, James T. *Grand Expectations: The United States, 1945–1974.* New York: Oxford University Press, 1996.

Patterson II Patterson, James T. *Restless Giant: The United States from Watergate to Bush v. Gore*. New York: Oxford University Press, 2005.

PCDR The Pennsylvania Constitution, Declaration of Rights. 1776.

PCS Paine, Thomas. *Common Sense*. Mineola: Dover, 1997.

Price Price, Richard. "Observations on the Importance of the American Revolution, and the Means of Making It a Benefit to the World." In *Political Writings*, edited by D. O. Thomas, 116–51. Cambridge: Cambridge University Press, 1991.

Rakove I Rakove, Jack. *The Beginnings of National Politics: An Interpretive History of the Continental Congress*. New York: Knopf, 1979.

Rakove II Rakove, Jack. *James Madison and the Creation of the American Republic*. New York: Longman, 2002.

Richards Richards, Leonard L. *Shays's Rebellion: The American Revolution's Final Battle*. Philadelphia: University of Pennsylvania Press, 2002.

RRA I Reagan, Ronald. "Farewell Address to the Nation." January 11, 1989. http://www.ronaldreagan.com/sp_21.html (accessed April 30, 2007).

RRA II Reagan, Ronald. "First Inaugural Address." January 20, 1981. http://www.yale.edu/lawweb/avalon/presiden/inaug/reagan1.htm (accessed April 19, 2007).

Rudalevige Rudalevige, Andrew. *The New Imperial Presidency: Renewing Presidential Power After Watergate*. Ann Arbor: University of Michigan Press, 2005.

SAL I Lincoln, Abraham. "Electric Cord." July 10, 1858. http://www.democracy.gov/dd/democracy_dialogues/keydocs/abraham_lincoln.html (accessed April 25, 2007).

SAL II Lincoln, Abraham. "Gettysburg Address." November 16, 1863. http://www.yale.edu/lawweb/avalon/gettyb.htm (accessed April 20, 2007).

Sandel Sandel, Michael J. *Democracy's Discontent: America in Search of a Public Philosophy*. Cambridge: Belknap Press, 1996.

Schlesinger I Schlesinger, Arthur M., Jr. *The Age of Roosevelt: The Crisis of the Old Order*. Vol. 1, *1919–1933*. New York: Mariner Books, 2003.

Schlesinger II Schlesinger, Arthur M., Jr. *The Imperial Presidency*. Boston: Houghton Mifflin, 1998.

Schwarz Schwarz, Frederick A. O., and Aziz Z. Hug. *Unchecked and Unbalanced: Presidential Power in a Time of Terror*. New York: New Press, 2007.

SFDR Roosevelt, Franklin Delano. "Before the 1936 Democratic National Convention." June 27, 1936. http://www2.austincc.edu/lpatrick/his2341/fdr36acceptancespeech.htm (accessed April 22, 2007).

Sherr Sherr, Lynn. *Failure Is Impossible: Susan B. Anthony in Her Own Words.* New York: Random House, 1995.

Sirica Sirica, John, J. *To Set the Record Straight: The Break-in, the Tapes, the Conspirators, the Pardon.* New York: Signet Books, 1979.

SJC Carter, Jimmy. "Crisis of Confidence." Speech delivered via television July 15, 1979. http://www.pbs.org/wgbh/amex/carter/filmmore/ps_crisis.html (accessed April 26, 2007).

SJM Madison, James. Speech to the House of Representatives on the "Proposed Amendments to the Constitution," June 8, 1789. http://www.let.rug.nl/~usa/P/jm4/speeches/amend.htm (accessed April 7, 2007).

SJW Wilson, James. Speech to the Pennsylvania Convention, November 24, 1787. http://teachingamericanhistory.org/library/index.asp?document=1714 (accessed April 7, 2007).

SMLK King, Martin Luther, Jr. "I Have a Dream." Speech delivered at the Lincoln Memorial, August 28, 1963. http://www.americanrhetoric.com/speeches/mlkihaveadream.htm (accessed April 20, 2007).

SPH Henry, Patrick. "Give Me Liberty or Give Me Death." Speech delivered before the Virginia House of Burgesses, March 23, 1775. http://www.bartleby.com/268/8/13.html (accessed April 24, 2007).

SRN I Nixon, Richard. "Acceptance of the Republican Party Nomination for President." August 8, 1968. http://www.watergate.info/nixon/acceptance-speech-1968.shtml (accessed April 30, 2007).

SRN II Nixon, Richard. "Annual Message to Congress on the State of the Union." January 22, 1970. http://www.presidency.ucsb.edu/ws/index.php?pid=2921 (accessed April 30, 2007).

SRN III Nixon, Richard. "President Nixon's Resignation Speech." August 8, 1974. http://www.pbs.org/newshour/character/links/nixon_speech.html (accessed April 15, 2007).

Stone Stone, Geoffrey R. *Perilous Times: Free Speech in Wartime, From the Sedition Act of 1789 to the War on Terrorism.* New York: Norton, 2004.

Suarez Suarez, Ray. *The Holy Vote: The Politics of Faith in America*. New York: Rayo, 2006.

Sunstein Sunstein, Cass R. *The Second Bill of Rights: FDR's Unfinished Resolution and Why We Need It More Than Ever*. New York: Basic Books, 2004.

SZ Szatmary, David P. *Shays' Rebellion: The Making of an Agrarian Insurrection*. Boston: University of Massachusetts Press, 1984.

TFC Farrand, Max. *The Framing of the Constitution of the United States*. London: Yale University Press, 1913.

TJA Jefferson, Thomas. "First Inaugural Address." March 4, 1801. http://www.yale.edu/lawweb/avalon/presiden/inaug/jefinau1.htm (accessed April 21, 2007).

TM I "Is Government Dead?" *Time*, October 23, 1989. http://www.time.com/time/magazine/article/0,9171,958814,00.html (accessed April 22, 2007).

TM II "Sound and Fury over Taxes." *Time*, June 19, 1978. http://www.time.com/time/magazine/article/0,9171,919742,00.html (accessed April 22, 2007).

TM III "Time for Healing." *Time*, August 19, 1974. http://www.time.com/time/magazine/article/0,9171,942967,00.html (accessed April 15, 2007).

U.S. Const. The Constitution of the United States of America. 1787.

VRC I "Virginia Ratifying Convention: June 5, 1788." The Constitution Society. http://www.constitution.org/rc/rat_va_04.htm (accessed Nov. 11, 2006).

VRC II "Virginia Ratifying Convention: June 27, 1788." The Constitution Society. http://www.constitution.org/rc/rat_va_23.htm (accessed April 7, 2007).

WAH Hamilton, Alexander. *The Works of Alexander Hamilton: Comprising His Correspondence, and His Political and Official Writings, Exclusive of the Federalist, Civil and Military*. Edited by John C. Hamilton. New York: Charles S. Francis, 1851.

Ward Ward, Geoffrey C., and Ken Burns. *Not for Ourselves Alone: The Story of Elizabeth Cady Stanton and Susan B. Anthony*. New York: Knopf, 1999.

Washington Washington, George. *The Writings of George Washington: Being His Correspondence, Addresses, Messages, and Other Papers Official and Private, Selected and Published from the Original Manuscripts; With a Life of the Author, Notes, and Illustrations*. Edited by Jared Sparks. New York: Harper and Brothers, 1848.

Wheeler Paine, Thomas. *The Life and Writings of Thomas Paine*. Edited by Daniel Edwin Wheeler and Thomas Clio Rickman. New York: V. Parke, 1908.

Wilentz Wilentz, Sean. *The Rise of American Democracy: Jefferson to Lincoln.* New York: Norton, 2005.

Wilson Wilson, Woodrow. *Congressional Government: A Study in American Politics.* Baltimore: Johns Hopkins University Press, 1981.

Wood I Wood, Gordon S. *The Confederation and the Constitution: The Critical Issues.* Lanham: University Press of America, 1979.

Wood II Wood, Gordon S. *The Creation of the American Republic, 1776–1787.* Chapel Hill: University of North Carolina Press, 1969.

WP Bernstein, Adam. "Consummate Lawyer Played Array of Roles." *Washington Post,* May 9, 2005.

Writings Rakove, N. Jack. *Madison: Writings.* New York: Literary Classics of the United States, 1999.

NOTES

Introduction: An Extraordinary Accomplishment

1   "America! America! God": Bates, p. 3.
3   "a blank sheet": Wheeler, p. 243.
3   "We have probably": LWJ.
4   "If men were angels": Federalist 51.
5   "conflict within consensus": Kammen, p. 29.
6   "defined by blood": Suarez, p. 2.
6   "more than any other leading democracy": Bok, p. 397.
6   "Our conviction about American greatness": Bennett, p. xiii.
6   "that the founders": Kammen, p. 398.
8   "We had slavery": SAL I.
10 "as too complex": Wilson, p. 57.
11 "A republic, madam, if ": Farrand III, p. 85.
11 "Liberty lies in the hearts": Hand, p. 190.
15 "Whatever its merits": FA, p. 127.
15 "an unqualified complaisance": Federalist 71.
15 "the growth of a politics": Frohnmayer, pp. 16–19.
17 "devised the most miraculous political document": Bennett, p. xiv.

1. The More Fatal Problem Lies Among the People Themselves

21   "A *people* is traveling": L-XII.

21   "Experience has taught us": LWJ.

23   "But what is government": Federalist 51.

23   "one of the great utopian movements": Wood II, p. 54.

24   "When virtue is": Montesquieu, pp. 118–19.

24   "a quarrelsome, litigious, divisive lot": Morgan, p. 4.

24   "almost as regularly": Ibid.

25   "Were these colonies": Ibid., p. 5.

25   "tameness and supineness": L-X.

26   He certainly is": L-I.

27–28   "My Dear Countrymen": L-XII.

28   "Cancer . . . too deeply rooted": Middlekauff, p. 313.

28–29   "We shall liberate": Ibid., p. 245.

29   "a leap in the dark": Ferling, p. 167.

29   "We have it": PCS, p. 51.

29   "Youth is the seed time": Ibid., p. 40.

31   "breathtaking boldness . . . separation": LWTP, p. 2.

32   "We are young": PCS, p. 40.

32   "Here Governments their last perfection take": Wood II, p. 55.

32   "Would any Man": Ibid., p. 92.

32–33   "If there is": Ibid., p. 119.

33   "A spirit of Liberty": Ibid., p. 102.

33   "sensible, hard-working, independent folk": Bailyn II, p. 44.

33   "A firm adherence": PCDR, Article XIV.

33   "As the possibility": Wood II, p. 102.

34   "necessary evil . . . restraining our vices": PCS, p. 3.

34   "The more simple": Ibid., p. 5.

34   "occasion delay": LHM.

34   "danger of an abuse": Ibid.

35   "confidence that the justice": Rakove II, p. 25.

35–36   "The Articles contained": Rakove I, pp. 172–73.

36   "that tried men's souls": LWTP, p. 50.

36   "Out of a population": KY, p. 8.

36   "A country overflowing": Ibid., p. 9.

36   "I wish I could say": Martin, p. vii.

37–38   "While we lay here": Ibid., pp. 87–89.

41   "regulators . . . moderating government": SZ, p. 56.

42   "Who can determine": Federalist 21.

42   "Leave them to themselves": Ketcham, p. 186.

42   "regal powers": SZ, p. 82.

42   "groaning under the intolerable burden": East, p. 85.

42   "mistrust, the breakdown": Wood II, p. 476.

43   "mistaken . . . sound policy": Writings, p. 72.

43   "We have probably": LWJ.

44   "Men love power" NDFC, pp.131–35.

44   "more fatal . . . lies": Writings, p. 76.

44   "Experience has taught us": LWJ.

44   "It is a just observation": Federalist 71.

44   "Most men indeed": Berkin, p. 163.

44   "united and actuated": Federalist 10.

45   "So strong is": Ibid.

45   "inflamed . . . with mutual animosity": Ibid.

45   "mortified . . . dissipation . . . excessive   jealousy . . . clashing   interests":
     Price, p. 151.

46   "What astonishing changes": LWJ.

46   "It is evident": Federalist 39.

46   "The citizens of the United States": SJW.

46–47   "The American war": Bailyn IV, p. 230.

47   "a republican remedy": Federalist 10.

2. *Approaching So Near to Perfection as It Does*

48   "Is it not time": Federalist 6.

49   "approaching so near to perfection": Farrand II, p. 642.

50   "Is it now time": Federalist 6.

51   "the other inhabitants": Ibid.

51   "ideas so different": LFD.

51   "mutual concessions and sacrifices": Elliot I, pp. 419–20.

51   "to secure the public good": Federalist 10.

51   "it must do harm": Ketcham, p. 190.

51–52 "Wise measures . . . to avert": LWJ.

52   "There is no maxim": Ketcham, p. 181.

52   "It is much more": Wood II, p. 413.

53   "true history of the making": Kammen, p. 184.

53   "I chose a seat": Koch, p. 17.

54   "the profound politician": Farrand III, p. 94.

54   "truth and lessons": Koch, p. xxii.

55   "Where we see": Ketcham, p. 184.

55   "The treasures of knowledge": Wood I, p. 16.

55   "expressed a doubt": Farrand I, p. 34.

56   "pivot": Federalist 63.

56   "the executive and judicial powers": Wood II, p. 598.

56   "The separation of this governmental power": Ibid., p. 608.

56–57 "policy of supplying": Federalist 51.

57   "ambition must be made": Ibid.

57   "In republican government": Ibid.

58   "small territory . . . in a large republic": Montesquieu, p. 176.

58   "thousand views": Ibid.

59   "In the extended Republic": Federalist 51.

59   "Temporising applications will dishonor": LMW II.

60   "different from each other": LWL.

60   "On the need": Berkin, p. 71.

60 "It was axiomatic": Brant, p. 11.

61 "Mr. Randolph opened": Farrand I, pp. 18–19.

61 "his regret . . . open the great subject": Ibid., p. 18.

62 "It is altogether possible": TFC, p. 89.

62 "contained no remedy": Farrand I, p. 319.

65 "As the States": Ibid., p. 196.

65 "If political Societies": Ibid., p. 491.

65 "what advantage the greater States": Ibid., p. 198.

66 "Mr. Sherman . . . admitted": Ibid., p. 35.

66 "national Legislature": Ibid., p. 192.

67 "information and are": Ibid., p. 48.

67 "the number of Representatives": Ibid., p. 197.

67 "that a question": Ibid., p. 201.

67 "at the existence": Ibid., pp. 177–79.

68 "It has given me": Ibid., p. 197.

68 "the muster rolls": Ibid., p. 497.

68 "lamented . . . instead of coming here": Ibid., p. 467.

68 "fate of America": TFC, p. 94.

69 "that a rupture": Farrand I, p. 462.

69 "the same causes": Ibid., p. 464.

69 "that some good plan": Ibid., p. 463.

70 "We were partly national": Ibid., p. 468.

70 "We are now": Ibid., p. 511.

70 "to take into consideration": Ibid., p. 517.

70 "that in the second Branch": Ibid., p. 524.

71 "the vote of this morning": Farrand II, pp. 17–18.

71 "no good government": Ibid., p. 20.

71 "Others . . . seemed inclined": Ibid., p. 20.

72 "double security . . . the rights": Federalist 51.

72 "This subject . . . the most difficult": Farrand II, p. 501.

72 "One great object": Ibid., p. 52.

72 "omnipotent . . . If no effectual check": Ibid., p. 35.

73 "with for and against": Ibid., pp. 191–92.

73   "may have been circulating rumors": TFC, p. 175.

73   "If he ought": Farrand II, pp. 54–55.

73   "The sense of the Nation": Ibid., p. 29.

73   "It would be as unnatural": Ibid., p. 31.

74   "the work of intrigue": Ibid., p. 29.

74   "he who has proved himself ": Ibid., p. 55.

74   "will never fail": Ibid., p. 29.

74   "In every Stage": Ibid., pp. 118–19.

75   "the danger of intrigue": Ibid., p. 500.

75   "the indispensable necessity": Ibid., p. 500.

76   "Monday Sepr. 17.": Ibid., p. 641.

76–77   "I confess that": Ibid., pp. 641–42.

77   "It appears to me": LWL.

77   "The founding fathers": Schlesinger II, p. vii.

78   "The Founders of ": Bailyn I, p. 4.

78   "You are not to enquire": VRC I.

3. That Poor Little Thing—the Expression We the People

80   "Is it not": Federalist 14.

80   "give me liberty": SPH.

81   "Is this . . . an association . . . most clearly": Elliot III, p. 44.

81   "that poor little thing": VRC I.

82   "You are called upon": Federalist 1.

82   "Conventions of Delegates": Elliot V, p. 567.

82   "the most audacious": Corwin, p. 106.

84   "There were some": Bailyn I, p. 107.

84   "Judging from the newspapers": Brant, p. 165.

85   "The proposed plan": Centinel.

85   "They had no plan": LMJ I.

85   "who either enjoys": SJW.

86   "We dissent": DMC.

86–87   "the omission of a Bill of Rights": Ibid.

87   "smelt a rat": Mayer, p. 370.

87   "Mr. Henry, who has been": LMW I.

88   "I have to lament": Mayer, p. 376.

88   "Here is a resolution": Elliot III, pp. 44–45.

90   "the single most": Bailyn II, p. 1142.

90–91   "When I reflect": SJW.

91   "that violence and outrage": DMC.

92   "adopted the system": Pamphlets, p. 20.

92   "The Public here continues": LMJ I.

92   "doubtful . . . the Constitution": Pamphlets, p. 176.

92   "Hearken not to the voice": Federalist 14.

93   "the experience of all mankind": Pamphlets, p. 117.

93   "own opinion has": LMJ II.

94   "I have not viewed it": Ibid.

94   "parchment barriers . . . overbearing majorities": Ibid.

94   "Wherever the real power": Ibid.

96   "I give my assent": Elliot II, p. 175.

96   "would remove the fears": Ibid., p. 130.

96–97   "exert all their influence": VRC II.

97   "for commencing proceedings": Elliot I, p. 333.

98   "It will be": SJM.

4. To Meet Extraordinary Needs

103   "It is patriotism": Stone, p. 46.

103   "Perhaps it is": Ketcham, p. 393.

103   "faithfully execute": U.S. Const., Article 2, Section 1, Clause 8.

103   "our long national nightmare": GFA.

104   "Hugh, it worked": TM III.

104–5   "Our Constitution is": FDRA I.

106   "nightmare": GFA.

107   "cunning, ambitious, and unprincipled men": GWFA.

107   "were made in": SRN III.

107   "republic, if you can keep it": Farrand III, p. 85.

107   "with luck . . . produce": Berkin, p. 8.

108   "mobocracy": Stone, p. 67.

109   "clearly recognized Federalist": Elkins, p. 415.

110   "the government can": Miller, p. 156.

110   "has inspired ignorance": Ibid., p. 59.

110   "our government": Stone, p. 35.

110   "to muzzle dissent": Chernow, p. 570.

111   "force and coercion": Miller, p. 74.

111   "ensure that the act": Stone, p. 67.

111   "To be the proconsul": WAH, p. 677.

111   "a free press": Miller, p. 72.

111   "most reprehensible act": Adams, p. 504.

112   "crowd[s] of spies": Stone, p. 37.

112   "It is patriotism": Ibid., p. 46.

112   "Perhaps it is": Ketcham, p. 393.

112   "By leveraging a moment": Stone, p. 29.

112   "put into the hands": LJM.

112   "entire Federal bench": Miller, p. 136.

113   "Information and communication": Ketcham, p. 402.

113   "calculation . . . oppressive exercise": Madison, p. 417.

113   "That the several states": KR.

114   "dissolve the union": Washington, p. 389.

114   "No State government": Stone, p. 45

114   "exclusively vested": Ibid.

114   "evil propensities of the government": Miller, p. 179.

116   "a Constitution is": Federalist 78.

116   "The opinion which gives": LWTJ, p. 378.

117   "great political importance": DTDA, chap. 6.

117   "most peculiarly American feature": Fiske, p. 332.

117   "a constitutional convention": Kammen, p. 265.

118   "With the utmost respect": LNS.

119   "skeptical of Dean's allegations": Sirica, p. 100.

119   "nervous": Ibid., p. 107.

120   "No judge wants": Ibid., p. 111.

120   "It's difficult to describe": Ibid., p. 121.

120   "My own instinct": Ibid., p. 118.

120–21   "That the Court": Ibid., p. 265.

121   "I was overwhelmed": Ibid., p. 138.

122   "embodies a set of values": Kammen, p. 389.

122   "Americans have bitterly disagreed": Ibid., p.123.

5. The Right to Alter the Established Constitution

123   "No country ever": Ward, p. 105.

123   "greater variet[ies] of parties": Federalist 10.

124   "a promissory note": SMLK.

125   "the People of America": LWL.

125   "right . . . to alter": Federalist 78.

127   "are not just words": Amar, p. 18.

127   "the very vision": Ibid.

127   "We had slavery": SAL I.

128   "truly republican government": Wilentz, p. 226.

128   "wicked design of demagogues": Ibid., p. 225.

129   "a hundred years": Amar, p. 352.

129   "The democratic proclivities": Wilentz, p. 767.

130   "a covenant with death": Stone, p. 85.

130   "The system almost died": Amar, p. 360.

131   "bank of justice": SMLK.

132   "New Frontier . . . looks": Patterson I, p. 474.

132   "the most systematically segregated city": Ibid., p. 478.

132   "Non-violence was losing": Ibid., p. 480.

133   "whether all Americans": Ibid., p. 481.

133   "Farce on Washington": Ibid., p. 483.

134   "Tell them about your dream": Ibid.

134   "Five score years ago": SMLK.

135   "A woman is": Ward, p. 42.

135   "A married woman": Ibid., p. 45.

135–36   "No country ever has had": Ibid., p. 105.

136   "If that government": Ibid., p. 41.

136   "For a quarter of a century": Flexner, p. 38.

136   "mission . . . is at home": Ibid., p. 142.

136–37   "Two million newly enfranchised black men": Ward, p. 103.

137   "This hour belongs": Anthony II, p. 59.

137   "Do you believe": Ward, p. 103.

137   "If that word": Ibid., p. 104.

138   "I will cut off ": Flexner, pp. 137–38.

138   "When women,": Ward, p. 119.

139   "Without having a lawful right": Ibid., p. 142.

139   "Well I have been": Sherr, p. 110.

140   "I could not see": Linder.

140   "The only alleged ground": Sherr, p. 114.

141   "Could I have spoken": Linder.

141   "The Court will not order": Anthony I, p. 85.

141   "If it is": Sherr, p. 117.

141   "unbearable burden": Flexner, p. 288.

6. A Mandate for Vigorous Action

147   "You cannot extend": Hofstadter II, p. 258.

147   "Ours has become": SRN II.

147–48   "There is no consensus": Patterson II, p. 10.

149   "distant, dim and motionless body": Kennedy, p. 30.

149   "if the Federal Government": Ibid.

150   "restrain men": TJA.

150–51   "Kindly separated by nature": Ibid.

151   "The age of machinery": SFDR.

151   "free, self-reliant, unencumbered": Friedman, p. 338.

152   "groupings which centered": Ibid., p. 339.

152   "Self-reliance gave way": Marone II, p. 366.

152   "position and power": Friedman, p. 339.

152   "bursting with class conflict": Marone I, p. 370.

152   "Here was": Morgan, p. 366.

152–53   DUE TO UNSETTLED BANKING CONDITIONS: Ibid., p. 373.

153   "The fog of despair": Schlesinger I, p. 3.

153   "The Country was": FC.

153   "No one can live": Leuchtenburg, p. 19.

154   "The United States Army": Burns, p. 217.

154   "The American experiment": Schlesinger I, p. 484.

154   "If we don't get": Leuchtenburg, p. 24.

154   "Unless something is done": Schlesinger I, p. 3.

154   "If we don't give": Ibid., p. 268.

154–55   "There is nothing": Ibid., p. 5.

155   "directorate of twelve": Leuchtenburg, p. 30.

155   "with dictatorial powers": Ibid., p. 30.

155   "genial and lighthearted dictator": Ibid.

155   "The situation is critical": Kennedy, p. 111.

156   "feasible under the form": FDRA I.

157   "You cannot extend": Hofstadter II, p. 258.

157   "overburden the shoulders": Burns, p. 549.

158   "to articulate and organize": Kennedy, p. 47.

158   "To the New Dealers": Sunstein, p. 43.

158   "a new despotism,": SFDR.

159   "opportunity to make": Ibid.

159   "We do not distrust": FDRA I.

160   "Energy in the Executive": Federalist 70.

160   "the President [was]": Rudalevige, p. 40.

160   "inertia": Schlesinger II, p. vii.

161   "The New Dealers": Leuchtenburg, p. 84.

163   "The Great Depression": Rudalevige, p. 40.

163 "The American home": Patterson I, p. 685.

165 "All you need": Ibid., p. 719.

165–166 "Ours has become": SRN II.

166 "It's time": SRN I.

167 "learned to their dismay" Patterson II, p. 90.

167 "Ask not": JFKA.

168 "second Bill of Rights": FDRA II.

170 "Social Gospel": Marone II, p. 18.

170 "Americans were much less sympathetic": Patterson I, p. 638.

170 "silent . . . forgotten . . . the non demonstrators": SRN I.

171 "The backlash represented": Patterson I, p. 676.

171 "mutual concessions and sacrifices": SJW.

171–72 "Conditioned to expect": Patterson II, p. 10.

172 "We wanted to create": Patterson I, p. 697.

172 "What you see": SJC.

7. *Government Is Not the Solution, Government Is the Problem*

174 "The separation of powers": FA, p. 127.

175 "Our political institutions": Ehrman, p. 41.

176 "In the present": RRA I.

176 "wounds . . . still very": SJC.

177 "we the people": RRA II.

177–78 "While fond of damning": Patterson II, p. 163.

178 IS GOVERNMENT DEAD?: TM I.

179 "No retreat. No surrender": DeLay, p. 9.

179 "broken branch": Mann, p. 13.

179 "The institutional rivalry": Ibid., p. 139.

181 "We're mad as hell": TM II.

182 "the strongest expression": Ibid.

182 "minimizing, even spurning": Marone I, p. 112.

183 "the restoration of ": Ibid.

184   "would put Madison": Ibid.

184   "would study the issues": Hofstadter I, p. 259.

184   "In ordinary circumstances": Lippmann, p. 41.

184–85   "Small and highly organized groups": Hofstadter I, p. 266.

185   "Government by initiative": Broder, p. 5.

185   "typically the result": CQ, p. 163.

186   "A commanding presence": WP.

187   "twisted and pulled": SJC.

187   "The separation of powers": FA, p. 127.

187–88   "they began": Ehrman, p. 41.

188   "through study and consensus": Ibid.

188   "a desire to avoid politics": Ibid., pp. 41–42.

189   "directly or indirectly": Schwarz, p. 56.

189   "The Enterprise, functioning largely at North's direction": Contra, Executive Summary.

190   "The Chief Executive": Ibid., p. 465.

192   "one of the most disgraceful": Ehrman, p. 130.

192   "Congress and the White House": Ibid., p. 131.

192   "when politicians acted": Ibid., p. 136.

192   "None of those": Ibid.

192   "In contrast, Gramm-Rudman": Ibid., p. 137.

193   "I do not think": Broder, p. 242.

193   "Senators were intensely loyal": Mann, p. 146.

194   "Members of the majority party": Ibid., p 155.

194   "Those institutions": Halper, p.70.

196   "failed to rebuild": Mann, p. 122.

196   "and both the presidency": Ibid.

197   "found that civic competence": Bok, p. 406.

197–98   "a growing danger": Sandel, p. 351.

198   "I am warning": RRA II.

198   "what holds us": Kammen, p. 398.

Conclusion: We

199 "A Constitution which . . . has brought": Dunn, p. 82.

199 "People revere the Constitution": NYT II.

200 "representative government bottomed": Ellis, p. 6.

200 "It secured": Dunn, p. 82.

200 "The United States is": Ellis, p. 5.

202 "an avaricious society": Wood II, p. 591.

203 "It is striking": Bok, p. 403.

204 "that the nation's citizenry": Farkas.

204 "Americans have expectations": Bok, p. 383.

209 "the most wonderful work": Kammen, p. 162.

210 "splended complacency . . . neglectful": Ibid., p. 18.

211 "People revere": NYT II.

211 "You must . . . oblige": Federalist 51.

211 "monarchial executive argument": Schwarz, p. 2.

213 "In short, our democracy": NYT I.

214 "suppose the President": Kammen, p. 383.

215 "Democracy is never": Wilentz, p. 236.

218 "Like the Bible": FC.

219 "This national feeling": RRA I.

219 "Younger parents aren't sure": Ibid.

219 "So we've got": Ibid.

INDEX

and need for compromise, 4–5; and New York state government, 34, 43; and presidency, 160; and ratification of Constitution, 82; and role of government, 113; and Sedition Act, 111; and self-interest, 44

Hancock, John, 96

Hand, Learned, 11

Harding, Warren G., 143

Hastert, Dennis, 212, 213

Hayes, Rutherford, 130–31

Hazlitt, Henry, 155

Henry, Patrick, 28–29, 78–79, 80–81, 87–88, 95, 96, 97, 157

history: detachment from, 16; importance of renewing connection with, 220; as informing decision making, 55; "what if" games in, 8

Hofstadter, Richard, 184–85

Hoover, Herbert, 143, 147, 153, 157–58

House of Representatives, U.S.: and appropriation bills, 70; and debate at Constitutional Convention, 64–71; and elections of 1800, 114; powers of, 57, 70; and ratification of Constitution, 86; representation in, 64–71; and separation of power, 56, 57, 216; size of, 86, 98; and Virginia Plan, 56, 57, 64–71. *See also specific member*

human nature: and adaptability of Constitution, 106; and adoption of Constitution by Constitutional Convention, 77; and anti-government sentiments, 201–2, 220; and Articles of Confederation, 3–4, 50–53; and challenges confronting framers, 201–2; change in framers' views about, 22–23, 43–47; and compromise, 4–5; and debate at Constitutional Convention, 65, 191, 220; and democracy, 3; and Federalists, 108; and

government as the problem, 176, 184; and initiative and referendum, 184; and ratification of Constitution, 82–83, 93; and reasons for success of U.S., 2–5

Hunt, Ward, 140, 141

Huntington, Ebenezer, 36

initiative, 14, 175, 180–86, 188, 193

intellectual revolution, American Revolution as, 22

Internet, referendums on, 193

Iran hostage crisis, 12, 218

Iraq war, 194, 206–7, 212, 214

Jackson, Andrew, 128

Jackson, Mahalia, 133

Jarvis, Howard, 175, 180–82, 185–86, 191, 193, 197

Jay, John, 43, 44, 82, 87–88, 109

Jay Treaty, 109

Jefferson, Thomas: and Bill of Rights, 112; and decision to rebel, 33; and definition of genius, 48; and Democratic Republicans, 108; and elections of 1800, 114; and judiciary, 116; Madison's letters to, 88, 92, 94; and need for refreshing of liberty, 217; press criticism of, 111; and role of government, 150; romanticized vision of Americans of, 150–51; and Sedition Act, 111, 113, 114; as vice president, 108; writings of, 25

Johnson, Lyndon B., 135, 163, 169, 197, 212

judiciary: activist, 169; and Bill of Rights, 112; and Congress, 115, 117; and Constitutional Conscience, 120, 121; and federal-state relations, 115; independence of, 105, 114, 115–18, 147; Jefferson's views about, 112; and new presidency, 161; power of, 56, 105, 115, 117, 119; and public opinion, 119; and rights revolution, 169;